WHERE THE MOUNTAIN
CASTS ITS SHADOW

Where the Mountain Casts its Shadow

The Personal Costs of Climbing

Maria Coffey

HUTCHINSON
London

First published in 2003 by Hutchinson

1 3 5 7 9 10 8 6 4 2

Hutchinson
The Random House Group Limited
20 Vauxhall Bridge Road, London SW1V 2SA

Random House Australia (Pty) Limited
20 Alfred Street, Milsons Point, Sydney
New South Wales 2061, Australia

Random House New Zealand Limited
18 Poland Road, Glenfield
Auckland 10, New Zealand

Random House (Pty) Limited
Endulini, 5a Jubilee Road
Parktown 2193, South Africa

The Random House Group Limited Reg. No. 954009

www.randomhouse.co.uk

A CIP record for this book is available
from the British Library

Papers used by Random House are natural,
recyclable products made from wood grown in sustainable forests.
The manufacturing processes conform to the environmental
regulations of the country of origin

Typeset in Bembo by MATS, Southend-on-Sea, Essex
Printed and bound in Great Britain by
Biddles Ltd, Guildford and King's Lynn

ISBN 0 09 179501 X

For Dag

There is no sun without shadow,
and it is essential to know the night.

Albert Camus

Contents

Acknowledgements

It was my husband Dag who first suggested I write this book. Throughout the entire project he gave me unstinting support and enthusiastic encouragement, and sustained me with his love, laughter, food and friendship. He listened patiently as I read out countless drafts, and made invaluable suggestions and editorial comments, many of which are now folded into the text. For all this, and much, much more, I can never thank him enough.

To Bernadette McDonald, Shannon O'Donaghue and the entire staff of Banff Centre for Mountain Culture, I owe huge thanks. They assisted me greatly with my research, generously providing contacts, welcoming me to the Mountain Festivals, facilitating interviews and always cheering me on.

I am also grateful to Bernadette McDonald, and especially to Jeff Long, for introducing me to Susan Golomb, my superb literary agent. Susan's belief in this book has buoyed me throughout all its stages, and her encouragement, advice and keen editorial eye have been invaluable. I am indebted to her for all of this, and for fearlessly lighting a fire underneath me when it was most needed!

Equally fearless is my editor, Isabelle Gutmanis. She came aboard the project when it had run into challenging waters, and with a firm hand helped to steer it safely to shore. I thank her for her thorough, passionate and insightful editorial work, and for her interest in to the book, which far exceeded the bounds of duty.

My thanks and deep appreciation go to Tony Whittome of Random House, for his commitment to this book, and his invaluable editorial work, enthusiasm, encouragement and constant support. I would also like to thank James Nightingale for his work on the text.

I was privileged to take part in the 2002 Cultural Journalism Program, at the Banff Centre, where I worked on parts of the book with the able and inspired assistance of faculty editors Ian Pearson, Alberto Ruy Sanchez and Moira Farr, and visiting lecturers Marnie Jackson, Lawrence Weshler and Ian Brown. To them, to my fellow participants in the program and to Kathy Morrison, Carol Holmes and all the faculty staff my thanks for such a stimulating, happy and memorable month.

Tom and Kathy Hornbein have been involved in this project from its inception, unwittingly becoming my mentors and generously offering advice, contacts, hospitality and friendship. Many thanks to them for this, and for painstakingly reading and commenting on two different incarnations of the manuscript. I am also very grateful to Geoff Powter for fact checking the final draft for mountaineering references, and for introducing me to 'flow'.

As always I am grateful to my community of friends and fellow writers. Carol Matthews was a huge source of inspiration, and intuitively referred me to exactly the right books at exactly the right times. Alison Watt shored me up on numerous occasions, and with her husband Kim Waterman read and commented on the first chapter. Karen 'Kaz' Connelly kindly read and commented on an early draft of the first four chapters. Valley Hennell assisted in writing the cover copy, and she and Rick Scott continued to share with us, over many a dinner, the trials and triumphs of the freelance life. Barb LeBrasseur most efficiently assisted with transcriptions of interviews. Roger Hubank, Julie Summers and Joan Skogan offered suggestions and thoughts on heroes. My thanks to them all.

My thanks to my mother for her love and encouragement.

I thank Jennifer Jordan and Theresa Girard for their hospitality, Sara Whitner for the understanding we share, Janet Rae Brookes for her interest in this project, Peter and Leni Gillman for their advice, and Ian

Wall for kindly sending me his dissertation. To the following people, who generously allowed me to interview them, I am enormously grateful. I was greatly touched by the honesty and courage many of them showed in sharing such deeply personal and often very painful stories. Although not everyone here is featured in the book, their stories resonate throughout it, informing and enlightening its themes. To each and every one of them my heartfelt thanks for their participation in this project.

Jean Allen, Bernard Amy, Conrad Anker, Pete Athans, George Band, Patrick Berhault, Beth (Burke) Bevan, Barry Blanchard, Dorothy Boardman, Chris Bonington, Wendy Bonington, Daniel Bonington, Rupert Boningron, Christine Boskoff, Peggy Bridwell, Helen Brown, Zoe Brown, Michael Brown, Carlos Buhler, Celia Bull, Lorna Burgess, Sara Burke, Carlos Carsolio, Tserin Cheesmond, Greg Child, Yvon Chouinard, Andréa (Harlin) Cilento, Dr. Charles Clarke, Julie Ann Clyma, Bee Coffey, Mick Coffey, Vance Culbert, Patricia Culver, Jim Curran, Steph Davies, Catherine Destivelle, Kurt Diemberger, Bill Dougherty, Ed Douglas, Annie (Wickwire) Dulucchi, Carolyn Estcourt, Tom Estcourt, Caroline Fanshawe, Jim Fotheringham, Gary Guller, John Harlin, Adele Harlin, Marilyn Harlin, Elizabeth Hawley, Jochem Hemmleb, Lynn Hill, Leo Houlding, Dr. Tom Hornbein, Dr. Kathy Hornbein, Dr. Charles Houston, Raymond Huey, Tomaz Humar, Sue Ibara, Cherie Bremer-Kamp, Andy Kirkpatrick, Mandy Kirkpatrick, Tami Knight, Goran Kropp, Bronco Lane, Cari Link, Robert Link, Bill Lockwood, Dottie Lowe, Jim Lowe, George Martin, Cecilia Mortenson, Greg Mortenson, Tara Mortenson, Beth Malloy, Jean MacIntyre, Andrew MacLean, Andy McNeigh, Ellen Miller, Catherine Mulvihill, Sam Naifeh, Hilary Nunn, Andy Parkin, Roger Payne, Gary Pfisterer, John Porter, Dean Potter, Geoff Powter, Paul Pritchard, Jane Pritchard, Alice Purdey, Gillian (Cheesmond) Quinn, Marcia Read, Hilary (Boardman) Rhodes, Sarah Richard, Rick Ridgeway, Rob Rowlands, Liz Robbins, Royal Robbins, Audrey Salkeld, Dr. Rebecca Saltonstall, Doug Scott, Jan Scott, Sharu Prabhu Scott, Dr. Ruth Seifert, Tom Shaw, Erin Simonson, Eric Simonson, Joe Simpson, Brummie Stokes, Steve Sustad, Deborah Sweeney, Lauren Synnott, Mark Synnott, Robina Thexton, Sue Thompson, Henry Todd, Mark Twight, Stephen Venables, Ed Viesturs, Paula Viesturs,

Ed Webster, Peter Whittaker, Tom Whittaker, Cindy Whittaker, Lizzie Whittaker, Jim Wickwire, Mary Lou Wickwire, Louise Wilson, Sharon Wood, Linda Wylie, Jane Yates, Simon Yates.

My condolences to the families of Goran Kropp and Jan Scott, who both passed away before this book went to press.

To anyone I may have inadvertently overlooked, my apologies and appreciation.

Introduction

The world needs risk-takers. They inspire, challenge and encourage. They set off sparks, igniting fires that burn long after their passing. They dare the impossible. But not without cost.

In 1999 I was invited to the annual Banff Mountain Film Festival to take part in a seminar on the personal costs of adventure. The organiser, Bernadette McDonald, told me that she had been trying to arrange this seminar for years, but so far had been unable to find enough people from the mountaineering community who would agree to sit on the panel. It is a subject most mountaineers avoid. Finally, she had assembled four 'insiders' willing to talk: two active alpinists; a man whose climbing career had abruptly ended when a rock smashed into his head, leaving him partially paralysed; and myself – once the girlfriend of a British mountaineer, Joe Tasker. During the two and a half years I spent with Joe, he went on four Himalayan expeditions. The last one was to Everest, where, along with Pete Boardman, he disappeared on the North-East Ridge.

Taking part in that seminar was a daunting experience. I sat in front of an audience of climbing enthusiasts and climbing stars, a witness to the costs of their passion. I described the intensity and excitement of my relationship with Joe, the gains it had brought me. But when I talked about his death, and expressed the opinion that climbers risked shattering the lives and breaking the hearts of those who love them the most, the room sharpened with tension. From the discussion that ensued, it was clear I had walked straight past a 'No Trespassing' sign and into carefully guarded territory. But there was also a sense of relief that this subject, long taboo in the world of high-end mountaineering, was out in the open. That a voice from the 'other' side of the mountaineering story was being heard.

The seminar in Banff was the seed for this book. During my research I talked to the families of cutting-edge climbers from all over the world: those left behind by mountaineering accidents and those who, luckily, have managed to avoid the worst outcomes of climbing. I went beyond the usual enquiry into why people climb, to ask why anyone would choose to love a person who repeatedly risks his or her life in the high mountains. What are the costs, and the gains, of such a choice? I also talked to the people who have no choice – the parents and the children of climbers. And through it all I found myself re-examining my own history, and the reasons I chose to share my life with a man who loved mountains.

Breaking a taboo is a risky business. It is my hope that this book sets off some sparks of its own, that discussions flame about the impact of climbing on people's lives. About the dazzling brilliance of risk, and the darkness of its shadows.

1

Moments of Perfection

Jim Wickwire lies in his bivouac sac on the edge of a crevasse, listening intently. A low rumbling as a boulder peels off the mountain. A distant, drawn-out creaking as the glacier creeps imperceptibly down the valley. Otherwise, nothing. Numbed by shock and exhaustion, he drifts into a brief sleep. On waking, he has a few moments of forgetfulness; a fleeting respite from reality.

He's on the north side of Denali, the highest peak in North America. This part of the mountain is rarely visited by climbers; there are no guided groups, no regular fly-ins, no one for many miles around. His line-of-sight radio is useless here; he can't call for help.

Twilight deepens to night. Stars appear. He imagines his wife, Mary Lou, and their five children asleep in Seattle, these same constellations above them.

Then, from the depths below him, the singing begins again. It's high and reedy, fainter than before, echoing eerily off the icy walls. A schoolboy's song, drawn from a slowly unravelling memory. A voice from a tomb.

The stars above Jim blur and waver through his tears. Twenty-five feet beneath him, a young man is trapped within the icy maw of the crevasse, freezing slowly, deliriously, to death.

Nine hours earlier, Jim Wickwire had been snow-shoeing in high spirits down the Peters Glacier. His climbing partner, Chris

Kerrebrock, was ahead, searching for a safe path through a field of crevasses. On the ropes between them was a heavily laden sled, which Jim was braking when it picked up too much speed. They were on their way to Denali's Wickersham Wall, hoping to put a new route up this treacherous, avalanche-prone face. It was their first trip together. The following year they planned to join an expedition to the north side of Everest, and this was a 'shake-down' climb, a chance for them to get to know each other. At forty, Jim was a veteran of Himalayan expeditions, while Chris, fifteen years younger, was just beginning his career in the world's biggest mountain ranges.

When they stopped for a rest, Jim offered to take over the lead, but Chris demurred. It was a decision that would cost him his life. An hour later, the snow crust gave way beneath him and he pitched into a crevasse, pulling the sled and Jim in after him. Their fall was abruptly halted when the walls of the crevasse bulged inwards, narrowing to eighteen inches. Chris's backpack wedged tight into the narrow slot, trapping his upper body beneath it. He was jammed face-downwards, staring into the void.

Two decades later, Jim sprawled across the living room floor of his house in Seattle, demonstrating Chris's position in the crevasse. 'Only his legs were dangling free,' he said. 'One arm came back up alongside his pack with just the top part of one hand showing. From the angle of the arm I suspect it was broken. I grabbed his hand; he had no feeling in it whatsoever. He was yelling at me to get him out.'

In the fall, Jim had broken his shoulder, disabling his left arm. For six hours he tried to rescue his friend. Urged on by Chris's constant panicked pleading, he managed to inch his way up the crevasse, and from the surface attempted to pull him out with the rope. When that proved impossible, he went back down the crevasse, and yanked at the backpack from every angle. It didn't budge. He tried to cut open the pack to empty it, but it was compressed so tightly between the glacier walls that it had taken on the consistency of stone. Jim worked to exhaustion, without success. Meanwhile, Chris was fighting the demons of intense cold and profound fear. 'He kept saying to me, "You've got to figure it out, Wick. You've got to figure out a way." He went through the stages psychiatrist Elisabeth Kubler-Ross writes about, when people are approaching death – denial, anger, negotiation, depression, acceptance. He went through them all in a matter of hours.'

By the time he reached the acceptance stage, Chris was making requests. He told Jim to climb Everest for him, and to put his trumpet mouthpiece on the top. He gave him messages to convey to his loved ones. And then he asked his friend to help him die speedily – something Jim didn't have the means to do. 'I asked him if he wanted to pray. He said he'd never been much for that. I said, "Chris, do you want to stay here or be taken out?" and he said, "Let my father decide."'

Jim stayed down the crevasse, comforting Chris, until nine thirty p.m. 'By then I was a basket case and he was becoming incoherent, but he was insisting I go up. The worst thing was the leave-taking, and going up the last time and just flopping into the bivouac sack, knowing he's still alive down there, knowing he's dying. Feeling this complete desolation at not having saved him. And then hearing him singing in the middle of the night . . .'

By two a.m., the crevasse was silent. Chris's struggle was over, but Jim's fight for life had only just begun. He was injured, on a remote glacier, with almost no food or water, and only a bivouac bag for shelter. His one hope was the pilot who had dropped them off a week earlier, promising that if the weather was good he would fly by to check on their progress. Thoughts of his wife and children overwhelmed Jim, filling him with regrets for what he was risking. This was his tenth expedition in nine years; he vowed to himself that if he survived he would withdraw from the Everest expedition and quit serious climbing.

For four days he lay on the ice. On the fifth day, hunger forced him to go back down the crevasse, and retrieve some food from the sled. 'The repugnance of that crevasse,' he said. 'It was like going into a grave.' He found crackers, margarine, honey and jam.

A week after the accident, he realised that to survive he had to move up the glacier and get over a pass to the West Buttress Route, where he might find help. He said a prayer at the side of the crevasse, and left a picket with a note attached to it, explaining what had happened, 'In case I didn't make it back.' For five days he staggered uphill, dragging his rucksack behind him in his bivouac sack. Sometimes he crawled on his hands and knees, probing ahead with his ice axe for crevasses. A storm moved in, bringing sub-zero temperatures and seventy-five-m.p.h. winds. It lasted four days, pinning him inside the bivouac sack, burying it in snow.

Eventually, the sky cleared. Two weeks after the accident, Jim heard a plane overhead. Turning on his radio, he made contact with the pilot. By the end of the day he was in the safety of the park ranger station, phoning his wife and promising to give up serious climbing.

I arrived at Jim Wickwire's house on a sunny autumn morning in 2001. It was the first time I'd met him or his wife, yet they welcomed me like an old friend and insisted I stay for lunch. One corner of their spacious living room was given over to children's toys, and Jim proudly showed me photographs of their eldest daughter's twins. He and Mary Lou, doting grandparents, cared for the toddlers two days a week.

Jim Wickwire admitted that he was a lucky man, for a mountaineer, having reached the age of sixty-one and still being around to enjoy his grandchildren. He didn't keep the promise he made to himself on Denali. He continued to go on expeditions, and just a month before we met, he had been on Everest as the leader of a team supporting Ed Hommer's bid to become the first double amputee to climb the mountain. While still at base camp, Jim suffered a sudden and extremely violent headache. Fearing it was the warning signal of a stroke or an aneurysm, he came home. Extensive tests revealed nothing sinister. He acknowledged this might have been his last expedition, but showed no signs of disappointment. 'Age is a great leveller, Maria,' he said. 'It has allowed those fires of ambition to burn less furiously than they did in my earlier years.'

I had come to him with questions about why some people choose to leave their families and the safety of their homes for a harsh, unforgiving environment where the risks are enormous. Jim Wickwire has made this choice repeatedly during his long mountaineering career. As a young father, for three consecutive years he went climbing instead of being at home for his small son's birthday. On the third occasion, he watched two friends, Al Givler and Dusan Jagersky, fall to their deaths in Alaska's Fairweather Range. He resolved to cut back on his expeditions. A year later he lay on K2, surviving a night in the open at 27,750 feet. Recuperating from the pneumonia, pleurisy and pulmonary emboli that followed, he considered giving up mountaineering for good. Then came the chance to climb Everest. Denali was the warm-up expedition. Lying on Peters Glacier, reeling from Chris Kerrebrock's death, he swore to himself, and later his wife, that he would withdraw from the Everest expedition, scheduled for the following year. He soon reneged on the promise, unable to resist the urge, as he put it, to 'embrace life and climb again'. On Everest, at 26,000 feet, he watched Marty Hoey slip from her harness and plummet to her death. That night he wrote in his diary, 'It is high time to start repaying my wife, family and society for the years I've spent pursuing this almost entirely self-serving activity. I must seek the "newer world" I promised to find a year ago, alone on Denali.' A few days after making this entry, he went back up the mountain for another try at the summit.

In an attempt to explain his longing for the mountains, Jim Wickwire wrote a book, *Addicted to Danger*. 'I picked the title and then I tried to get the publishers to change it,' he told me. 'I didn't like the "addiction" part, I didn't like admitting that directly. I thought my climbing friends would find it ridiculous. I don't back away from anything that I describe in the book as an addiction, just the title itself.'

Some of his friends and peers, however, say much the same. '[Climbing] is an addiction,' wrote Linda Givler, a climber herself, two years after her husband's death in Alaska. 'We are far worse off than any drug addict could ever imagine. Our curse takes us to physical and mental highs and satisfies some urge to challenge ourselves. We feel healthy and happy and we don't see that it could ever be wrong to do what we do.'

In the introduction to his collection of mountaineering essays *Eiger Dreams*, Jon Krakauer wrote about his attempts to cut back on his climbing: 'Today I feel like an alcoholic who's managed to make the switch from week-long whiskey benders to a few beers on Saturday night.'

Reinhold Messner uses a similar analogy. 'Endurance, fear, suffering cold and the state between survival and death are such strong experiences that we want them again and again. We become addicted. Strangely, we strive to come back safely and being back, we seek to return, once more, to danger.'

On Everest in May 1997, while waiting for the winds to drop, the filmmaker David Breashears light-heartedly founded 'Everest Anonymous', a self-help group for climbers unable to resist the lure of this mountain. The dozen or so charter members, realising they had spent far too long on the slopes of Everest for their own good, agreed that when they felt its pull again they would call each other up for support in fighting the temptation. In 1999 a system of fines was created for back-sliders. When Pete Athans cracked, the group waived his fine, but warned that if he went back again it would be reinstated, and doubled. In the spring of 2002 he summited Everest for the eighth time. Payment of his fines, now up to $2,000, is still pending.

What exactly is it that climbers find so addictive about climbing? 'There are many sides to it,' said Jim Wickwire. 'One side is physical.' He cited the research done into the role of dopamine, a chemical that, along with adrenaline and endorphins, floods the system during times of stress or high excitement, acting as an analgesic and leaving behind a feeling of well-being. Studies in the 1980s suggested that this feeling was addictive, and the phrase 'runner's high' was coined for those people who became slaves to the pleasurable sensation they experienced following vigorous exercise. Extreme sports are one way to keep the dopamine flowing.

Calling something 'addictive', however, suggests that it is patho- logical, and climbing, quite clearly, is not a sickness. For people at one end of the scale it is a recreation, a way of getting exercise and enjoying the outdoors. For those at the other end of the scale it is a deep need, something they can't live without. A desire so strong it is like a calling. In 1961, an eighteen-year-old in Poland went rock climbing for the first time. 'I was totally possessed,' wrote Wanda Rutkiewicz, who became one of the world's top mountaineers. 'The experience was like some inner explosion. I knew it would somehow mark the rest of my life.'

Sometimes the signs are there much earlier. 'He was always going upwards, from the time he was eighteen months old,' said the mother of UK mountaineer Pete Boardman. She recalls him starting with chairs and tables, progressing to the garden fence, the laburnum tree and then, when that started to bend under his weight, the taller sycamore. Hills, cliffs, mountains – on and on it went, until he stood on the top of Mount Everest. And even then, the need wasn't satisfied.

For Jim Wickwire, the obsession with climbing began through books, and most particularly Maurice Herzog's *Annapurna*, the account of the first ascent of an 8,000-metre mountain in 1950. Along with Louis Lachenal, Herzog was trapped by a storm on the way down from the summit, and forced to spend the night in a crevasse. Both men suffered terrible frostbite, and the resulting amputations meant they never climbed again. 'There are other Annapurnas in the life of men,' are Herzog's famous closing words in the book. Jim Wickwire admits that on many occasions during his long climbing career he has recalled those words, and tried to heed them by turning away from climbing, but with little success.

In February 2003, I talked to Jim Wickwire again. Within six weeks he was returning to Everest, hoping to climb it from its northern side. What, I asked him, had rekindled those 'fires of ambition' he thought had all but burned out? Strangely, it was the death of a good friend. The previous September, Jim had been climbing on Mount Rainier. He was leading a team that included Ed Hommer, who was training for his second attempt on Everest. A rock 'the size of a football' flew down the slopes towards them. Jim heard it coming and called out a warning. As Ed spun around to move out of the rock's trajectory, it hit him on the crown of his head, killing him instantly. A month and a half later, Jim was firming up his own plans for Everest.

'In ways I can't fully articulate,' said Jim, 'once I got through the depression and the sadness and the early stages of grief over Ed's death, it made me come to life again. It was the utter randomness of it, the fact it happened on Rainier, on that particular route, that's normally so safe. It made me realise that I don't want to just slip into old age. If I've still got the ability to climb Everest, if I can do it safely and not take unnecessary risks, why not go do it? And so it's a gift from Ed Hommer. That's the way I look at it.'

He insisted he had nothing to prove. That he didn't have to get to the summit of Everest; that trying for it was what mattered. He insisted he would be careful. For the sake of his wife, his five grown-up children and, most important of all, his twin granddaughters.

'Those girls, they're five and a half now. I want to be around to see them grow up. To find out how they turn out at twenty or thirty. They are my greatest constraint against doing something stupid up there.'

In the West, we live in relatively safe times, cocooned from most of the perils our ancestors faced. Some people miss the element of risk and uncertainty; they seek it out, and if necessary, create it. Dr Ruth Seifert, a psychiatrist, has pointed out that the Italian and British mountaineers of the nineteenth century were wealthy, titled people who had everything they needed for a comfortable life. 'So what were they doing, climbing dangerous mountains? They couldn't just sit and enjoy what they had at home, they were moved to go out and explore. There's some instinctive thing in mankind, that such comfort is just not enough for the soul.'

In the summer of 2001 I attended the Outdoor Retailers Convention in Salt Lake City, Utah. This enormous trade show offers the newest clothes and the latest equipment for every high-adrenaline sport, and is a testament to the modern need for adventure. Among the famous alpinists representing their sponsoring companies at the show was Conrad Anker. In 1999 he discovered the body of George Mallory, who with Sandy Irvine disappeared high on the slopes of Everest in 1924. A few months after that discovery, Conrad survived an avalanche on Shishapangma which swept away Dave Bridges and Alex Lowe, his closest friend. Since marrying Lowe's widow and becoming the stepfather of her three children, Conrad has vowed to reduce the risks he takes in the mountains, but he admitted that this was no easy commitment to make. The need for adventure, he believes, is hard-wired into some human beings, part of our natural evolution.

'That's why risk-takers have to go out on the hunt,' he said, 'but they're not hunting animals any more, they're not providing game for the table, they're going out and proving themselves against a challenge. It goes right to the ego of men.'

What about the women? Steph Davies, from Moab, Utah, has tackled some of the most challenging big-wall climbs in the world, and in early 2002 she became the first woman to climb the major peaks in Patagonia's Fitzroy massif. For her, ironically, the mountains are the place where she feels most safe and in control. Growing up in Washington DC, and attending the University of Maryland, where women were advised not to walk around alone at night, she remembers existing in a climate of constant fear for her personal safety. 'I feel safe in the mountains because nothing heinous is going to happen to me. The risk with climbing is nothing in comparison to always worrying if someone is going to abduct you and kill you. My worst fear is ending up locked in a basement for ever by some evil person. Wouldn't you rather get hit by a rock on the side of a mountain than have that happen?'

Fears of human predators also haunted Wanda Rutkiewicz. During her childhood in Poland, just after the Second World War, her little brother was blown up by a landmine while he was playing in the rubble of a bombed house. In 1972, her father was murdered by a couple who had rented half his house. They attacked him with knives and an axe and buried his body in the garden. These events fuelled Wanda's deepest fears. The woman who had been on over twenty expeditions and climbed eight 8,000-metre peaks, including Everest and K2, was afraid to go into a dark cellar by herself or be alone at night in a big apartment. 'People frighten me,' she admitted to friends. 'I'm forever scared that something terrible might happen to me.' In 1992 she set off on the Caravan of Dreams Expedition, her objective to climb eight 8,000-metre peaks in one year. On the first, Kangchenjunga, she disappeared.

Over the past twenty years, the number of female rock climbers has soared. But mountaineering remains a male-dominated activity, with female climbers of the calibre of Wanda Rutkiewicz and Steph Davies still in a minority. Steph believes it is the mountaineering culture that turns many women off it initially. 'You walk into a place where it's all male climbers. First of all it gets really juvenile and stupid, so you're not interested and you leave. Or all they are talking about is equipment, and you think, this is boring. Or it's competitive and macho and aggressive. But for me that stuff falls away, I love climbing so much I ignore it or refuse to accept it.'

Ellen Miller, a Colorado-based mountaineer, in 2002 became the first North American woman to summit Everest from its south and north sides. On most of her expeditions, she has been the only female climber, a fact she attributes partly to the nature of mountaineering itself. 'It's very abrasive and harsh, especially in the zone where you need to start using supplementary oxygen. It simply doesn't appeal to the mass of women.' The issue of children is also something she believes affects the gender imbalance. Ellen is presently working on a book about the women who have summited Everest – a total of seventy-five up to the end of 2002. 'So far I've interviewed about sixty of them, and almost all of them did not have children when they climbed Everest,' she said. 'For me personally, and I think for many women, either you want to climb or you want to have a family. I don't think many women can do both very well.'

In California's Yosemite Valley, on El Capitan's 3,000-foot face, is a route called The Nose. Traditionally, climbers spent days scaling it, hauling up gear behind them in sacks, whacking bolts into the rock to aid their progress and sleeping in tiny tents pinned to the face. In 1994, the American rock athlete Lynn Hill became the first person to 'free' climb The Nose, using a rope and equipment only to protect herself from falling, and scaling it in twenty-three hours straight. It was a feat that, to date, no one has repeated. With such skill, nerve and determination, there's little doubt that, had Lynn Hill wished, she could have become a leading mountaineer. But she has always been wary of that side of the sport. The death of her close friend Hugues Beauzile on Aconcagua, fifteen years after her brother-in-law Chuck died on the same route, in almost exactly the same place, brought home the high costs that alpinists and their loved ones face.

A year after Hugues' death, Lynn was invited to join a climbing trip in the mountains of Kyrgyzstan with a group of highly experienced American alpinists including Alex Lowe, Kitty Calhoun, Conrad Anker and Greg Child. She would be climbing rock walls, they told her, not going to high altitude. There wouldn't be too much ice or snow. The area was enchantingly beautiful, and largely unexplored by climbers. Intrigued, and reassured by the calibre of her companions, she agreed to go. During the month-long expedition, an avalanche carried her eighty feet down a slope, depositing her inches from the edge of a crevasse. She dodged falling rocks, moved unroped across steep snowy slopes knowing that one slip would be fatal, curled up fearfully on a high ledge while an electric storm buzzed around her. She was constantly aware that their remoteness brought a whole new element of risk – so far from help and the possibility of rescue, even a broken ankle could spell disaster. Her final climb of the trip was the first all-free ascent of a 4,000-foot wall, which she and Alex Lowe completed in three days. She stood on the summit, exulting in her sense of accomplishment and the grandeur of the landscape, but also thinking of Hugues, Chuck, and all the other friends she had lost in the mountains. This, she decided, was as far as she ever wanted to go towards the extreme edge of alpinism.

'I loved the challenge,' she said, 'but I don't choose to go to those places any more. For me there's so much more excitement and beauty in the touch and feel and the aesthetics of warm rock. It's alive. The high mountains are dead places. Nothing lives up there. I understand the adventure and the pristine beauty of going to them, but it's not worth the risk and the discomfort – or the hurt that it brings to the people who are close to you if you die. And the chances of dying are so much higher in places like that.'

There was another reason for the decision she made on that remote summit. When Lynn was in Kyrgyzstan she had begun to think about having children. 'And to do that,' she said in the autumn of 2002, when she was four months pregnant, 'I've got to be around. Alive.'

High-altitude mountaineers frequent an environment which, if they are not skilled, attentive and in control, or if they are unlucky, can kill them. To hard-core climbers, such risk comes with the territory, and is a necessary part of the game. 'You know it's dangerous in the first place, and the ironic thing is that when there's a mountain on which people died, getting up that mountain alive has a greater value,' said Royal Robbins, one of the pioneers of big-wall climbing in America. 'If climbing was totally safe it wouldn't have the same draw.'

Over the past decade, however, more climbers have begun publicly to question the costs of mountaineering. A voice frequently heard on this subject is the British climber and author Joe Simpson, whose best-selling book *Touching the Void* recounts his epic escape from a crevasse in the Peruvian Andes. 'The defining thing about climbing is that it kills you,' he said. 'Not many people publicly question the fatality rate because it opens up a very nasty Pandora's box. Your rather fragile rationale for why you are climbing might not stand up to a close examination, and so you'd rather not talk about it. People feel uncomfortable and think, no, no, it's not like that. But you only have to look at the facts.'

According to figures collected by Elizabeth Hawley, an historian based in Kathmandu, the death rate on foreign climbing expeditions to the Nepalese Himalaya between 1950 and 1990 was 2.5 per cent, and during the last decade has declined to 1.9 per cent. These figures reflect a whole spectrum of mountains in terms of size and difficulty, and a wide range of objectives among the various expeditions. Zero in on people doing new routes in the high Himalaya, however, and the statistics change dramatically.

A survey on all British expeditions to mountains over 7,000-metres between 1968 and 1987 recorded eighty-three expeditions involving

535 climbers, of whom twenty-three died; most were killed in falls, struck by rocks or caught in avalanches. Excluding the deaths of Sherpas and porters, this added up to a fatality rate of 4.3 per cent – at least one death every fifth expedition. 'The percentage now is almost exactly the same,' said Dr Charlie Clarke, a co-author of the survey report. 'If that was Formula One, and more than one out of every twenty-five drivers were killed over this time span, it would be crazy. The level of risk would never be accepted. Looking at the details from our data, it was difficult to prise anything out except that climbing at this level was exceedingly dangerous.'

Many fatalities occur when people are on their way down from the summit. A survey in 2000 calculated that the 'death rates on descent' from the summit of most 8,000-metre peaks averaged 2.3 per cent, but that on Annapurna and K2 the rates were 7.3 per cent and 11.6 per cent respectively. 'Reaching the top of K2 and contemplating that you have a 11.6 per cent chance of not getting down alive must be disconcerting,' said Raymond Huey, who was involved in the survey. 'After all, 11.6 per cent comes perilously close to the odds of dying in Russian roulette (16.7 per cent).'

Joe Tasker used to say he was as likely to get killed in a car crash as on a mountain, and many climbers echo his sentiment. 'Driving is super-scary, people are always getting killed,' said Steph Davies. 'But because it's accepted by our society it's considered normal, while climbing is considered weird. If you look at the numbers, driving is much more of a killer.'

According to 2001 figures, in the US approximately 41,000 people are killed every year in motor vehicle accidents, and three million more are injured. Out of a population of 272 million, that's approximately one death in 7,000. When I asked Steph Davies, who is thirty, how many of her friends have died in climbing accidents, she added up four or five. The US alpinist Mark Twight, who is in his early forties, says that thirty-seven people he knew have died climbing. Joe Simpson has lost, on average, a friend a year to the sport, over the past fifteen years. How many people of their age have lost that many friends in car crashes?

When I arrived at Joe Simpson's cottage in Sheffield, he was perched on a ladder in his kitchen, trying to attach a light fixture to the wall above the sink. 'Pass me that screwdriver, would you?' he asked, and promptly stuck its metal end into the inner workings of the electrical outlet. I gasped, anticipating sparks, a cry of pain, a body slumping to the floor. Joe has a reputation for being accident-prone, and over two decades of climbing he has racked up an alarming number of injuries. I was relieved when eventually he descended the ladder and was sitting safely at the table. As well as doing home renovations, he told me, he was in the last stages of writing a book to explain why he was giving up mountaineering. Most of the reasons had to do with his disquiet over what he calls the 'slaughter' of alpinists in climbing accidents and his growing conviction that if he didn't stop climbing soon, he would be the next to go.

The previous summer he and a friend had attempted the North Face of the Eiger in Switzerland, a place where to date over sixty climbers have perished. 'There was a horrendous thunderstorm,' he recalled. 'We took shelter in the Swallow's Nest and these two other climbers ahead of us carried on. The whole face turned into a waterfall. The leader slipped at the top of the second ice field, and pulled his mate off. They flew straight over the top of us and fell two thousand feet.'

He paused, and inhaled on a cigarette.

'I tend to find that sort of thing slightly distressing. My desire to carry on climbing evaporates. I just thought, Fuck it, we'll go home.'

Despite his British understatement, it's clear the incident distressed him deeply, bringing back painful memories of a long fall he took on a Nepalese mountain, Pachermo, that left him with a badly smashed ankle and facial injuries. 'I kept thinking about these lads falling eight hundred feet down an ice field and then launching off into space. I know what that would have been like.'

The leader slips on some soft snow. A slow, casual, tired slip. He goes down on his right side, rolls on to his stomach and takes a blow with his ice axe to self-arrest. It doesn't work, he's still falling. Another futile blow, then a desperate third but now he's coming off the band of soft snow and on to the ice and WHOOSH – Joe clicked his fingers in emphasis – he's accelerating, it's like going over a hump-backed bridge, he's doing about eighty m.p.h., his elbows are thrumming on the ice, things are happening so fast, there's so much information coming into his head he doesn't have time to be scared, and yet his thought processes are clear and slow and he registers, almost calmly, that he's probably falling to his death . . .

'On Pachermo,' said Joe, 'I remember thinking, if I put the axe in, it won't work at this speed, but I might as well try.'

In the force of its planting, the adze hit him in the face and rearranged his features, but the axe itself held. The men on the Eiger were not so lucky.

'What did my head in about their accident wasn't really to do with their deaths,' Joe admitted. 'It was to do with mine. It was the inevitability that scared me.'

He went home and started writing *The Beckoning Silence*. It was almost complete, and he showed me his draft of the final pages. After I'd read it I asked him what his plans were once the book was finished.

'I'm going back to the Eiger in September,' he said.

'But I thought you said—'

'I do want to stop climbing,' he interrupted me, 'but on my own terms. And I want to climb the North Face of the Eiger first.'

For serious mountaineers, climbing transcends sport or hobby. It is self-expression, it defines their friendships, their personas and, sometimes, their professions. Cecelia Mortenson, a young American alpinist and mountain guide, described how hard it is to step out of that definition even for short periods. 'Your climbing friends ask, "So what are you up to?" If you answer, "I'm climbing this, I'm going there to climb that," it's a very positive exchange. Whereas if you say, "I'm going back to school," they say, "Oh," and lose interest. That's definitely something I've struggled with. If I have defined myself as a strong woman, climbing and travelling all over the world, and suddenly I haven't done any of that for the last three months, and I don't have any immediate plans, does that make me a failure?'

For some climbers, like Joe Tasker, defining themselves as mountaineers is a happy alternative to the other roads they might have taken in life. Between the ages of thirteen and twenty, Joe was in a Jesuit seminary training to be a priest. By his mid-teens he had begun to rebel against the strictures of the institution. Childish pranks, like stealing a Christmas tree from a nearby plantation, led to confrontations with the Fathers and threatened his future in the school. When Joe discovered climbing, he found a socially acceptable channel for his teenage rebelliousness. In this he was not alone.

'I was a wild kid,' admits the Canadian alpinist Barry Blanchard. 'I stole things, some of them as large as automobiles. The first climbing rope I got, I used to rappel off the tops of warehouses so I could break in through the windows.'

A sobering visit to a friend in prison, and the discovery of climbing, redirected his ambitions. Before long he was constructing his entire life around alpine climbing, and admits to having taken extraordinary risks. 'As a young man I frequently pushed past the point of lethal consequences. I think that is a rite of passage that a lot of young alpinists probably seek out.'

Now in his early forties, he is still considered one of the 'hard men' of North American mountaineering, but claims that he no longer pushes at his outer limits. His actions don't always back this claim. In an article for the *Canadian Alpine Journal*, he describes his attempt on Howse Peak in the Canadian Rockies, which he undertook with Steve House and Scott Backes in celebration of his fortieth birthday. At 11,000 feet, the mountain is not high by the standards of these climbers, but its east face is formidable, lined with precariously thin ice systems. They climbed for two days, then spent two more days storm-bound in a snow hole. On the fourth morning, they peeked out to see 'a Niagara Falls of snow'. Despite this, Scott Backes suggested they continue their ascent, and Barry agreed. Steve House was amazed by their decision – both men were older than him by a decade and he had presumed they would be more cautious. They headed up, into a whiteout and terrifying unstable conditions.

'Snowflakes the size of postage stamps filled the air like exploding down and monstrous spindrift avalanches roared from the gully every several minutes as if something malevolent within the mountain was loosing the gates of a white hell,' writes Barry. 'I was terrified . . . Climbing up into it was like climbing into a waterfall, and the weight of the slides stacked kilograms on to my bowed head and shoulders and arms . . . I knew that if I got to the top of the bulge and started to pull over and took one of the slides in the chest, it would take me off. What I was doing bordered on madness, yet in my heart, where real decisions are made, it remained, to me, a fine kind of madness.'

One of the luxuries of youth is a sense of immortality. For most people, the illusion begins to fade when the responsibilities of adulthood loom large, and as the years go by, caution increasingly replaces carefree abandon. This isn't necessarily the case, however, for climbers. 'I won't die,' the Swedish mountaineer Goran Kropp told me, in the summer of 2001. 'So I don't write a will, because if I do, maybe I think I will die climbing, then I should have to stop.' A year later, he fell to his death from a cliff in Washington State.

'I had this notion,' Jim Wickwire said, 'that if I was out there on the edge, willing to push the limits, then I was somehow pushing back the limits of mortality. That by looking at death, and then coming back to normal life, I had made that mortality recede.' He was forty years old and the father of five small children when he lay on the edge of a crevasse, listening to Chris Kerrebrock slowly die. One of the resolves he made then, and quickly broke, was to reset his priorities. 'As a climber,' he wrote in *Addicted to Danger*, 'I had remained in a kind of perpetual adolescence, often neglecting my primary responsibilities.'

Perpetual adolescence; the Peter Pan syndrome; eternal youth; in Latin, *puer aeternus*, the term used by Ovid in *The Metamorphoses* to describe the child-god Iacchus. Jung adopted the term to describe someone, most often a man, who remains too long in adolescence. Marie-Louise von Franz, the author of *The Problem of the Puer Aeternus*, describes such men as being charming, unconventional, full of interesting ideas and ever in pursuit of their dreams. They get bored easily, and always have to have a new plan. They have difficulty with commitment, particularly to anything they see as mundane; they are horrified by the idea of a 'normal' life and yet they are able, when enthusiastic about a task in hand, 'to work twenty-four hours at a stretch or even longer, until [they break] down'.

To mountaineers, and anyone who has lived with one, these characteristics may have a familiar ring. 'You're never too old to have a happy childhood,' says Ace Kvale, a climber from Colorado. Von Franz claims that such men are often attracted to dangerous sports, especially flying and mountaineering, because these are symbolic of getting above the earth, away from the confines of ordinary life. 'If this type of complex is very pronounced,' she writes, 'many such young men die young in airplane crashes and mountaineering accidents.'

According to von Franz, a classic *puer aeternus* when earth-bound for too long becomes depressed and irritable, a trait mountaineers sometimes admit to. 'I have quite big mood swings and I can get very depressed at home,' said Chris Bonington, Britain's most famous climber, 'but when I'm in the mountains I live on a very even keel and I feel very attuned. I think that's one of the reasons I like them so much.'

Many climbers are fascinated by flying. John Harlin, a US alpinist who was killed on the Eiger, trained as a fighter pilot. Seattle-based Christine Boskoff, the owner of the Mountain Madness guiding company, is a trained pilot as well as a Himalayan climber. Ed Hommer, who lost his legs after his small plane crashed in Alaska, carried on climbing after the accident and also became a pilot for American Airlines. Eric Simonson, the leader of the expedition which found George Mallory's body on Everest, has taken up flying small planes and has already crashed a Cessna. Carlos Carsolio, a Mexican mountaineer renowned for audacious ascents in the Himalaya, has given up climbing temporarily to be close to his young family, but goes paragliding almost daily. 'I love so much this being in the clouds,' he said. 'To traverse, to feel you are the mother of your decisions.' A whole phalanx of British alpinists have taken up paragliding, including Joe Simpson, who waxes lyrical about the sheer aesthetic beauty of the sport – travelling for many miles through the air without power, flying in the company of eagles, feeling like another bird in their midst. 'It's not like mountaineering because it's more immediate,' he said. 'It scares the shit out of me when it goes wrong. You suddenly get a sense of this huge elemental power and you go, "What the fuck are we doing, this is stupid." And then you get out of it alive and you go, "Well that wasn't too bad, was it?" You start using the same rationale as when you're climbing.'

For all her criticisms of the *puer aeternus*, von Franz admits that such characters usually have a joyous enthusiasm that invigorates people around them; if forced to grow up and accept life's mundanities, inevitably some of this would be stripped away. 'How can one grow up,' she writes, 'without losing the feeling of totality and the feeling of creativeness and of being really alive, which one had in youth?'

Every mountaineer at some point says about their climbing: 'It makes me feel alive.' Some describe moments of transcendence in the mountains, claiming, as Pete Athans put it, 'a sense of intimacy with the infinite'. Barry Blanchard recalls the times when he has been stretched to his absolute limits on a climb. 'It's when your senses are cranked up

like they've never been before. It's all related to risk, if you screw up
you've got a really good chance of getting killed.' His wife Catherine
Mulvihill often climbs with him. She calls such instances their 'narrow
moments of perfection'.

The spiritual teacher George Ivanovitch Gurdjieff described that
fleeting feeling of being utterly alive as 'a reintegrative moment',
which, he said, occurs in times of great intensity, in danger or when
engaged in the throes of a new and exciting experience. In Zen
Buddhism it is reached through meditation, and named as Zensho,
the moment when the divine is present. In Christianity it is the
concept of epiphany, a moment when God is made manifest. For
Reinhold Messner, who pioneered climbing the world's highest
peaks solo and without oxygen, it is the moment that comes on
descent from a challenging route. 'Before reaching base camp, only
halfway to civilization,' he wrote in 2000, 'there is something special.
Between wilderness and civilization – at the end of the exposure –
that's it!'

In 1977, the veteran British mountaineer Doug Scott broke both
legs in a fall just below the summit of the Ogre, a 7,285-metre
mountain in Pakistan's Karokorum Range. For eight days he wormed
down the mountain through a storm, hauling himself along with his
arms and dragging his useless legs behind him. 'It was strangely,
intrinsically interesting at the time, to have to solve this new problem,'
he said. 'To accept, first of all, new rules – how am I going to get out
of this one? And then sort it out. It always brings the best out of you
if you do totally commit, you get like a second wind, an extra
superhuman burst of energy. You do everything right almost without
knowing it.'

The experience of 'doing everything right almost without
knowing it' is what the US psychologist Mihaly Csikszentmihalyi
calls 'flow'. It happens when all one's attention is focused on a clear
goal, and when difficult challenges are matched by finely tuned skills.
It is when, with a sudden sense of effortlessness, an ice skater
executes a perfect triple jump, a surfer rides down the face of a giant
wave, a trapeze artist flies from one bar to another, a mathematician
finally solves an incredibly complex equation, an alpinist moves
flawlessly up a wall of ice on crampon points and ice tools. In each
case, the depth of concentration on the task in hand is so intense that

everything else in life falls away; unaware of the passage of time, one moves beyond normal consciousness into a short-lived state of 'flow'.

It was such an experience that set Sharon Wood on the path to becoming the first North American woman to climb Everest. In her early twenties, she was in South America, and trekking alone for a few days in the Peruvian Andes. She had not intended to do any climbing, but when she reached the end of a valley and saw a mountain face looming above her, she suddenly changed her mind. 'I said, I'm going to climb that. It was just a need, a drive beyond any conscious thought. I did the approach walk, I slept on the glacier below the face, and all night I was awake, churning with anticipation. And when I was soloing that face, I have never felt more present, more in my body, more in the moment. The fear was right on the edge of either paralysing me or putting me into this place of being fully engaged – that magic moment when you're performing better than you ever have before. You're out of your head, you're away from your thoughts, you're out of your fears, you're just in this zone. When I experienced that climb I realised, Ah! This is part of me, I'm hooked on this, I'm doing this because there is a reason that goes beyond ego and beyond anything except what I need as an essential ingredient. Two days later I went right back up on another face and soloed it. It was such a contrast to ordinary life. It was just totally the opposite place, out there on the very edge of my ability.'

Focus, peak experience, epiphany, the reintegrated moment, flow, in the zone – different names but the same meaning: the sense of being intensely alive. The moment when life is NOW, without past or future, beyond earthly mundanities. An intoxicating state. A fleeting sense of immortality. The state that Jim Wickwire sought, throughout his forty years of climbing, and hopes to find again, at the age of sixty-three, high on the north side of Everest. 'We're captives to the past and the future,' he says. 'We're so distracted, and that's why a lot of people are unhappy. One of the addictive aspects of climbing is that it allows you to be in the present moment in ways that are impossible in ordinary life.'

In *The Evolving Self*, Csikszentmihalyi affirms what mountaineers so often claim, that the enjoyment of risk-taking derives not from the danger itself, but from managing it, from the sense of exercising control in difficult situations. In the long run, this adds up to a sense of control over one's life. And this, he claims, 'comes as close to what is usually meant by happiness as anything else we can conceivably imagine'. But he warns that flow has its negative sides. 'The goals to which it can be applied,' he writes, 'can make life either richer, or more painful.'

To the onlooker, to the non-climber, what Jim Wickwire describes in *Addicted to Danger* might seem like madness, the punishment of Sisyphus, endlessly pushing a stone uphill. In his version of the myth, Albert Camus called this an 'unspeakable penalty, in which the whole being is exerted toward accomplishing nothing'. Yet he concluded that Sisyphus must have been a happy man. 'Each atom of that stone, each mineral flake of that night-filled mountain, in itself forms a world,' he wrote. 'The struggle itself toward the heights is enough to fill a man's heart.'

The Russian mountaineer Anatoli Boukreev insisted his partner, Linda Wylie, join him on an expedition in his native Kazakhstan. They climbed Myramornya Stena and from there traversed to Khan-Tengri. Setting out very early one morning, they climbed to 6,800 metres, where Anatoli said they should stop. Ahead of them, the full moon was slipping towards a horizon of jagged peaks. Behind Khan-Tengri, out of their sight, the sun had begun to rise. As the stars disappeared and darkness seeped away, a vast shadow, like a giant pyramid, was cast against the dawn sky. The shadow of the mountain. 'It was a perfect moment,' said Linda. 'I was overwhelmed by the beauty of it all. Toli turned to me and said, "I had to show you this. If something happens, you have to know why I would risk everything just to be here."'

If something happens. All the climbers I talked to were happy to discuss the reasons they climb, and the good things climbing has brought to their lives. But when asked about its personal costs, the impact on the people waiting at home, their tone changed. The ebullient Slovenian alpinist Tomaz Humar, after talking nonstop for an hour about all his adventures in the Himalaya, suddenly paused for breath. 'This is the hard question,' he said.

Doug Scott started shifting around in his chair. 'You're asking questions that perhaps most of the guys put into the back of their minds,' he said.

Only Royal Robbins was unflinching in his reply. 'We have to remember that if we're talking about true risk,' he said, 'occasionally there has to be a price paid.'

'By whom?' I asked. 'The people left behind?'

'Yes,' he said. 'That's part of the largeness of the price.'

The nature of that price, and if it is worth the gains, is what this book sets out to discover.

2

High Times, Hard Contract

The glacier stretches away, its flat, white expanse shimmering with reflected sunlight. A desert, he thinks. So what is a shark doing here? It swims towards him, a blue-grey streak, fast and sinuous. He stops, holding up his ice axe to fend off its attack. Light glares from the snow, dazzling him. He blinks against it, and the shark is suddenly gone. In its place is a crevasse, deep and shadowy, a few steps away. He stares at it for a while. Where's Dick? Vague memories of their descent from the mountain drift around his brain. Digging in the snow to make a ledge for a bivouac. The wind gusting around him. Snow stinging his eyes. Losing his grip on an ice wall. Sliding off. Dangling above 4,000 feet of space, the rope holding by a single peg. Dick's frozen, black-tipped fingers. How many days had they spent climbing down? Five? Six? No fuel left to melt snow. Nothing to drink. Their mouths so dry that swallowing the little food they had left was impossible. Moving like robots. Inching silently down the mountain, abseil after abseil.

He hears voices. A family wanders by, a father, mother and two children. Garish shorts, T-shirts, baseball caps, running shoes. They must be on holiday. Did they see the shark? He looks around for it. When he looks back, the family has gone.

The crevasse worries him. He skirts its far edge, carefully turning around to make sure it isn't following him. He is tired. So tired. He lies down on the *snow, leaning against his rucksack. Dick. Now he remembers. He wanted to go down that steep rocky gully that led to base camp, instead of taking this glacier route. Unable to agree, they separated. Stupid decision, he thinks. You should never do that. Wandering about a glacier alone is utter folly.*

'Why is he just lying there, Dad?' That family again. Struggling to his feet, he lifts his rucksack to his shoulders. It's a huge effort and he resents the family for not helping him, for just standing there, staring. He staggers on; they trail behind. Minutes later he stops to rest. So tired. Too tired to deal with the rucksack. He flops over in the snow with it still on his back. Staring at the clear blue sky, he thinks how stupid it would be to die here, a few hours from the safety of base camp.

From the corner of his eye, he notices a dark form. A stone, large and flat like a table, atop a column of ice. At the base of the column, melted by the sun-heated rock, is a pool of water. Instinct drives him to his knees. Scrabbling through his rucksack he finds a few oats, a piece of chocolate, some sweets. Quickly he grinds them together in his mug, then scoops water on top. He slurps the mash too fast; some of it runs down his chin and the family hoots in derision. He doesn't care about them. He doesn't care about anything except the intense, blissful sensation of liquid sliding down his parched throat.

The man on the glacier told me this story as we drove in darkness from Wales to Manchester. I remember the warmth of the car, the beat of the windshield wipers, the way the beams of light stretched ahead of us carving mesmerising tunnels in the rain. Most of all I remember his hands, strong and capable on the steering wheel, and how sometimes he would lift one to emphasise his words.

We had met the day before, in the kitchen of a friend's house in Wales. I'd walked in while he was recounting how he and Dick Renshaw had climbed Dunagiri, and then, without food or fuel to melt water, begun their epic five-day descent. He was slim and wiry, with blue eyes and rather pinched features. He wore jeans and a fisherman's sweater. A web of fine lines ran across his forehead and his hair was thinning. Had I passed him on the street, I doubt I would have given him a second look. It was his story that entranced me. He was describing Dick's fingers, blackened with frostbite, but my presence distracted him. He stopped talking, and met my gaze. 'Don't you two know each other?' my friend asked. 'Maria, this is Joe Tasker.'

★

I already knew a little about the climbing world. My eldest brother Mick had been a climber, and I shared a house with a young mountaineer, Alex MacIntyre. I had watched their girlfriends suffer the stress of separation when they left on expeditions, and I felt sorry for them. It wasn't the sort of life I wanted. But I was craving change, a respite from the routine of my teaching days. Recently I'd sat through the retirement speech of a fellow teacher who was about to leave the high school after working there for twenty-eight years – longer by a year than I had been alive. He proudly listed the number of times he had passed through the school gates, the number of school lunches he had consumed, the number of detention periods and playground duties he had supervised, the number of school reports he had written, the number of staff meetings he had attended . . . It went on and on, a long list of routines that obviously gave him comfort. The hypnotic horror of it all quieted even the most fidgety students and a strange silence settled over the assembly hall. I stared in dismay at the man as he recounted his lists, his life story. His past. My future.

Before that day in Wales, and Joe. He offered me a lift back to Manchester, and as he drove he told me his story. It was a story of danger in remote places, of life on the edge of human experience. Dunagiri had been his first Himalayan expedition. In the four and a half years since then he'd climbed Changabang, joined expeditions to K2 and Nuptse, and reached the summit of Kangchenjunga. Already a 'name' in the climbing world, he described how hard it was to juggle all the different aspects of his life: organising expeditions, raising sponsorship, pursuing his writing and photography, giving lectures, and running his climbing equipment store, The Magic Mountain.

'I'm so busy, and gone so often, most women won't put up with me,' he said, giving me a flirtatious glance. It was a clear invitation.

Like wealth and power, danger is very attractive. In his book about the daredevil climber Dan Osman, Andrew Todhunter wrote, '[Dan] was just standing there on the sidewalk . . . but there was something in the air around him, a kind of glimmer.' Dan Osman developed the sport of rope jumping – tying into a climbing rope attached to the top of a cliff, and then diving off. His father believed the glimmer was his son's unusually strong concentration of *chi*, or life energy. That energy ran out in 1998 when his rope broke during a 1,200-foot jump off Yosemite's Leaning Tower.

A daring *wunderkind* of the British climbing scene, Leo Houlding, once told a journalist that he is 'surrounded by good *chi*'. It sounds like a boast, but beyond his physical grace, beneath his breezy, carefree persona is something strong and still, a strange mixture of energy and control. Joe had that same 'glimmer' in abundance. He also had a fine intellect, a sharp wit and a determination to focus on what he wanted until he got it. Now he turned that focus on me; despite my reservations about relationships with climbers, I was drawn, irresistibly, into his life story.

As Joe Tasker's new girlfriend, I received instant membership to the mountaineering tribe. It was a heady place to be in the early 1980s, on the arm of one of its stars. I found myself in the company of some of the world's elite climbers, people with big personalities and strong egos. People who were always on the move, making plans, zipping off to remote mountains to do audacious climbs, and returning with wild stories. Nothing was static, nothing was certain. And the parties – especially the ones just before expeditions left – were outrageous, as extreme as the climbing. A naked man dancing madly to ear-splitting punk music in the tiny living room of a Welsh cottage. A food fight in a kitchen, cheesecake and lemon meringue pies flying through the air. A couple making love in the bathtub, heedless of people using the toilet right next to them. Alcohol, marijuana, hash, magic mushrooms, all strongly laced with laughter and the heady sense that life was endless, and ours for the taking. 'It was a great life, wasn't it?' reminisced a friend from those days. 'I never had to think, What will we do this weekend? We partied like rock stars.'

Joe relished such craziness, but more as an observer than a participant. He was careful how he spent his energy, always keeping enough in hand to maintain his focus. His single-mindedness and his discipline were astonishing, and even after a heavy night in the pub, he would get up early the next day to work on one of his projects. Though he refused to discuss the risks he took in the mountains, he seemed driven to cram as much into his life as possible, as if he accepted it could be cut short at any time. I soon learned that at least one of his previous girlfriends had grown tired of always waiting around for him to find time for her, and had walked away. But, at the beginning at least, I was thrilled by the pace of his life, and relished the vicarious excitement, the reflected glory and the touch of glamour our relationship brought me.

The ability to withstand long, uncertain separations is a desirable attribute in a climber's partner. Joe admitted that he had been drawn to my independence, and he was proud that I maintained my own interests and friends. He knew I was not going to curl up in a ball when he left on expeditions. For my part, our relationship gave me a chance to flex my emotional muscles. Compared to the other people left at home, though, I had it easy. During Jim Wickwire's annual expeditions, his wife Mary Lou had the sole charge of their five small children. Yet she claims to have taken such responsibilities in her stride. 'It wasn't all that bad. There were times when they were all crying or there was a flood in the basement and it would be "Damn him, why isn't he here?" But I was young and I had a lot of energy, and for the most part I could handle it. I really enjoyed the authority I had when he was gone.'

Whenever Dr Charlie Clarke joined an expedition, his wife Ruth Seifert became the solo parent for their two daughters as well as working full-time as a consultant psychiatrist. She, too, was up to the challenge. 'I've preferred to have a life where I've not been the little wifey, where I've had to be the man and the woman,' she said. 'I know what I did at home was much harder than what he did in the mountains. It took me to my extreme. I thought, good, I know who the strong one is.'

And you need to be strong. Six weeks after Joe and I became lovers, he left to climb K2, the world's second highest mountain. I'd been spellbound by his stories of quest and adventures, but suddenly the magic was stripped away. This was real life, filled with what climbers refer to as 'objective dangers'. A sérac, or ice pinnacle, that falls without warning, an avalanche that sweeps down in seconds, obliterating all in its path, a fast-brewing storm that traps climbers in the 'death zone' above 8,000 metres, a snow bridge across a yawning crevasse that collapses under the weight of a footstep, a single stone that wings down a mountainside and wipes out a life. Each of these, I knew, had killed at least one friend or acquaintance of Joe's.

Pete Boardman, Dick Renshaw and Joe were camped at 26,500 feet on K2 when they were hit by an avalanche in the middle of the night.

Joe was buried in the tent. While the others were digging him out, the mountain unleashed another avalanche, trying to sweep them away. They spent the next three days struggling through blizzards and thigh-deep snow, down avalanche-prone slopes. When finally they reached the safety of base camp, they sent messages home. This was long before the days of emails; a mail runner was about to leave the camp, and Joe scribbled a hasty letter to me. It had been, he wrote, the most profound experience of his life. 'I know I haven't come to terms with its implications, and last night I went to sleep twitching at the slightest rustle of the tent, or rattle of a stone outside, imagining rocks plying away from ice, and slipping into dreams of hospital wards and personal apocalypses.'

I stood in my sunny living room on a hot August day, clutching his letter. Over the past three and a half months, since he left for K2, his friends had been reassuring me. He was 'the safest mountaineer' they knew. He had 'consummate skill and judgement'. He was 'near-invincible'. Gladly, I had believed them, ignoring the fact that no one had mentioned the word 'luck'. At the end of the letter, almost as a postscript, Joe added that he, Pete and Dick had decided to go up the mountain for another try at the summit. 'We will be all right this time,' he wrote. Trembling, I leaned against a table for support as waves of panic and desperation surged through me. This time? Did he mean this time there would be no avalanches? No blizzard? I stared at his familiar handwriting, its loops and dashes, imagining his fingers holding a pen, his hand moving across the flimsy blue paper. 'Love, Joe.' Folding up the aerogram, licking the strip of glue. Sealing the message inside – this mountain is more important than anything else in my life. He wasn't invincible. He could die. The letter I held was almost three weeks old; he might be dead already. I ran next door, crying to a bewildered neighbour. I phoned Doug Scott, one of the mountaineers who had reassured me months before. 'Nothing to be done, love,' he said, when he'd heard me out. 'But no news is good news.' It was nine more days before Joe reached a telephone and called to say he was safe, and on his way home.

Driving to his flat to see him for the first time in four months, I was as excited as a child at Christmas, my stomach churning in anticipation. When I walked into his living room, he was sitting on the floor, talking on the phone. His eyes lit up as I entered. Shy, eager, happy – one embrace and my mountain of worries slid away. He had survived; we were together.

Physically and psychologically, he was ravaged by his experiences on K2. In the days following his return, I cherished my nurturing role, happy to feed him, to ensure he got some rest and to look after the trivia of his life. In the midst of a love affair with a man who put the mountains before me, at this moment I felt needed. And though he claimed he didn't expect such devotion from me, it was clear he revelled in it.

Four months later, Joe was getting ready to leave again, on a winter expedition to Everest. As his departure date approached he became increasingly frenetic, throwing his life, and our relationship, out of balance. In the evenings, while he struggled through an impossibly long 'to do' list, I would hang around his flat, trying to help wherever I could and hoping to catch a few minutes with him between tasks. I sensed how much even my accommodating presence placed unwanted demands on him. He longed for the simple, uncluttered existence he would find in the mountains. It was a place where he was happy – in some ways much happier, I suspected, than he ever was at home. Yet he often despaired of the fact that he had to go so far, and to so much trouble, to find peace of mind. 'I wish I could be like other people,' he once said to me, 'content with rock climbing at weekends, and short trips to the Alps. Life would be so much easier. What's wrong with me?'

But if I expressed concern about how little time we had together, he became defensive, repeating what had become his leitmotiv: 'You were attracted by my drive and ambition, and if I changed you might not like me any more.' I loved him for who he was, but the strain of our separations, and the worry that he might not come back, began to take their toll. I started to wonder why he wanted to be away so often and for so long, and why he didn't miss me in the way I missed him.

According to the psychologist and mountaineer Geoff Powter, my complaint is common. Geoff has a practice in the town of Canmore, the hub of the Canadian mountaineering scene. During therapy sessions, he often hears those left behind bemoan the fact that settling down or having a child hasn't made their climbing partner want to pull back from risk-taking. 'I signed on for the journey,' one of his clients put it, 'but a part of me really thought the journey would be over pretty soon.'

In Joe's case, he had set his course before I met him, and I knew he was determined to stay on track, no matter what else happened in his life. One year and two expeditions into our relationship, I was struggling to find ways to block out the worry when he was climbing. Some women, like Doug Scott's wife Jan, coped by denying the possibility of her husband's death. Despite Doug's numerous narrow escapes, including an avalanche on K2, Jan had developed a simple, implicit belief that he would always return safely. 'I completely obliterated any thoughts that Doug was going to get killed,' she said. 'I just wouldn't have it. I would have gone barmy otherwise.'

I just stopped asking too many questions, choosing ignorance as my defence. I was deliberately vague beforehand about which route Joe would be taking on a mountain, and I preferred not to hear too much afterwards about what he had been through. It was enough that he was home, and safe. Acknowledging the import of his risk-taking was, for both of us, emotionally forbidden territory. In his posthumously published book, *Savage Arena*, Joe wrote with typical understatement about the start of our relationship, 'I had become friendly with a girl called Maria, whose brother was a climber but who had never appreciated the full implications of having a boyfriend who was committed to climbing mountains.' That was true, but now I was learning quickly, taking a crash course in those implications, and the unspoken contract whose terms I had accepted.

One of those terms is accepting the spectre of widowhood, which always hovers over the partners of mountaineers. For the lucky ones, it is an ever-present shadow. For Linda Wylie, it is all too real. A nurse practitioner from Santa Fe, New Mexico, she developed a ten-year friendship with Greg Gordon, a local oncologist. They shared a passion for the outdoors and went on climbing and river-rafting trips in the southwestern mountains. Finally, the friendship evolved into romance, and by 1993 they were discussing marriage. Greg, who was forty-seven, admitted that he had always wanted to climb a Himalayan mountain, that it was something he felt he had to do before he got married again, or grew too old. He joined a private American expedition to Pumori, a 7,145-metre peak close to Everest. Previously he had climbed on ice and snow only to an elevation of 4,000 metres, but this didn't hold him back; he reached the summit of his mountain. On the descent, just above Camp One, at 6,000 metres, there was a place where the climbers had to move from one section of fixed ropes to another. No one knows why – perhaps he lost his footing, perhaps the weight of his pack unbalanced him – but Greg fell from here. He hit a rock head first, bounced, then fell another 600 metres down a couloir, a steep gully. The next night, in the States, Linda received the news of his death in 'the first of those terrible phone calls that come in the middle of the night'.

One of Greg's team members, Billy Pierson, along with Henry Todd, a guide from another expedition, accepted the gruesome responsibility of burying Greg's body. Using a pulley system from ropes, they dragged him from the avalanche-prone slope to a more level, protected area. Here they wrapped him in his tent, laid him flat and covered him with boulders.

Before burying Greg, Henry took photos of his body. An experienced mountaineer, he knew that without conclusive proof of Greg's death, legal problems could ensue for his family. When Linda Wylie called Henry to thank him for what he had done, on behalf of Greg's children she asked him for the photos, to pass on to lawyers. Months later, when Henry was in the States, he stopped in Santa Fe. He offered to take Linda to the grave, saying he felt the climb to 6,000 metres on fixed ropes would be possible for her. It was a gesture, he admitted, that would mean as much to him as to Linda. He told her he had lost many friends in the mountains whose bodies were never recovered. It was very unusual to be able to bury someone, and he had buried Greg. Taking Linda to the grave would be like finishing the circle for all the people he had lost. 'I'd be handing it on,' said Henry.

Linda had never been to mountains outside of America, and knew nothing of the mountaineering world. But she accepted Henry's offer, and was hugely grateful to him for making it. 'He was the last person who touched Greg. For a woman in extremis, that person becomes so important. I was insane with grief. He was offering to do something for me that I could not do alone.'

In the autumn of 1994, Linda flew to Kathmandu. From there she set off on the ten-day walk-in to Everest Base Camp, where she had arranged to meet Henry Todd. In the village of Pheriche, she stopped for a day to acclimatise to the altitude. Around three in the afternoon she was sitting in a tea-house, doing some embroidery and drinking tea, when a tall man stepped through the door. Despite the cool wind, he was wearing shorts and a light top. He was impossible to ignore. 'There was this composure, this sureness about the way he moved, a grace that was animal-like. We were across the room from each other. I watched him until he raised his gaze; it was so intense, I had to look away. Every time I looked up he was there, gazing mercilessly.'

Presently, the man nodded to her and left the tea-house. The next day she continued with her trek, through a landscape that overwhelmed her in its scale. 'I was crossing giant rivers, roaring under the trail, there were great icy monoliths protruding from the rubble, it was like some Nordic fairytale, the land of the frozen giants. The last two hours before base camp went on for ever.'

At last, climbing to the top of a rocky ridge, she saw the village of tents that make up Everest Base Camp. Close to the trail, a man lay on a carefully constructed platform of rocks. He was sunbathing, wearing only a pair of shorts, a nose guard and sunglasses. It was the man from the tea-house. He sat up, and in a deep Russian-accented voice asked, 'Are you Linda?'

Anatoli Boukreev, a mountaineer from Kazakhstan, had been asked by Henry Todd to watch out for Linda when she arrived. Henry walked down from Camp Three that day to greet her but it would be a week before he could guide her to Greg's grave. 'During those first few days at Base Camp, everyone spoiled me,' said Linda. 'The Sherpas, Henry, Anatoli and the other climbers, they were all so kind.' Particularly Anatoli. He spent hours in conversation with Linda. He shared his precious cache of mandarin oranges with her, he entertained her with stories of his expeditions. And he answered her questions about why Greg had died. 'He told me Pumori is not a hard mountain. I was stunned. Greg was a fine athlete, he paid attention to things, he was strong. I had thought it would take something big to kill him. Anatoli said, "Linda, a man here does not escape his destiny. For six days you will get up, you will walk outside your tent, you will put on your gear and go out to climb. And then on the seventh day, one thing will be different and you will be away down the slope. It will be an avalanche or a rock. You cannot look for blame. And you cannot look for reasons."'

Eventually, Anatoli left for Namche Bazaar to meet clients he would guide up Island Peak. And Henry Todd interrupted his Lhotse efforts for the Pumori journey. Starting off early one morning he and Linda crossed the glacier. By noon they were ascending the sections of fixed rope to the ridge above the grave. Belaying down to the mound of stones that covered Greg made death in the mountains 'a fierce reality' for Linda. In her backpack she was carrying tokens of her life with Greg – arrowheads they had found on river-rafting trips, bundles of sage, a pot from Acuma Pueblo in New Mexico that she had given him as a gift, a bottle of gin that one of his friends had sent, with instructions to pour the contents over the cairn. She sprinkled the sage, poured the gin, placed the pot in a rock cleft. Then she sat and looked at his view – across the sculpted chaos of Khumbu Icefall and up the snow fields and rock ridges of the South Col route on Everest. There was no sound, save for the rattle of an occasional falling rock. 'I had come asking, Why?' she recalled. 'This man who was so full of purpose and promise, why did he die? He had started the Cancer Treatment Center in Santa Fe, he had helped so many people. We were wonderful together. Such long-time friends, real partners with so much to share. And he was gone. It was staggering. Losing him was like having the door shut on love. But I had to stop asking. I realised that I was going to have to let go and accept that he was here, for ever, in this beautiful place.'

Her pilgrimage complete, Linda returned to Everest Base Camp. Anatoli Boukreev was preparing to leave for Island Peak, a relatively easy mountain close by. He invited her to join his group. And on the first night of the trip, he asked her if she would share his tent. Linda refused.

'I had seen Greg's grave, I had finally accepted that he was dead. But Anatoli was not a man you could have a casual affair with, he was serious, intense. And I felt it so keenly that people could die up there. I was not ready to take that on.'

Anatoli was hurt by her refusal, and she spent the next two weeks trying to make it up to him in other ways. 'I served him first at dinner. I doted on him. Henry Todd just rolled his eyes.' Their long con-versations continued. Weeks later they said goodbye in Kathmandu. Anatoli took her to the airport, and on the way he asked her to do 'all these domestic chores' for him once she got back to the States – a list of people to call, parcels to mail. And he wrote down her address and phone number.

Recently, I talked to the American mountaineer Carlos Buhler, who has been climbing in the Himalaya for twenty-five years. We'd never met, but he knew of me through my association with Joe Tasker. He asked how my life had turned out since Joe's death, and was astonished to discover I was married to a man who doesn't climb. 'Really, Maria?' he said. 'I thought you'd be a lifer.'

I laughed at his presumption that I'd seek out another mountaineer, yet I understood the reasoning behind it. The mountaineering tribe is a comforting place for the partner of a climber. Its protective circle shuts out the questioning eyes of the outside world. There's no need to explain why someone would choose, again and again, to put himself in danger – this is understood, accepted as normal, seen as admirable. Should something terrible happen, the tribe offers you support, solace and, if you wish, a choice of other strong and daring individuals as potential partners.

A few years after her boyfriend died on Everest, Sharu Prabhu became the second wife of Doug Scott. Tomaz Humar's wife, Sergeja, met the Slovenian climber while she was living with his close friend Danilo Golob, an alpinist who loved free-soloing frozen waterfalls. When Danilo skied to his death off the edge of a cliff, she married Tomaz. And months after the US climbing star Alex Lowe died on Shishapangma, his widow was living with his best friend Conrad Anker, the only survivor of the avalanche that swept her husband away.

Why would these grieving lovers forge a new relationship with another risk-taking man? The San Francisco psychiatrist Sam Naifeh offers one possible explanation: that the bereaved mates miss the intensity they enjoyed in their former relationship with a risk-taker. 'It's a systemic thing,' he said. 'It's about the sense of being in the moment that ordinary life doesn't bring. The climber seeks it in the mountains and the partner in the relationship. Both of them have some investment.'

Dave Cheesmond's widow Gillian admits that even now she sometimes misses the excitement of her life with Dave. A cutting-edge alpinist, Dave disappeared on Mount Logan in 1987, along with the American climber Catherine Freer. Two years after the tragedy, Gillian married his best friend and frequent climbing partner Choc Quinn. They had known each other since Gillian and Dave first emigrated from South Africa to Canada in 1981. Choc was a dyed-in-the-wool Irish bachelor, but Gillian and Dave had always kept a lookout for a suitable girlfriend for him. In the confused weeks after Dave's disappearance, the devastated friends turned to each other for support and understanding. 'He was like a comfortable old shoe,' said Gillian, about the start of their romance six months later. 'Just always there.' After two years they married, but not before seeing a counsellor. 'We wanted to sort out exactly why we were doing it,' said Gillian. 'For me it was a mixture of everything. It was a way of holding on to Dave, and it was scary to be alone. Choc is solid, like the Rock of Gibraltar. And he's a great storyteller – he made me laugh again.' And for Choc? 'He doesn't talk about his emotions. So I don't really know. He was probably holding on to Dave, too.'

The climbing tribe deeply mourns its dead. Those who have disappeared without trace are immortalised, frozen in memory as romantic heroes. Their partners, wittingly or not, enshrine their memory. When Joe Tasker died I sensed his climbing friends were sorry that what they did, what they were so passionate about, had caused me to suffer. They wanted to help me, to protect me in whatever way they could. But they also seemed to need me, as if I encompassed a little part of Joe, a lingering memory that they welcomed in their midst. For a year after Joe died, his closest friend took me under his wing. We went to parties, we went skiing together, we shared countless bottles of wine. Finally, we had a very brief affair. It began, perhaps, because we were seeking something of Joe in the other. It ended messily, wrecking our friendship. Beyond Joe's memory, there had been nothing to find, but I understood the comfort that such a surrogate love could offer. Days after the accident on Shishapangma, in October 1999, Conrad Anker wrote in a dispatch to MountainZone.com, 'For whatever reason, I didn't become an angel in this avalanche – I walked away from it and I'll never know why . . . Now that I've gotten another chance to do something in life I'd really like to help people out.' The first thing he did was help Alex Lowe's widow and three boys cope with the tragedy. Jenny Lowe, a long-term member of the mountaineering tribe, surely understood his gesture. When love grew between them, and they married, Conrad started easing out of the high-altitude arena – a luxury that not all second-time-around climbing wives enjoy.

Linda Wylie was a newcomer to the mountaineering tribe when Anatoli Boukreev offered physical comfort after Greg's death. Later, he would say he always remembered the sadness on her face when he first saw her in a tea-house on the trail to Everest. After they parted in Kathmandu, he kept in touch, writing to her over the next year from his base camps on Everest, Dhaulagiri and Manaslu. On 1 January 1996, he called her from his family home in Korkino, Russia, to tell her his father had died. He wanted to see her. She was planning to return to the Himalaya in March, to trek up to Everest Base Camp again. He was due to be there at the same time, working for Scott Fischer's guiding company, Mountain Madness. When she arrived in Kathmandu, he was waiting for her at her hotel, with an invitation to dinner. 'She is happy to see me, she is attracted to me,' he wrote in his diary. 'I can read it in her eyes. I like her as well.'

Days later Linda trekked into Namche Bazaar with the Himalayan Guides expedition. Once again, Anatoli was waiting for her. The setting was exotic: rain falling on bright, wet streets, the buildings coloured with Tibetan symbols, bells ringing in a nearby temple, a smell of incense in the air. He wooed her with melancholy Russian songs, with old-fashioned chivalry and with constant attention. For a while she resisted. 'Finally, I asked myself not just how, but why I should refuse the affections of such a man.' The contract was made – Linda was willing to gamble, to be there for Anatoli. 'You are not sad anymore,' he observed after they became lovers. 'You have survived and now you are a present to me from Greg.'

As they trekked together to Everest Base Camp, Linda was exultant. 'When you adjust to the altitude there's some lightness of being that comes. The thin air is actually intoxicating. It's as though everything is finely etched in your view, as though you're focussing on the space between molecules. It's the best feeling I know, to be above 4,000 metres and acclimated, and strong. You feel like you're on another planet.' The last time she was on that trail she was in mourning; now she was newly in love. She and Anatoli spent a romantic month together at Base Camp. On many nights, Anatoli could be heard singing Linda to sleep in his Russian tent, an improbable bright blue affair printed with flowers. 'It was a delightful time,' she said. 'A sweet time, in the most dramatic setting on earth.'

It was also, quite literally, the calm before the storm. Linda recalls watching Anatoli, Scott Fischer and Rob Hall striding around base camp together, three strong, beautiful and confident men. 'We were in the Throne Room of the Gods. None of them looked like they were going to die. They were full of hubris, in front of this mountain. Scott was always saying, "Hey Toli, why don't we climb K2 with a Russian team?" And Toli would say, "First we must live through this." He was so careful. And he wanted so much to do a good job for Scott.'

She left during the third week of April. Anatoli trekked out of Base Camp with her as far as the settlement of Gorak Shep. In a tender goodbye, he filled her pockets with sweets and set his camera on auto-timer, posing with his arm around her for a dozen photographs. 'To remember,' he said.

On 10 May, back in Santa Fe, she received the first of a series of phone calls from Everest Base Camp. A tragedy was unfolding – twenty-four climbers were trapped near the summit by a ferocious storm. Reports were muddled, it was chaos up there, but Linda knew Anatoli was high on the mountain. She sat by the telephone, numb, waiting for news. 'I remember getting the call that Anatoli was all right, and thinking, It's not me this time. Then feeling so bad that I was relieved. It's terrible. You know that somebody else's life is in shambles.'

Two days later, Anatoli called her. He had gone out into the storm, time and time again, bringing three people to safety. Eight more died, including his close friend Scott Fischer and the New Zealand mountain guide Rob Hall. 'He said, "Oh Linda, I'm crazy. The things that happened, it was terrible. But I have to tell you, I'm going to climb Lhotse. I'm sorry."'

To ease his grief over the events on Everest, he had decided to speed-climb Lhotse, an 8,511-metre mountain, solo. 'It was difficult to hear that,' said Linda. 'It was awful. But I understood.'

By the end of May, Anatoli was with Linda in Santa Fe, resting before Scott Fischer's memorial. He was exhausted, and racked by terrible nightmares. He slept through the days, waking sporadically and wanting to eat, waking in the middle of the night and needing to talk, for hours on end. By mid June he was beginning to recover, but new nightmares soon followed. News came from Kazakhstan that his mother, who had had a heart attack on the day he was trying to save Scott Fischer on Everest, had died. An article about the Everest disaster, written by Jon Krakauer and published in *Outside* magazine, questioned Anatoli's behaviour as a guide on the Mountain Madness expedition and suggested that his actions may have added to the tragedy, sparking a storm of controversy. While travelling through Tajikistan in late 1996, he was in a bad bus accident. The person in front of him was decapitated and Anatoli injured an eye. As if to fight off these problems, he continued to climb at a frenetic pace, mostly in the Himalaya – Everest and Lhotse again, Cho Oyu, Shishapangma, Broad Peak and Gasherbrum II. 'During that period of our relationship we faced one challenge after another,' said Linda. 'It was like having to live out some myth.'

Between his climbs, he returned to the peace of Linda's world and her solicitous attentions. 'I spoiled him and made him laugh. He loved my house, how quiet it was. He would get up every morning and make a fire and make oat meal. One evening we were sitting by the fire and he said, "This is like a harbour for me. You are like a lake and the water is very still. And I can rest here." He used me a lot for that.'

And for Linda, what were the rewards? She relished the drama of their lives. 'Like a latter day Ulysses, he journeyed in a world of cataclysm and giants,' she wrote later, 'armed only with wit and strength, to meet destiny unafraid.' He gave her his trust, which she regarded as a great honour. Their love together was 'happy, exciting, passionate, full of funny moments'. And intense. 'He came back from the mountains transparent. Every minute I was with him, every time I looked at him, I was grateful he was alive. I wanted to touch him, make sure he was happy.'

They spent the spring of 1997 in Nepal, and took a six week climbing trip in Kazakhstan. They worked on his book *The Climb* together. They wasted no time. 'For those two years,' she said, 'the world was our oyster. That intensity is addictive and hard to leave behind.'

By the end of 1997, barely two years into their love affair, Anatoli lay dead on Annapurna, buried by an avalanche. Linda Wylie insists that the pain of her loss has been worth the joy of knowing and loving him. 'You struggle with letting go of them and that's really the higher calling of being a mountaineer's lover. Always releasing them to their fate and their destiny, knowing that there's a possibility that they won't come back to you. Yet you don't want to spend your time saying that you're afraid or that they shouldn't go, because you know they love it. In a way, all mountaineers are married first to the mountains and second to their families. So it requires a kind of sacrifice in a woman that is either foolish or beautiful, or a little of both.'

It wasn't a sacrifice I was prepared to make again. After Joe Tasker died, I stayed within the tribe for a time, grateful for the comfort and support it offered. But over the course of the next few years, several friends of mine died in the mountains, their glimmer, like Joe's, suddenly reduced to a shadow. I vowed I would never let myself fall in love with another mountaineer. To avoid the possibility, I moved to the opposite side of the world, and stepped outside the boundaries of the tribe. Sometimes I missed the vicarious excitement, the wild times, the sense of life renewed after long, uncertain separations. Sometimes I remembered the silence when Joe went away. How it stretched and stretched, to the point where I knew it had to break. Anticipating that moment, stepping towards the ringing phone, hoping with every cell in my body that it would be his voice on the other end, saying he was safe and on his way home.

3

In Thrall

ineteen ninety-two, Panch Chuli V. In a tiny tent pinned to a narrow ice ledge above a thousand feet of space, he waits for his friends. Four of them. Gone twenty-two hours now. They should have made the summit long ago, and been back on the ledge, drinking tea, exulting in their success. Dread gnaws at his gut. The deaths almost always happen at the end of an expedition. The final trip through the icefall. One last push for the summit. Now, one more peak before going home. Yesterday, crossing that slope beneath an overhanging tower of ice, he tried to get the others to turn around. The fear – he rarely felt it so sharply in his youth. But they were determined to carry on, just like he would have been at their age, twenty-odd years ago.

He leans out, stares up into the darkness. No pinpricks of light. No human sound. Only the flicker of a distant electric storm, the patter of snowflakes on the tent. No sign. If they don't make it back . . . They took all the ropes. The descent is a chaos of icefalls, huge crevasses, crumbling snow bridges. Alone. A long, dangerous haul to reach help. To reach a phone. Tears prick his eyes. He can't face it. Not again. Especially not with four of them. Delivering news that will shatter lives. Going home to face the ones left behind, looking into their eyes, finding the right words. He's done it too many times already. Betty, Beth, Carolyn, Hilary, Maria. And now – if they don't come back – who else? Rosie.

Jan. Maggie. Rose. He sits on the ledge, in the darkness, huddled in the tiny tent, counting the widows.

He's due back soon. Is she worried? Not that she'll admit to. For her these expeditions are like walking a tightrope. She must concentrate to keep her balance; worrying is the same as looking down. Something she'd rather not do. . . .

Nineteen ninety-two was a good year. Chris Bonington made it back from Panch Chuli V, a remote Himalayan mountain, and so did his four companions, although not without mishap. One of them, Stephen Venables, fell on the descent from the summit, breaking both legs. During their efforts to bring him to safety, Chris also fell, over a thousand feet, but survived. By then Wendy Bonington had been walking her tightrope for thirty years. Number of expeditions – more than fifteen, not including all the forays to the mountains of the Alps. Number of friends lost on those expeditions – seven. Number of friends killed on other mountains – too depressing to count. Number of times Wendy tended the emotionally wounded – innumerable, and ongoing. Each death was like a stone thrown into the pool of her life, the ripples never-ending.

The first was John Harlin in 1966, plummeting from the North Face of the Eiger. It was Chris who skied to the base of the wall to identify the body. It was Wendy who drove the icy roads to carry the news to Marilyn Harlin and her two children. She was spared the task; others got there just before her.

Chris has never had to break such news, not directly. There's always been a buffer. Someone else on the front line. Wendy. His secretary, Louise Wilson.

Louise's first job for Chris was to help him organise an expedition to the South West Face of Everest, in 1975. It was a big effort – a team of eighteen, sixty high-altitude porters, tons of gear – which Chris ran with military precision. On the expedition committee, in an advisory role, was Lord Hunt, who had led the first ascent of Everest in 1953. During one of the meetings in London, Hunt took Louise aside. He explained that high-altitude mountaineering was very dangerous, and fatalities were common. 'You must be aware of what might happen,' he said, 'and you must be prepared for all the administration it will involve.'

Louise collected the names of the climbers' next of kin, and numbers where they could be contacted, day and night. With Wendy's help, she lined up friends, acquaintances, local clergy, reliable people who were willing, if necessary, to be the ones to go round and knock on the door, to make the phone call. And to do it fast. 'I realized that if some bad news came through we've have maybe a couple of hours before the press got hold of it,' she said. 'So it had to be someone we felt confident in.' They also listed others they could ask to go in a little later, as back up support.

To some extent, Wendy was prepared. By then, as well as John Harlin, there had been Ian Clough on Annapurna, young Tony Tighe on Everest. But Louise was new to this. 'Until Lord Hunt talked to me, I hadn't really considered the dangers.' she said. 'But then I began to look into it more deeply, and I saw that he was right. After that I was on tenterhooks, always aware that something could happen.' At the very end of the South West Face of Everest Expedition, Mick Burke disappeared without trace. Three years later, Nick Estcourt was swept away by an avalanche on K2. Four years after that, it was Joe and Pete who died. Lord Hunt had been right; dealing with death was part of her job description.

Usually, it was the embassy who called with the news. Only once was it Chris. 'I was at home. It was breakfast time,' Louise recalled. 'I don't know where he was calling from, maybe Lhasa. He just said, "It's terrible, it's terrible, Joe and Pete have been killed." We cried and cried. Then I had to pull myself together and go straight over to Badger Hill to start phoning, to help Wendy.'

What Chris had to do in the wake of the tragedies wasn't easy. Visiting the families, attending the services, delivering eulogies. Offering kindly hugs, an apologetic sadness. But after all the condolences were delivered he knew, and the families knew, that he was going back to the mountains, risking it all again.

For a time after Joe died, Wendy was an island of peace for me, a place I could swim to through the confusion. I remember wailing in her kitchen, phoning early in the morning to tell her my dreams, walking the dogs with her in my insatiable need for her kind ear. And I was just one in a long line of many. Daniel, her eldest son, remembers how as a child he wondered about 'all the women coming to stay with Mum . . . the crying and tears'.

Recently, I asked Wendy about the emotional toll of mopping up so much sorrow. 'It's not a toll,' she said. She refuses to cast a negative light over her experiences; she stays aware of the past but 'it's not useful to look back and count it up'. What she did was listen, and share with the bereaved her own hard-won understanding of grief.

After John Harlin died on the Eiger, while Wendy was comforting his widow and children, Chris and the rest of the team went back up the mountain, in deteriorating weather. They were storm-bound for days. Chris got frostbite and spent six weeks in hospital. Shortly after his discharge, he left to climb Sangay, an active volcano in Ecuador. In his absence, Wendy took their two-year-old son Conrad to Scotland, to visit a friend. At the bottom of the friend's garden was a stream, a harmless trickle that children had played next to for years. A sudden cloud burst swelled its waters; Conrad wandered away from his playmates, and fell in. It was Wendy who found his body.

Wendy has a rule about not sending Chris bad news when he is in the mountains. She fears it will distract him, disturbing the focus that keeps him safe. This time she broke that rule. She needed to reach Chris, to share the burden of pain. But in the wild reaches of Ecuador, Chris was out of easy contact. A week later, just as he was about to climb Sangay, the message from Wendy arrived on foot, handed to him by a man who came running into camp. All these years later, neither can speak of that time without tears.

By the time Wendy Bonington was twelve years old she was announcing to friends that she would never marry someone with a nine-to-five job. Her perfect mate would be 'an outdoors type, a hunky man in a lumberjack shirt'. A decade later, hearing that a mountaineer was going to be at a friend's party, she decided to check him out. The slender and baby-faced Chris Bonington didn't fit her physical image of a future mate, but she was attracted by his enthusiasm and warmth. The only potential hitch was that he was working at the time as a margarine salesman.

'If he'd stayed doing that, I'm not sure how long our relationship would have lasted,' she said. 'Having to be the wife of a businessman with a regular life could have rocked the boat badly.' She got her wish – life with Chris has been far from regular. 'I appreciate having chunks of time alone,' she said, of their frequent separations. 'I love Chris being around, but when he's absent physically I can explore my private thinking.' She has her own passions, including teaching the Alexander Technique and playing golf, which appears to be as addictive for her as climbing is for Chris.

Not long after Conrad's death, Wendy became pregnant again; within a few years she had two more sons. She stayed at home with them while Chris went away, year after year, to the mountains. The boys are now in the thirties, and married. Chris continues to climb, with great enthusiasm. Wendy seems wary of speaking her fears about him out loud, careful of what she offers of herself for public consumption. And she is always supportive of Chris. 'Love to me is the whole plant,' she said recently. 'Once we put conditions on something, that is cutting off one branch of growth. There are very often things about another person that you cannot understand, but to me that does not change whether you love them or not.'

When I first entered the climbing tribe, I looked to the 'veteran' wives and girlfriends of mountaineers, hoping to find ways to cope with the challenges of my new relationship. Around many of them, I sensed a wall of silence. They didn't seem to want to question the life, or complain about it. The implicit understanding was: you knew he was a climber when you met him, you know what climbers do, take it or leave it.

Jan Scott admitted that when Doug first left on an expedition, shortly after they were married, she was so sick with worry, 'I literally took to my bed.' By the time their first two children came along, Doug was away climbing more than ever, and his determination to get to the mountains seemed to Jan 'like a rejection of me and the kids'. To make it bearable, she decided that she was the one who would have to change, as Doug offered no compromise. She threw herself into her teaching job, developing a life that could function with or without him. This, she wrote in 1975, won her his respect, 'so when I'm screeching at him because he's going off for three months and hasn't paid the phone bill, he doesn't think of me as the idiot wife'.

There were other things she had to do in order to survive in the relationship. Never tell him not to go to the mountains. 'Doug's need to go climbing was like a rat in his gut. I didn't feel I had any right to keep that rat there. It would have just been gnawing away at him. He used to go off and do his own thing and come back much happier.'

Make some choices. 'When I first started teaching I was told I was
head teacher material. I knew that was a thing I could not possibly do
as long as I was married to Doug. I was already at the limit of what I
could do, being a class teacher and being married to him.'

Hang in. 'It took me the first seven years of being married to Doug
to come to terms with being happy and content within our
relationship.'

Those seven years stretched from when she married him at barely
twenty, through the birth of their son, and until their first daughter
arrived. Years when Doug was away climbing and travelling in the
Alps, Afghanistan, Chad and the Himalayas, and she was at home, with
a baby, no car and very little money. Gradually, as his fame grew, their
financial situation improved and Jan was able to start accompanying
him on lecture tours in North America. When the last child, Rosie, was
nine months old, the whole family trekked to Everest Base Camp. For
Jan, this was one of the 'enormous pluses' of her life with a
mountaineer. Sharing some of the excitement and the travel. The
stimulating friends who flowed endlessly through their house, the
frequent parties.

At the peak of his climbing career there was always a buzz around
Doug Scott. His strength and ability to survive in the most extreme
circumstances were the stuff of legend and this, along with his air of
quiet, steady wisdom, his quirky brand of spirituality and his generosity
of spirit, won him many followers. To some, he was a guru; people
were enchanted by him, and Jan basked in the glow of that enchant-
ment. 'Before I met him I was just an ordinary person,' she said. 'My
parents went through the Depression and it had a lasting effect on their
lives. Until he joined the army, my dad couldn't get any other job
except a bell-pusher on a tram. He has always lived with that. He's
always been very conservative. Our family never went abroad, and it
was years before we had a car. With Doug, life was exciting. I was quite
happy to go along on his coat tails. There is something magic about
climbers. If you are prepared to let yourself, you can be taken along that
path by your partner in a positive way.'

A friend of the couple, the US climber Greg Child, remembers them
in the 1970s as 'wild and fun and very beautiful'. Years later, that is how
Jan liked to remember herself and Doug, too. She didn't want to linger
on the rest. The times when she was driven crazy by the long

separations, the worry, the emotional uncertainties. Or how Doug eventually left her for another woman. She forgave him all that. They remained good friends, and right up until her death from cancer in early 2003, she looked back fondly on their past.

Not all the 'veteran' wives were so supportive. 'Climbers are very single-minded and unspeakably selfish,' said Ruth Seifert. 'There is no compromise in what they do. No compromise whatsoever.'

Ruth, a consultant psychiatrist, is married to Charlie Clarke, who has frequently accompanied Chris Bonington to the Himalaya, usually in the role of doctor and base camp manager. Although he's not a mainstream mountaineer, expeditions took Charlie far away from his family and his career as a consultant neurologist almost every year, for twenty years. Their house was a London 'base camp' for many climbers, and among them Ruth's hospitality and outspoken wit was legendary. Joe Tasker adored her, and they were good friends. During my time with him, and especially after his death, she also became an important touchstone for me, always ready to offer support and wise counsel. But there was no 'take it or leave it' attitude with Ruth. No wall of silence. 'I don't see why mountaineers need to be protected. What? They're going to have absolutely everything? Plus the dear faithful wife who's never to say anything horrid about them? Well, that's too much to ask frankly.'

Ruth met Charlie at a London medical school when they were both in their twenties. Charlie was already mountaineering, but at first Ruth thought it was just a hobby. Then they got married, and he persuaded her to go to Kashmir for their honeymoon. She realised he couldn't live without climbing, and she soon understood the reasons why. 'Charlie's father had been a very successful doctor, a geneticist, a professor of medicine, the president of the Royal College of Physicians. Charlie could never compete with that. I think it left him with a deep sense of inadequacy. I think that they all have that, somewhere. I think that every single person that does this sort of thing doesn't feel whole, they feel they have to go on proving and proving and proving, filling in a massive gap and helping themselves survive their feelings of not being good enough. I don't think they feel real unless they're taking themselves to extremes.'

Charlie, she realised, came into his element in the mountains. He was a different person when he went away, more lively and confident. Like other mountaineers he felt alive in high wild places. It was a feeling that home life couldn't provide. 'So Chris left Wendy with babies. Charlie left me with babies and a full-time job. They thought, What's such a big deal? I'm a brave mountaineer, I'm doing something incredibly dangerous here and all you have to do is look after the house and family. Let's get this into proportion.'

It's three decades since Ruth and Wendy were at home with their babies. Has anything changed for the next generation of climbers' wives?

'Well, I can't really complain,' said Paula Viesturs flatly, the day before her husband returned from an attempt on Annapurna, in the spring of 2002. 'I guess I knew when I married Eddie that this is how it was going to be.'

Paula met Ed Viesturs at a barbecue in Seattle. The fact that he was a highly regarded mountaineer and had climbed Everest didn't impress her much, nor was she particularly excited when he asked for her phone number. 'I had moved to Seattle just four months before,' she said, 'and I was enjoying being single.' He didn't phone, but two days later she was out walking with a friend when they bumped into Ed, who was on a training run. He asked her out on a date. 'After that, we were inseparable.'

Ed taught Paula how to climb and together they did ascents of Mount Rainier and other peaks in the Pacific Northwest. In 1995 she accompanied him to Everest Base Camp. The following year, two weeks after they got married, they were heading there again. Ed was part of a team led by David Breashears that was planning to make an IMAX movie on Everest. Paula was their base camp manager, a job that included supervising the menu planning and cooking. In a remote, barren campground, 17,600 feet above sea level, for a large group of climbers. On her honeymoon.

On the afternoon of 9 May, Paula paused from making soup, stepped out of the cook tent and looked at the mountain. As usual at this time of the day, clouds were forming, and streaming up the flanks of Everest. But these clouds were much bigger and darker than usual. At base camp, it was snowing hard; further up the mountain, conditions would be far worse. Her husband, along with the rest of the IMAX team, was at Camp Two. Earlier in the day they had decided to hold off going for the summit, until the crowds there cleared. Around fifty people were on their way towards the top of the mountain. Among them were Ed's good friends Rob Hall and Scott Fischer, both leading commercial expeditions.

Over the following twenty-four hours, a series of factors quick-brewed into a disaster that Jon Krakauer later brought to world attention through his book *Into Thin Air*. A large number of inexperienced climbers going for the summit beyond the usual turnaround time, paring down their already sliver-thin margin of safety. A human bottleneck forming at the Hillary Step, as climbers waited their turn to negotiate the fixed ropes. Oxygen running out. Hypoxia setting in. The onset of a storm, bringing brutal winds and blinding blizzards.

At base camp, someone from the New Zealand expedition came to tell Paula that things were going very wrong on the mountain. She went over to their main tent. 'I pretty much stayed there after that. A lot of us gathered there, sleeping on the floor, listening to the radio calls.' The storm had trapped a number of climbers near the summit. Those who escaped it were staggering into Camp Four on the South Col, at 26,000 feet, in various stages of shock, exhaustion, hypoxia and frostbite. People were dying. Doug Hansen, one of Rob Hall's clients, perished just below the summit, after becoming too weak to move. Hall had stayed with him all night, in the open, at 28,000 feet. Now it was his turn to be incapacitated, and he was calling for someone to bring him oxygen and water. All of this news Paula relayed to Ed and the IMAX team, who were moving up the mountain, hoping to help the survivors on their way.

On the evening of 11 May, Paula, and many other people on Everest, listened in to a heartbreaking radio exchange between Rob Hall and his pregnant wife Jan Arnold, whose call had been patched through to him from New Zealand. A group of Sherpas had tried to mount a rescue from Camp Four, but were beaten back by the ferocious winds. The sun was slipping away, another night was about to close around Rob, bringing its deadly cold. Jan was an experienced mountaineer. She had stood on the summit of Everest; she understood the full import of her husband's situation. Hearing his slurred, hypoxic voice, she knew he could not survive another night in the open. 'I just know you're going to be rescued,' she said. 'I'm looking forward to making you completely better when you come home.' Rob told her he loved her, bade her to sleep well, and said she should try not to worry too much.

Try not to worry too much. By the time the storm over Everest had passed, eight people were dead, including Rob Hall and Scott Fischer, and others were badly injured. All Paula Viesturs wanted for herself and her new husband was to cut this honeymoon short, pack up and go home. In a radio call to David Breashears, she suggested that the team should think about what happened next, once they got back to Base Camp. 'In my eyes,' she said recently, 'after having gone through those days, after losing Rob, Scott and everyone else, the expedition was over. Then all of a sudden David's saying, "No. Hey, we're going to go up."'

According to David's book, *High Exposure*, what he actually said was far more blunt. 'This isn't your decision. You're not part of that debate . . . You can either support us or you can leave.'

She left. She walked out of Base Camp as far as Namche Bazaar with the New Zealand team, who had lost several members in the storm, including their leader, Rob Hall. She spent a few days alone. Then she returned to Base Camp, telling Ed that she supported his decision to go back up the mountain.

'It was hard,' she admits. 'I was on the edge of my seat when they were going for the summit.'

Why would anyone offer such support? 'There is a divine child in all of us – a symbol of the self, the core of who we are,' says the psychiatrist Sam Naifeh. 'It is sacred and lovely, something no one wants to destroy. You think, How can I tell him not to go, if he's so alive? The look in the eye will go dead. What am I doing? You'd be taking someone's life away, that's the feeling of it.'

And you would be trying to change the person you were drawn to in the first place – something that Joe Tasker often reminded me of. Something that other climbers' partners often attest to. 'The risk-taking is so much a part of his nature, if he stopped going away on these trips, I'm not sure he'd be the man I want to live with,' said Sue Ibara, about her husband Mark Jenkins, a columnist for *Outside* magazine. 'To tell you the truth, when he's here at home, telling me about an impending trip, I think, That's okay. But when I'm taking him to the airport, it's a different tune. The minute I'm seeing him off my knees go weak and I'm thinking, Please be safe. Please be the one to come home.'

Over the last few years, Ed Viesturs has been trying to become the first North American to climb the world's fourteen highest mountains without using supplementary oxygen. So far he has done twelve of them. Two remain, Nanga Parbat and Annapurna, which he has attempted twice. Ed has a reputation for being a highly cautious climber, willing to turn back if conditions aren't exactly right, or if his gut instinct tells him it's best not to carry on. Annapurna has a reputation for being a killer mountain; one out of every fourteen of the climbers who have reached its summit has not made it down alive. In the spring of 2002, after giving up his attempt on Annapurna, Ed told Paula that he might not try again 'But he said that two years ago when he didn't get to the summit,' she said, 'and here he is again.'

Paula doesn't accompany Ed on trips any more. She stays at home looking after their small son Gil and their baby daughter Ella. Now she has a double responsibility – as well as dealing with her own concerns for Ed's safety, she has to manage her children's. While Ed was on Annapurna in 2002, four-year-old Gil sometimes asked Paula what would happen if his daddy got hit by an avalanche. 'He's understanding more of the dangers now,' she said. 'He hears people talking. He's looked at books. He's getting a feeling for the whole thing, even though he's never seen a mountain that big. He got Ed on the satellite phone the other day, when he called from Annapurna and said, "Daddy, when you come home will you teach me how to mountain climb?"'

Ella was too young to understand how long her father was away, but Gil felt the absence keenly. Paula tried to structure the time for him – every day they would go to the calendar and mark off the date. As the number of marks increased, Gil's excitement about his father's return grew. The day before Ed was due to fly back to Seattle from Kathmandu, Paula woke Gil in the morning and told him that tomorrow they would be picking up Daddy at the airport. 'He said, 'Can we just go back to sleep right now and when we wake up we can go and pick him up?' He was so excited, it was like Christmas Eve.'

Charlie Clarke's daughters were nine and six in 1982, when he was in Tibet with the British Everest Expedition. On learning from their mother that Joe Tasker and Peter Boardman had died on the mountain, they became worried that their father, too, might not come home. Reticent to promise something she herself was unsure of, Ruth Seifert struck a bargain with the two girls. 'What they had always wanted since they were very little was a white flat with a white carpet and a white rabbit. So I said, 'If Daddy doesn't come back we'll move into a flat and we'll have a beautiful white sofa and a white carpet and a rabbit.' They were so happy. A few days later, I heard from Charlie. I said to the girls, 'Daddy's fine. He'll be back soon.' They went 'Aaaaw . . .' They were slightly disappointed because we'd sat and talked about all these lovely things we'd do if he didn't come home.'

Privately, Ruth was in a fury. 'I thought, What a bloody bastard for doing this to me. Can't he stay by his post and behave like other men? Why do I have to look after everything? If he'd died, I'd have been left with that anger. The other awful thing was that when I heard that Joe and Pete had died, the first thing I felt was relief that it wasn't Charlie. And that is the most poisonous thing – to put anyone in the position of being relieved when two people you're incredibly fond of have died.'

In 1982, it took three weeks for the news of Joe and Pete's death to reach Ruth, and the rest of us, in Britain. Back then, the only communication with an expedition was via letters, which arrived sporadically, long after they had been written. Most of us managed the separation, and the worry, by splitting the expedition into stages. The first couple of weeks were easy – we imagined the climbers walking into base camp and facing little danger. Then they were establishing lower camps – not so bad. The really anxious time set in as they got higher up the mountain, preparing for the summit push. Then came the longest, most nerve-racking silences.

These days, some expeditions have satellite phones, send out emails and post regular dispatches on their websites. The silences are few and far between – if climbers have the technology, they can contact their families on an almost daily basis. But this doesn't necessarily decrease the worry factor. 'Sometimes I think it's easier when I can't talk to him,' said Lauren Synnott, the wife of an alpinist sponsored by the American outdoor clothing company The North Face. 'You're always thinking it may be him when the phone rings. You don't want to be gone from home in case you miss a call. Life is just easier if you put him on the back burner and do your own thing one hundred per cent until he gets home.'

For several months of each year, while Mark Synnott is away climbing, Lauren is at home alone in New Hampshire with their two children, a toddler and a baby. The possibility of becoming a climbing widow crystallised for her in 1999 when Alex Lowe was killed on Shishapangma, a month after he and Mark were in Pakistan together, climbing Great Trango Tower. 'It really brought it home to me. I just have to block the worry out. It does affect our marriage because I put up an emotional wall when he leaves, and when he comes back it's hard to instantly tear it down. I always have a wall up, to be honest, because he's gone so much – it never comes all the way down. The wall is preparing myself for if I ever did have to deal without him.'

When Ed Viesturs leaves on a trip, his wife, too, finds that her thinking changes. 'I trust his judgement, but there's always a chance of something happening. Suddenly I'm responsible for everything, and I think, What if he doesn't come home? What would I do?'

His regular website dispatches provide little reassurance. Paula knows that he gives them an optimistic, upbeat spin, and that later she will learn the full truth about the conditions – and the dangers – he faced. And like Lauren Synnott, she's not crazy about the satellite phone connections. 'It helps that I hear his voice, that I know he's okay,' she said. 'But the connections aren't that good and sometimes you can't complete a sentence before you get cut off. I find it to be terribly irritating. And there's nothing intimate about our conversations. He's in such a different place than me, so to talk about how my day was, well, it's just too much of a contrast. We have a hard time relating. He tells me he thinks about me all the time, and that he loves the kids, but when you don't really talk for two months, a lot of things go unsaid. That's one of the hard parts of him coming home.'

Another hard part is breaking through the 'exclusive club' that forms during Ed's expeditions. The members of the club are his team, and particularly his regular climbing partner Veikka Gustaffson. For months at a time these men inhabit a special world, far above the confines of daily life, that no one on the outside can ever fully understand, or share. When Ed called Paula from Kathmandu, on his way home from Annapurna in 2002, she raised this issue with him. 'I was actually kind of mad. I said, "Eddie, it's going to take a while before we get to know each other again." Veikka's like his other wife. I find myself being kind of jealous of that whole relationship. They're in their raw state together for weeks at a time, surviving, risking their lives. I read his last dispatch, "We've really become a family up here. I'm really going to miss all these people." I know that's a huge part of what he loves about climbing – the joking, the camaraderie – and I think that's really great, I want that for him. On the other hand I felt like saying, "You've got a family at home too."'

The return home can be a rude awakening for the climber. For weeks or months he has had a singular focus, and a simple, uncluttered life. He has been out fighting dragons, moving through landscapes of mythical proportions, dealing with fundamental issues of courage and survival. Suddenly he is back in the slow river of domestic life, a never-ending flow of chores, demands and small, mundane concerns. And a wife used to being without him.

'Re-entry time' is what Erin Simonson calls her husband Eric's return from his expeditions. 'It's as if you're trying to get the gears to re-engage, but the clutch is slipping. The gears don't automatically mesh right away, and there's a time where you hear them grinding constantly, trying to get all the teeth to lock smoothly.'

It used to take Jan Scott weeks to adjust to Doug being back in her life after a long expedition. While he was away, she had everything well organised, and his return upset the whole schedule. Other wives recognised this pattern. 'Charlie was a nuisance,' said Ruth Seifert. 'He just wrecked the whole well-oiled machine. And so I resented it. Also, I had to then fit into his schedule. Why should that be? He never fitted into ours. They come back and expect that the whole universe of their home is going to revolve around them . . . God, I hated him when he came back. He was so full of himself. And then, after every expedition, he became depressed. And so I wasn't adequate – none of the wives could ever supply the real love and the enormous romance that they have with the mountains.'

Part of that romance follows them home, particularly if they were involved in high-profile expeditions. When the Everest IMAX movie was released, Ed and Paula Viesturs were invited to many openings and dinners. Inevitably, the spotlight of attention was focused on Ed, and

Paula stood in his shadow, answering all the usual questions about him. 'In the end it was like, okay, he isn't Gandhi,' she said. 'I don't show up at things like that any more.'

After the first all-British ascent of Everest in 1975, the climbing team and their families were invited to Buckingham Palace to meet the Queen, and to Downing Street to be hosted by the Prime Minister. Ruth Seifert remembers basking for a while in reflected glory – and then tiring of being sidelined socially by people wanting to talk to Charlie, and not her. 'You're subsumed underneath their umbrella. You start disappearing. The way I dealt with it is that, because I'm bossy and loud anyway, I became more bossy and loud when we went out. I overshadowed him and never let him say anything. If anyone said, "Charlie, do tell us about your last expedition," I'd go, "NO! Fuck off! It's boring, I'm not listening, I'll leave the dinner party." And when people said to me, "It must be marvellous being married to a mountaineer," I wanted to die. "I'M HERE!" I was shouting. "Look what I've done!" And I didn't want to listen to his stories and I never wanted to read his books because I'd lived through it.'

The 'glimmer' around Joe Tasker that I had found so attractive was especially intense right after his expeditions. Inevitably, other women were drawn to it. Joe enjoyed the public attention his exploits brought him, especially from female quarters. He loved women and was an inveterate flirt. Often the flirting was harmless; at other times, it was the prelude to an affair.

'A lot of climbers see affairs as being almost as compulsive as the climbing,' said Jim Curran, a filmmaker, and an old friend of Joe's, who was on the Mount Kongur expedition with him in 1981. 'They've given themselves permission because they've put their lives on the line. Having the odd shag here and there seems a lot less dangerous than what you're doing on the mountain.'

Within the mountaineering tribe the stories abound. The climbing guide writing passionate letters to his wife from base camp, omitting to mention that another woman is keeping him company. The deeply devoted husband who turns up from time to time to give climbing lectures with a strange woman on his arm. The climber who offers to sleep with a friend's widow, the night of the memorial service. The climber who comes home after a long expedition, and starts an affair.

'After expeditions, they were ordinary again,' said Ruth Seifert. 'So they needed to break new ground. And they were very easily flattered. None of us wives say, "Oh, you're so wonderful, I want to hear everything. Tell me everything." But other women do. "Oh, you're so brave and so wonderful!" they say. And out puff the men's chests and up go their pricks. So predictable. I used to watch, and without being able to hear the woman's words, I could tell by Charlie's demeanour that she was saying he was a wonderful brave man, and how does he do it. And I'd be thinking, You stupid cow, why aren't you talking to me, asking me how I do it?'

So why did she do it? Why stay married to a mountaineer for all those years? Ask Ruth Seifert this and she laughs and says she was too busy to leave him. 'It's sort of true. I just had about enough energy to do a massively demanding job and bring up the children. If I had to start leaving him – oh God, I just couldn't bear the thought of it really.' But she admits to what is obvious to everyone else – that, despite their ups and downs, she and Charlie 'basically really like and love each other, and always have done'. Admiration, too, seeps through. 'Mountaineers aren't disappointed people. They don't feel they are wasting their lives. They've gone out there and done something.'

There is a pattern that the psychologist Geoff Powter calls the 'repeating personality syndrome', the need for constant change to create excitement. Climbers exhibit it in their restlessness – at home they long to be away on an expedition, and as soon as they get to the mountains, they long to be home again. Their partners exhibit it in their choice of a mate, and the lifestyle that goes along with that person.

'To a certain extent, Eric going on these long expeditions is a positive thing for our relationship,' said Erin Simonson. 'It's like this process of constant renewal. Just about the time we're getting on each other's nerves he goes out the door for a couple of months and it gives me time to reflect on the things I really like about him.'

Four years into her relationship with Mark Synnott, Lauren left him and became engaged to her high-school sweetheart. A regular guy with a regular job, he came home to her every night and weekend, he never went away without her, he wanted to spend all his spare time with her. It should have been a perfect match – Lauren is a self-confessed homebody, with no desire to travel, or even venture far from her small

New Hampshire town. But that wasn't the case. 'The life was so boring,' she said. 'I kept comparing him to Mark.' Soon she had dumped her fiancé, returned to Mark and married him. 'Everyone loves an adventurous spirit, especially if you're not that way yourself. I kind of live vicariously through him.'

Wendy Bonington is clear about why she chose Chris, and what that choice has meant for her. 'If you want to ride an exciting horse,' she said, 'you can expect some bruises and a few narrow moments.' After four decades of marriage, the repeating personality syndrome obviously works for the Boningtons. They behave like love-struck teenagers, flirting with each other, holding hands and cuddling shamelessly in public. I witnessed one of their farewells, as Chris left home to spend a day and a night in London. Wendy and I were sitting at their kitchen table, drinking tea. When Chris appeared, computer case in hand, they clung to each other like barnacles to rock, exchanging long kisses and murmuring endearments. After he had gone, I teased Wendy about it. She smiled, radiating contentment. 'It's long-term glue,' she said.

In 1924, after her husband George was lost without trace on the North-East Ridge of Everest, Ruth Mallory wrote to a friend, 'It was his life I loved, and love.' It's the life Lauren Synnott returned to, after trying to settle for a man with no desire for adventure. The life Paula Viesturs walked back to, in Everest Base Camp. The life Wendy Bonington chose when she was twelve years old. The life that took Ruth Seifert to her extremes. The life that Jan Scott, living alone and battling cancer, looked back on, despite her broken marriage, with delight. None of these women chose ordinary men, or ordinary lives. They chose a life of drama; they chose men enchanted by the mountains, who in turn enchanted them.

A year before Joe Tasker died, he gave a lecture at a prestigious hall in London. Standing at the back of the auditorium, I watched him cast his spell. As he spoke, pictures were projected on a huge screen behind him. Precipitous snow slopes. Knife-edge ridges. Summits soaring into the sky. Places that most people never go, except in imagination. Joe stood before us, brimming with hubris, spinning stories of daring, danger, death. By then I knew his faults, his contradictions, the weaknesses behind the brilliant image. But like everyone else in the audience that night, I was enthralled. I envied him the certainty of his calling. I longed to be so strong, so brave, so focused. To plumb the depths of human endurance, to experience the perfect moments he found on the tops of snowy peaks. He was the hero I could never be, the hero I thought I needed – without any real inkling of what that would cost.

4

The Transcendence Zone

Nanga Parbat. Its summit guarded by the Rupal Face, the biggest mountain wall in the world. A murderous wall: sheer, beset by storms and avalanches. Four Japanese men are attempting it. They enter a long chute called Miracle Gully. A storm breaks. The men do not return. At base camp the rest of their team wait . . . and wait . . . Before abandoning the mountain they climb the fixed ropes to 22,000 feet and leave a duffel bag filled with equipment, food and shelter. A gesture beyond hope; an offering to the dead.

Some years later, four North American men attempt the same mountain, by the same face. They are in Miracle Gully, 1,200 feet from the summit. One man is suffering from altitude sickness. A storm breaks. They retreat. Spindrift avalanches pour over them in waves. One, far bigger than the rest, sweeps them off the face. Their rope holds by a single ice screw. Dangling in panic from the mountain, choked by rushing snow, they expect the screw to fail at any moment, and death to follow. When the avalanche ceases, the sick man's face points upwards, his eyelids frozen shut. 'I was going to unclip,' he tells his friends, 'and get it over with.'

Hour after hour, they fight their way down. Around ten at night, they emerge from Miracle Gully and reach a protective overhang. Two of the men remove the ropes from the final section of the gully. 'I'm letting go of the ropes,' shouts the *man at the top. The wind blows away some of his words. His friend misunderstands. He hears a command. He obeys it. 'Okay, I let go,' he shouts back. Their ropes – their umbilical cords to the mountain, to life – sail away through space.*

They have two choices. To stay where they are and freeze to death. Or to attempt the impossible – descending the Rupal Face without ropes.

Morning. Four specks cling to a mountain by a few slivers of steel – crampons and ice axes. No safety net. A single slip, and they fall 10,000 feet. Chances of survival: negligible. Then they see it . . . a duffel bag, clipped to the wall. Sunbleached. Tattered. Emblazoned with Japanese writing. They cut it open. Sixty pitons spill out. A dozen ice screws. Chocolate bars. A tent. A stove. Two new fifty-metre ropes. An offering from the dead.

Four men on a chosen journey, facing great trials, confronting death, and surviving. An heroic story that stayed with me long after I heard it.

'Heroic?' Mark Twight, a US alpinist, and one of the four men on the Rupal Face, was sceptical. 'I don't think so. When I was younger I was dying to have my accomplishments treated as heroic, but now I don't see it like that. No one was putting a gun to our heads and forcing us to do it. And we weren't doing it for the good of anyone else.'

Most mountaineers willingly admit that climbing is of no benefit to anyone but themselves. 'It's super-selfish,' said the British mountaineer Joe Simpson. 'It has to be. You can't do it otherwise.' And yet their exploits are lauded as heroic, particularly when the mountain in question is Everest. In 1924 George Mallory and Sandy Irvine disappeared on the North East Ridge of Everest, while they were attempting to make the first ascent of the mountain. A memorial service held for the two men in St Paul's Cathedral was attended by representatives of the royal family. In their honour, an eternal flame was set on a plinth at Merton College, Oxford; a plaque was erected on a chapel wall in Shrewsbury; two streets were renamed after them in Birkenhead, Liverpool; memorial windows were placed in Chester Cathedral and in the church in Mallory's home village of Mobberly. 'At last in the flower of his perfect manhood he was lost to human sight,' the Mobberly inscription reads, 'between heaven and earth on the topmost peak of Mount Everest.' In the official expedition book, Geoffrey Bruce was quoted as saying, 'It was worth dying on the mountain to leave a reputation like that.'

With all the great peaks of the world claimed, the days of climbing mountains for the sake of one's country are largely over, but mountaineers continue to be celebrated. For their efforts on Everest, Britain gave Ed Hillary a knighthood; Tenzing Norgay the George Medal; John Hunt membership of the House of Lords; Chris Bonington and Doug Scott the Order of the British Empire, as well as, in Chris's case, a knighthood. On the other side of the Atlantic, the members of the first successful American expedition to Everest in 1963 were invited to the Oval Office to shake hands with John F. Kennedy. Erik Weihenmayer, the first blind climber to scale the mountain, was there in 2001 to meet George Bush. *Time* magazine, covering Weihenmayer's feat, trumpeted it as 'A Hero's Ascent'. What is it about mountain climbing that transforms a fundamentally useless, selfish activity into a heroic act?

The *Oxford English Dictionary* defines a hero as one who 'exhibits extraordinary bravery, firmness, fortitude or greatness of soul in any action'. Mountaineering offers countless opportunities for this definition of heroism. During the spring of 1999, Alex Lowe was preparing to climb the Upper West Rib on Denali, Alaska, when the park service asked him if he would help in the rescue of three Spanish climbers who were trapped on the mountain. Together with Mark Twight and Scott Backes, Alex was helicoptered to 19,500 feet. From there they had to down-climb to the Spaniards and get them back to the waiting helicopter, in a turnaround time of two hours.

When they reached the beleaguered climbers, they found that one had already fallen to his death. For 200 vertical feet they pushed, shoved and hauled the survivors up the fixed ropes. Finally, one of the Spaniards collapsed. Moving him any further seemed impossible, until Alex Lowe announced he would carry him. Mark Twight remembers Alex saying, 'Take my pack. And take off his crampons so they don't rip my jacket.' Hoisting the man on to his back, he carried him up the thirty-five-degree slopes of ice and snow, for another 100 vertical feet, and over a third of a mile. Piggybacked the dead weight up the steep, slippery mountain – a Herculean feat. 'It was one of those things you do because you have to do it,' he said later.

But he didn't have to do it – he could have left the man behind. On the morning of 11 September, 2001, some people stopped racing wildly down the stairwells of the burning Twin Towers in order to help others who were trapped. Imagine such a moment – when you make a split-second decision that affects the chances of your own survival, when the basic instinct of self-preservation is overridden by concern for another human being. Schopenhauer, a nineteenth-century German philosopher, would have called this a breakthrough of a metaphysical realization. He claimed that separateness is an illusion, that our true reality is an interconnectedness with all forms of life. When the four men on the Rupal Face looked into each other's eyes, wondering which of them would survive, it was as if the answer was of no consequence, because in the extremity of their situation they had left behind their individual selves, and become as one. Barry Blanchard claims such moments are 'timeless and the truth.' Schopenhauer would have agreed – such a breakthrough, experienced under certain moments of crisis, is the truth of life. And the hero is someone who is willing to risk his physical life for – albeit it subconsciously – the realization of that truth.

Alex Lowe's phenomenal strength, drive and talents as a climber were legendary. *Outside* magazine called him 'arguably the best climber on the planet'. Fellow mountaineer Tom Hornbein said that his ability 'was like the difference between Horowitz and some ordinary concert pianist. When you watched him climbing there was a flow and a virtuosity that made things look easy that were impossible for most human beings.'

Months after his spectacular rescue effort in Alaska, Alex Lowe died in an avalanche on Shishapangma. The climbing world was stunned. 'Alex's death hit everyone really hard,' said Pete Athans, a fellow North Face-sponsored climber. 'I think we all believed that he was always going to emerge unscathed from his endeavours in the mountains, come back to corporate headquarters and do 500 pull-ups in an hour as usual. It was a serious psychological blow when he died.'

Part of the shock surrounding his death, according to the psychologist Geoff Powter, stemmed from the nature of the accident. Alex was walking on a glacier, across relatively easy ground, out of apparent danger, when an avalanche unleashed thousands of feet above him. He ran in the wrong direction. If he'd followed his friend, Conrad Anker, who was walking just behind him, he might be alive today. 'We want our great heroes to have more noble deaths than that,' said Powter. 'Like falling off some hugely difficult technical pitch – it would have been easier to accept.'

The fact that Alex Lowe left a wife and three sons raised eyebrows among the US media, and led to subsequent questioning of his heroic status. When it became public knowledge that Lowe's widow had begun a relationship with Conrad Anker, the eyebrows went up even higher. '*Outside* magazine published an article from this woman,' said Conrad Anker bitterly. 'It said something like, "Jenny, wake up. You're going out with another self-centred, risk-taking bastard and the real losers are your sons."'

When George Mallory disappeared on Everest in 1924, he too left a wife and small children behind, yet this did nothing to dent his public image. In the wake of the horrors of the First World War, the deaths of Mallory and Sandy Irvine seemed, according to the climbing novelist Roger Hubank, 'like a sacrifice . . . the recovery of something trampled under the mud of Flanders, now made clean again, and simple, like a fire . . . and who would have given a thought then to Mallory's widow and children, in a land filled with widows and fatherless children?' For today's mountaineer, however, heroism is a more tenuous affair. Alison Hargreaves was the darling of the British press in the spring of 1995, when she became the first woman to climb Everest alone and without oxygen. 'Alison of Everest!' one headline trumpeted. The following August, she was on K2, making her final push to the summit. It was late in the day and threatening clouds were forming to the north, but she kept going. At six thirty p.m., she stood on the top of the world's second highest mountain. The sky was clear, the air still. A moment of triumph. But thousands of feet below her, those clouds were generating storm-force winds. 'When wind strikes the bottom of a mountain it has nowhere to go but up,' wrote Ed Douglas and David Rose, in their biography of Alison Hargreaves. 'And as it searches for escape, it accelerates.' About two hours later, winds of approximately 100 m.p.h. struck the upper reaches of K2. Alison, along with five Spanish climbers, was plucked off the mountain, like a speck of lint. She was slammed down again so brutally that her jacket, her harness and one of her boots was ripped off. After the storm subsided another climber found these items. Linking them, a trail of blood led down the mountain to where her body lay, unreachable.

Back in England, media veneration quickly turned to vilification. The fact that Alison was the mother of two small children was seized upon by the press, and used to knock her off the hero's pedestal.

Had Alison turned back from the summit, she, and many of her public, would have considered this a failure. Caution in mountaineering is rarely celebrated, or seen as heroic, but Ed Viesturs – and his sponsors – are managing to shift this perception. Ed has reached the summits of twelve of the world's fourteen highest mountains, without supplementary oxygen. He's also the father of two small children. 'I always felt as a climber that I don't want to do anything ultra-dangerous in the mountains,' he said, 'and now that I have a family I feel that more so. If I fail on a peak because I feel it's too dangerous, I'm happy to walk away.' There's no doubt that he walks his talk. In 1993 he reached the Central Summit of Shishapangma; the true summit was twenty feet higher and 300 feet away, across a knife-edge ridge. Ed was alone, and the ridge was mined with cornices, unstable masses of wind-blown snow. He turned around. On Broad Peak, he turned back 150 feet away from the top because the slope leading to it was too heavily laden with snow. Twice on Everest, in 1987 and in 1995, he stopped at the South Summit, because conditions didn't seem optimum for going to the top. On Annapurna, in 2002, he retreated from an avalanche-prone slope en route to the summit, even after two of his team members had climbed it ahead of him without mishap. In a website dispatch from the mountain he admitted to being 'disappointed that we didn't climb Annapurna. It's one of these things where there are some risks involved . . . but at the same time it's ultra important that you have a very conservative attitude.' After the expedition, a full-page magazine advertisement for one of Ed's sponsors, a manufacturer of woollen garments, showed him on the summit of Manaslu, triumphantly holding his ice axe aloft. 'When Ed Viesturs climbs,' the caption reads, 'he never moves out of his comfort zone.'

The responsible, family-minded mountaineer is but one of the new breed of climbing hero. Another, fast growing in public popularity, is the handicapped mountaineer, a hero driven by the need to overcome a disability, who along the way provides a role model for others. 'When a fifty-year-old man with an artificial leg climbs Mount Everest,' said Arizona-based mountaineer Tom Whittaker, 'it makes a statement – for baby boomers, for people who are infirm, for all kinds of folk who are making excuses for doing less. Maybe it helps to invigorate them to say, "Damn, I really don't have to give up on my dream."'

Whittaker was an experienced alpinist, with ambitions of becoming 'a brand-name mountaineer', when a drunk driver ploughed head on into his van as he was driving to Sun Valley on Thanksgiving Weekend, 1979. Though he lost his right foot and left kneecap to the accident, he was determined to climb again. Within two years, he was scaling the big walls in Yosemite Valley, and had set his sights on becoming the first disabled mountaineer to scale the Seven Summits – the highest peak on each continent. In 1998 he became the first disabled person to climb Mount Everest. This certainly made him a hero in Nepal. The local media dubbed him Bravest of the Brave, Emperor of the Disabled World, and he became patron of a group home in Kathmandu that trains children with disabilities. 'When a person loses a foot in Nepal, his life is as good as over; all he can do is beg,' said Tom. 'For the Nepalese to see someone with one foot not only scale Everest but also lead the expedition – it was huge. There are two and a half million disabled people in Nepal, and suddenly they were seeing me as a champion of their cause. I couldn't ignore that.'

In 2002, Tom Whittaker was beaten in his bid for the Seven Summits by Erik Weihenmayer, who has been blind since the age of thirteen. The year before, Erik climbed Everest. His expedition had been underwritten by the National Federation of the Blind, which hoped to use the attention generated from the ascent to publicise the fact that more than 70 per cent of blind Americans are unemployed, and to change negative attitudes towards blindness. 'It's nice to have a broader cause attached to the climb,' Weihenmayer said. 'It might shatter people's perceptions about blindness, which are often more limiting than the disability itself.'

A ten-man team helped get him up Everest. There was always a climber ahead of him, signalling with a bell and giving him descriptions of the terrain that he had to negotiate. The climber behind him gave course corrections and additional directions. Higher up the mountain, when the team started using oxygen, they communicated with Erik via throat mikes. One of the biggest challenges they faced was the Khumbu Icefall, a 2,000-foot jumble of constantly shifting ice, at the start of the South Col Route. Negotiating the icefall involves crossing crevasses via a series of ladders, and walking beneath huge, unstable séracs. Because the risk increases exponentially with time, climbers endeavour to get through it as fast as possible. The average time is four hours. Erik's first traverse of this obstacle took him and his team thirteen hours. Many more traverses followed as they set up camps at different levels on the mountain. By the end of the expedition they had reduced their time to five hours. 'I was just so happy to get down through the icefall for the last time,' said Michael Brown, a filmmaker on the team. 'I came down quickly, ahead of everyone else, so I could get footage of them coming off the mountain. I was really nervous until the last person stepped out of the icefall. It's a really grim place.'

Erik generously credits his climbing team for the part they played in his successes, but it is on his forehead that the wreaths of honour are placed. After summiting Everest, he was invited to the White House, led the Pledge of Allegiance at the 2001 Republican Party Convention, and carried the Olympic torch for both the summer and winter Games. He won national awards for courage and achievement, was featured in most major US magazines and on many high-profile television shows. His achievements have also provided him with a new career. Once a high-school teacher and wrestling coach, he is now a professional mountaineer who stars in a documentary film of his Everest climb. He is sponsored by Aventis Pharmaceuticals and the National Federation of the Blind, and is company spokesperson for Freedom Scientific Inc., which develops assistive technology products for people with sensory impairments and learning disabilities. He has already written his biography. And of all the mountaineers on the US corporate speaking circuit, he is rumoured to be one of the most highly paid.

The corporate world, eager to maintain the efficiency and enthusiasm of their employees, has created yet another type of hero – the motivating mountaineer. Many climbers are happy to draw analogies between climbing a mountain and becoming successful in business. Carlos Buhler, a US mountaineer whose CV includes twenty-five years of Himalayan climbs enjoys 'trying to create a common language' with corporate executives. Their challenges, he believes, 'are equally as intense and interesting as anything I did on K2. When I give these corporate lectures I understand people have their own mountains. Not much separates us. There's the level of risk, the level of human loss – but other than that, the problem-solving challenge is not so different from the problem of trying to sell fibre-optic cables or invent software.' Some climbers find the business analogy difficult to understand, even as they profit from it. Joe Simpson, whose corporate presentations are largely an account of how he crawled out of a crevasse in the Peruvian Andes, admits with some incredulity that groups of successful business people gladly listen to his tales of 'what a mess we made of our first mountaineering expedition'. And pay him royally for it.

Two of the men on the Rupal Face, Mark Twight and Barry Blanchard, often give talks and slide shows about their climbs. They recognise that their stories are entertaining and sometimes greatly inspiring to others, but they steadfastly refuse to fashion them into corporate motivational speeches. 'I don't buy the analogies between climbing a mountain and putting together a successful business plan,' said Barry. 'I don't think it rings true, and I don't want to have it coming out of my mouth.'

On a number of occasions, Mark Twight has been encouraged to use the story of their epic on the Rupal Face as a business model. One businessman suggested that he could follow up with the account of an expedition that ran like clockwork because of all the lessons they'd learned. 'I told him I just couldn't stand there and talk that shit with a straight face,' said Mark. 'I see it as preying on the sensibilities of people who are at a time in their life where they are saying, "What if?" I really don't believe in feeding on that kind of insecurity as a way of making a living. And even if it is relevant as a source of motivation and team building, how long does it last? Every prescription drug lasts six to eight hours, and I think the motivational speeches are probably similar to that.'

Not all companies would agree with him. In 2002 Aventis Pharmaceuticals invited Erik Weihenmayer to speak to their employees at the launch of a new sales campaign. Named 'Over the Top', the whole campaign was given a mountain-climbing theme. On a website known as Base Camp, the sales staff were encouraged to monitor their goals and track their progress against each other. As incentives they received sporty gifts, such as a carabiner key ring with a compass attached, and encouraging emails and voicemail messages from Erik Weihenmayer. At the end of the first three months, sales quotas were up 22.1 per cent compared to the first quarter of the previous year.

Helping people to set and reach goals and to effect change in their lives are worthy outcomes, but aren't there more profound benefits to be gained from the adventures of mountaineers? Surely they have a deeper appeal, something fascinating and unsettling, with a mythic resonance?

In 2001 I met the Mexican mountaineer Carlos Carsolio, the fourth and youngest of only a handful of human beings who have reached the top of all fourteen of the world's 8,000-metre mountains. One of the hardest was K2, which he climbed in 1993, in gruelling conditions. 'We slept on the side of the mountain, just below the summit,' he told me. 'We were frozen. The storm was so hard, coming down the mountain was a little bit crazy.'

'A little bit crazy' meant battling through a blizzard so intense that after hours he and his three team mates had only progressed 300 metres down the mountain. A pair of climbers on their way up offered them shelter in their two-person tent. Six men inside a tiny space. Six desperate men. Two had developed cerebral oedema, one had pulmonary oedema, one was snow blind, one was badly frostbitten. No one had any supplementary oxygen. Outside, the storm clawed at their fragile nylon shell, trying to rip it away. They had to go down, or die. As the strongest, Carlos and his partner went first, breaking trail through deep snow, and fixing ropes. In the whiteout conditions, they lost sight of each other. Mistakenly Carlos headed south, down a slope that grew increasingly steep. Suddenly he stopped. Snow was whirling so thickly around him he could see no further ahead than his hand, but some instinct warned him that he was on the edge of a precipice. 'I had not the energy to go up again. I was completely drained. I sat down in the snow. In such a storm, I could not see anything, but I could feel something. I sensed there was a void below me, an empty space, but I was sure there was something beyond this void. I concentrated a lot, I took many deep breaths. I reached a moment that was clear, a moment without worries. And when I reached this point – I jumped.'

I stared at him. 'You *jumped*?'

'It was a one-way ticket,' he said. 'This was a jump to the life or the death. I don't know how long it was, but it took time. Then I crashed into the snow, I started to slide, I braked with my ice axes. I stopped. And my legs were hanging in space. There was a shot of adrenaline and I crawled up and lay there for a long time, feeling alive again. It was a fantastic moment.'

As I listened to Carlos tell his story, part of me was thinking, This man is *insane*. But another part was spellbound, eager to know more about that leap into the abyss, about entering the zone between life and death. A zone that the men on the Rupal Face stepped into when they made the decision to climb down the mountain without ropes. A zone Joe Simpson vividly describes in *Touching the Void*.

While Joe was descending Siula Grande, a 21,000-foot mountain in the Peruvian Andes, he fell, and broke his leg. His climbing partner, Simon Yates, spent hours lowering him down the mountain. During one abseil, Joe went over a cliff, and found himself hanging above a huge crevasse. Higher up the mountain, out of sight and beyond calling distance, Simon faced the terrible choice of being pulled off with Joe, or cutting the rope that bound them. He cut the rope. Joe plummeted into the crevasse, landing on an ice shelf fifty feet below its surface. Too badly injured to climb up, and terrified of the yawning depths below him, he spent a long night fighting off madness and cold. When morning came he made the decision to abseil further into the depths of the crevasse. Deliberately, he dropped the rope without a knot. If he found no way of escape he would rather slide off the end than return to that ledge. A hundred feet down, he reached a snow floor – not the bottom of the crevasse, as he first hoped, but a thin ceiling above another great chasm. For five hours he gingerly hopped and pulled himself along this ceiling, which sloped steeply up towards a shaft of light, until suddenly his head popped out of the crevasse. His overwhelming relief was short-lived. Base camp was still six miles away, across a wild landscape of glaciers and rocky moraines. After crawling and hopping for three days, he arrived to find that Simon, presuming him dead, had burnt all Joe's belongings and was preparing to leave.

Touching the Void is an international bestseller. First published in 1989, it has been translated into twenty-five languages, and sold millions of copies world wide. And the reason? Besides being a gripping adventure story, it embodies an ancient fear of being buried alive, a terror echoed throughout history in religion and myth. Jonah was swallowed by a whale. Persephone was dragged down a deep, dark fissure into the Underworld. Joe Simpson's lifeline was severed and he plunged into the bowels of the earth. The stories of mountaineers are new versions of old myths.

In *The Hero with a Thousand Faces*, American author Joseph Campbell states that one of the purposes of mythology is to convey 'the symbols that carry the human spirit forward'. Among these symbols, the hero and his quest are key. Mountaineers willingly set out on dangerous quests, their Holy Grail the adventure itself. They fashion their own odysseys, leaving the known for the unknown, venturing into high places where suffering and trials await them. If they are lucky, they return home victorious, bearing stories that enthral the less adventurous. Stories of altered states of mind and body, of going beyond the limits of ordinary human knowledge and experience. Of stepping into the zone between life and death. The transcendence zone.

In 1939, in a speech to the Alpine Club, the climber-poet Michael Roberts said of mountaineering, 'The sacrifice is not necessary. The risk brings no material gain, but it offers something – the exhilaration, the sense of clear vision – which partly excuses the risk. And then, for the rest, the risk excuses itself. It is a demonstration that man is not wholly tied to grubbing for his food, not wholly tied by family and social loyalties; that there are states of mind and spirit that he values more highly than life itself on any lower level.'

Sixty years later, Mark Twight wrote in *Extreme Alpinism*, 'On certain routes I achieved a mind/no mind state of mystical connection to the mountain so powerful I knew I could not fall or make mistakes. I could read my partner's mind. I was not affected by gravity. I lost myself on those days. I became the mountain . . .'

For the Slovenian mountaineer Tomaz Humar, considered by many to be the world's most daring high-altitude climber, this altered state of mind is linked to his belief in a higher power. 'I am the chosen one,' he said. 'I strongly believe in Him. We must just follow when we have the sign. We are too small to ask why. If you believe in the Spirit, you will be blessed and nothing will happen.'

Close to his house in Slovenia is a mountain where he frequently goes to meditate, to talk to the faces of the mountain, to ask questions of it and to receive answers. Even from inside his house, he insists he can still have this communication. 'If it happens at night-time, nobody can sleep in our house; it's so strong a connection. It's like a telephone, buzzing. It's not a voice; it's energy. After two or three hours, my wife kicks me. She says, "Hey, I want to sleep." So I take a blanket and I go outside. I'm a little strange.'

At Himalayan base camps, when the time for his climb approaches, he retreats from all social contact. In a ritual reminiscent of the samurai's *misogi*, a symbolic cleansing of the spirit, he bathes and dresses in clean clothes. Then he finds a place to meditate, focusing all his thoughts on the face he wants to climb. 'I wait for the face to call me. It's like a relationship. I understand the mountains, not with my muscles but with my third eye. This is my secret weapon.'

His 'secret weapon' has helped him perform superhuman feats. Summiting Annapurna I, solo, in blizzard conditions. Descending Nuptse alone, in the dark, after his climbing partner was blown off the top. Forging a new route up the South Face of Dhaulagiri, a deadly place of overhanging séracs and loose rock. Tomaz spent eleven days on the South Face, alone, surviving icefalls and avalanches, running out of food and water, sometimes climbing without protection – no ropes, no pitons, no ice screws. The climbing world was dazzled by what is considered the most audacious and brilliant achievement in mountaineering for a decade.

Tomaz Humar is a hero not just among his peers, but in his own country. Returning to Slovenia from Dhaulagiri, he was swamped by admirers at the airport. Honour, fame and sponsorship were heaped upon him. Eventually, he did fall to earth. While building a house for his family he stumbled into a construction pit, shattering bones in both legs. It was only a temporary respite from heroism. Now he's back in the Himalaya, more determined than ever. 'Sometimes . . . I simply flash up into the heights . . .' he writes in *No Impossible Way*, '. . . for an infinitesimal interval of time I feel all the magnitude of eternity.'

Their drive to go above the clouds leads mountaineers to heights both physical and metaphysical. Some return having glimpsed eternity, having 'touched the face of God'. Like Icarus, they risk all for this. Like Icarus, they ignore the warnings: 'Fly too high, my son, and the wax will melt on your wings.' Like Icarus, often they die young.

Despite the costs, society needs its risk-takers, those who dare to make huge leaps into the unknown, stretching the imagination of the time beyond its previous limits. Columbus set sail on exploratory sea voyages, facing the possibility that he might fall off the edge of world; Neil Armstrong took the first step onto the surface of the moon; Phillipe Petit walked a high wire strung between New York's Twin Towers. Like them, extreme climbers venture to the very edge of existence, discovering new physical, mental and spiritual territories. Their mythic stories give us a window on to our deepest concerns, and point towards the potentialities of human experience. They tap into what Joseph Campbell calls 'the inconvenient or resisted psychological powers that we have not thought or dared to integrate into our lives . . . These are dangerous because they threaten the fabric of the security into which we have built ourselves and our family. But they are fiendishly fascinating, too, for they carry the keys that open the whole realm of the desired and feared adventure of the discovery of the self.'

But these 'psychological powers' quickly dissipate when the climber returns to earth. The memory of transcendence fades, the experience can only be captured in story. Or by returning to the mountains.

'What possible difference could climbing Everest make?' wrote Tom Hornbein after his legendary and never repeated traverse of the mountain with Willi Unsoeld, in 1963. 'Was I any greater for having stood on the highest place on earth? Within the wasted figure that stumbled weary and fearful back toward home there was no question about the answer to that. It had been a wonderful dream, but now all that lingered was the memory . . . Everest must join the other realities of my existence, commonplace and otherwise . . . The questions, many of them, remained. And the answers? It is strange how when a dream is fulfilled there is little left but doubt.'

Tom and Willi had had a chance to be among the first group of Americans to summit Everest, via the South Col route. But the route had already been climbed so often it was 'almost paved'. Instead, they opted for a 'leap into the unknown'. They would ascend the mountain by way of its virgin West Ridge, climb down to the South Col route, and so make the first traverse of Everest. Quite literally, they would go over the top. 'The challenge is to see if we can pull it off on a shoestring,' Tom wrote to his wife, just before setting off. 'Our hope is lightness, speed and a hell of a lot of luck.'

On 17 May, they were camped at 25,000 feet when winds blasted their tent down the mountainside, with them still inside it. Scrambling out just in time, they watched one of their sleeping bags get sucked out through a tear in the fabric, fly upwards 'like a giant green wind sock' and disappear into the blizzard. Everest had tried hard to shed them, but they refused to give up. Four days later, before dawn, they left their last camp at 27,200 feet, for the summit push. After hours of climbing, they reached the top of the Yellow Band, an area of crumbling, treacherous rock. Getting up the Yellow Band had been so hard, they knew that climbing down it would be too difficult. There was no going back.

'Home, life itself, lay only over the top of Everest and down the other side,' wrote Tom Hornbein later. 'Suppose we fail? The thought brought no remorse, no fear. Once entertained, it hardly seemed even interesting. What now mattered most was right here: Willi and I, together on a rope, and the mountain, its summit not inaccessibly far above. The reason we had come here was within our grasp. We belonged to the mountain and it to us . . .' They had crossed a line, closed a door behind them. They had entered the zone beyond life, in clear sight of death.

At six fifteen p.m. they stood on the top of the world. They hugged each other, and cried tears that quickly turned to ice. As the sun set and their shadows grew ever longer, they began their descent of the south side of Everest. Destination: Camp Six, established by their team members above the South Col Route. A thousand feet above the camp, they met two of that team, lying in the snow, exhausted after summiting the mountain earlier in the day. Tom and Willi tried to coax them down to the camp. But their progress was slow; in the darkness the way was perilously uncertain. They had no choice but to spend the night in the open, on the side of the mountain. No one had ever bivouacked at such a height – 28,000 feet – and survived. They took off their rucksacks, curled up like commas, and waited for the night to pass.

It was an endless night of profound isolation, of deeply penetrating cold. Tom Hornbein 'floated in a dreamlike eternity, devoid of plans, fears, regrets . . . Death had no meaning, nor, for that matter, did life.' Around four a.m., the sky to the east began to lighten. The next hour stretched on interminably as the frozen men waited for the sun. 'Not till after 5.00 did it finally come,' wrote Tom, 'its light streaming through the South Col, blazing yellow across the Nuptse Wall, then on to the white wave crest of peaks far below. We watched as if our own life was being born again. Then, as the cold light touched us, we rose.'

Carlos Carsolio leapt back to life, Joe Simpson crawled to life, the men on the Rupal Face found life hanging on a precipice. In confronting their mountain, each broke through boundaries in himself, discovering new reaches of mind, body and soul. These 'missionaries of transcendence', as the psychologist James Hillman calls such adventurers, returned with their stories, reminding us that there is more to life than the everyday. That leaps into the unknown are vital for the human spirit. Sometimes, like Tom Hornbein, they survive all their quests, and live into old age. But all too often they are shooting stars, dazzling the world for a while before burning up fast. 'They make their mark early,' writes Hillman, 'disturb the commonplace, and then vanish.'

5

Voices I: The Shadow Falls

T he man walks towards a house in Manchester. He's hurried here from two hundred miles away, but as he turns into the quiet avenue, his pace slows. He stops to check the address, to look for street numbers. He knows she has a blue car, a Volkswagen. It's parked outside the house; she's home. Pushing open a small wrought-iron gate, he takes a few steps to the front door. From inside he hears laughter, and a hubbub of voices. He pauses for a few moments, composing himself, thinking of what he will say.

The woman is having a small party to celebrate the renovations on her house, completed today when new carpets were laid. Smiling, she moves from person to person, pouring wine into their glasses. She's clad in a short summer dress that shows off her tanned limbs. There's a lightness about her, an innocence. Young for her thirty years, childless, she's unencumbered by responsibilities. She can't see beyond the imminent return of her lover, a mountaineer who for the past three months has been away on Everest. Anxiety for his safety is quietly ticking in the back of her mind, but she buries this beneath the happy anticipation of their reunion. When the phone rings she rushes to answer it, hoping it will be the long-awaited news that he's off the mountain and on his way home. But it's only a friend, saying she can't make it to the party.

Through the frosted-glass window of the door the man sees a figure come into *the hallway and pick up the phone. He hears the woman talking cheerfully, and registers when she replaces the receiver. He presses the doorbell.*

I've often wondered what went through Dick Renshaw's mind that afternoon, when I opened the door, greeted him cheerily, and welcomed him in to join the party. Given the circumstances, there could have been only one reason why he had travelled so far to visit me without prior warning. But the defence mechanisms of shock, activated the instant I saw him, allowed me to usher him into my living room, introduce him to a couple of people, pour him a glass of wine and finally, after what must have been minutes of torture for him, to ask, 'What brings you here?'

Dick had recently been on Everest with Joe, as part of a British expedition attempting the then unclimbed North East Ridge. After suffering two minor strokes at altitude, Dick had been forced to leave the expedition early. His departure, and Chris Bonington's realisation that he was too exhausted to go for the summit, had reduced the climbing team to two – Peter Boardman and Joe. Despite their understanding that if anything went wrong there would be no hope of rescue, they decided to make a bid for the ridge. 'There is a big job for Pete and me to do,' Joe wrote in his last letter to me, 'but hopefully it could go well . . . and if fortune, weather and spirit favour us, we could be up the mountain in a few days from when we start.'

Just before they set off, there was a party at Advance Base Camp for Joe's thirty-fourth birthday. A photograph I saw later captures him laughing as a bottle of champagne is uncorked and a stream of frothing liquid shoots across the cook tent. The cards I had sent him, one funny, one romantic, did not arrive in time. They were returned to me later, unopened.

Following Joe and Pete's departure for the ridge, there was silence from the mountain. No more letters came. The newspaper and television dispatches stopped. The silence stretched for over two weeks, until a representative from Jardine Matheson, the Hong Kong-based company that was sponsoring the expedition, finally rang around to say they had received a telex. 'Expedition about to leave Base Camp,' it reported. A few days later came another. 'Team arriving in Hong Kong, June 09.' I began contacting the wives of the other team members. 'Maria, they are all dead,' said Ruth Seifert. Wendy

Bonington was less dramatic, but quietly admitted that something seemed amiss. 'The longer the gap in hearing from them,' she remembered recently, 'the more you could feel yourself holding things together, holding time back. There was a containment of possibilities until you got the information. And then of course, the containment burst.'

My way of containing the possibilities was by becoming ridiculously optimistic. On a warm Sunday morning in mid-May, I sat outside the cottage my friend Sarah Richard shared with her mountaineering boyfriend, Alex MacIntyre. Like Joe, he was away climbing in the Himalaya, and she was worried about him. I reassured her that he would be fine. 'Everything looks bright,' I said. 'There's plenty of happiness ahead.' She was soon to remind me of how wrong I had been.

Days later, I dreamt I was running down a street, screaming and crying, because I had just been told that Joe was dead. When I woke up, I persuaded myself that the dream was simply a manifestation of the fears that I had been tamping down for weeks. From then on, however, shards of truth kept slipping into my conscious mind. While I was writing out a cheque to pay Joe's electricity bill, I had a sudden feeling of dread. A few hours before my party, a thought flashed through me: 'What if he doesn't come home?' Instantly, I chased it away.

So I knew. Of course I knew. But even when Dick said, 'I've got some tragic news,' still I blocked it out. I led him into my tiny back garden, where we could talk privately. An old green easy chair that I'd moved outside while the carpet fitter was at work stood in one corner. I retreated into it as Dick began to talk. 'Last seen on the sixteenth of May . . . climbing for fourteen hours that day . . . twenty-seven thousand feet or so . . . moved behind a rock pinnacle as night came . . . Chris thinks a cornice might have given way . . .'

Time slowed. The world around me crystallised into fine details. Jewel-hued petals of pansies moving in the breeze. Sheets on a neighbour's washing line billowing and flapping. Clouds, long and streamlined against the blue sky, their ends flicked up like tails.

'Probably down the Kangshung Face . . . a long fall . . . no hope . . . I'm sorry.'

I asked Dick to leave me alone. From inside the house, I registered a sudden cessation of laughter. Sarah appeared in the doorway, her face torn, her eyes full of horror. With her arms around me, the stillness began to shatter irreversibly. A wave of pain crashed down, dragging me under so that I had to fight for breath, gasping at the terrifying realisation that the future I had looked forward to was wiped out; that Joe was never coming home.

The big green chair stayed in my yard. During those first days, I took refuge in it as people came and went with kind words, flowers, cards of condolence. Later that summer, during long, heart-sore nights when I couldn't sleep, sometimes I curled up in it with a blanket around me, like a child. I watched it through the kitchen window as the seasons changed, dusting it with leaves, soaking it with rain, covering it with snow – a friend who had helped me through the worst of times, and whom I couldn't discard. A year passed before I could bear to let it be taken away.

'Inshallah, we will rest in the spring,' Anatoli Boukreev promised Linda Wylie, when he called from Pokhara, on his way to Annapurna. He had been away in the mountains so much that year. It was a hard winter in Nepal, he wrote later, the snowfall was unusually heavy. A recent storm had brought three and a half metres of new snow. Its weight destroyed two of their tents at base camp. By mid January, he hoped to have climbed the mountain. In February he would return to her.

I had a bad feeling about Annapurna. When Toli was here with me, usually I'd get up and run in the morning, while he did yoga breathing exercises. One morning in the spring of 1997, he woke me up and he said, 'Linda. Don't go running today.' He was quiet for a while. Then he said, 'I've had this dream. I dreamt I died, in an avalanche.' He described it in exact detail, only the name of the mountain was missing. He said he wasn't afraid.

Everything was speeding up that year. He climbed so much, it was like he couldn't stop. He'd say, 'My body can't do this for ever.' So he had to do it all now. Why didn't I tell him not to go to Annapurna? I could have said, 'You climbed all summer, stay here. Who cares about the ticket, we'll buy another one.' But I didn't.

Once he said to me, 'If I love you too much, the gods will be angry.' The night before he left for Annapurna, he told me that for twenty years he had never thought of women when he was climbing in the

Himalayas. Then he said, 'But now, Linda, you are my habit.' And I've often wondered about that – whether that jealous mountain knew I was in his thoughts. I faxed him a letter. I told him he had to be very careful with Annapurna. I knew she was the Harvest Goddess, but I didn't know about the other things, not until after he was dead. That before Westerners came, women were not allowed past a certain stone. That when the shepherds went up there they didn't mention a woman's name because the mountain would be jealous. She would toss her head in anger, and send snow and ice falling down her sides. Toli must have known. I found out later that some friends had sent up a piece of beef to their base camp. But local custom forbids anything but mutton there, so Toli sent it back down, with some money for a *puja*, in atonement. He tried to respect those things.

On Christmas Day, I was having dinner with my family and someone said, 'It's too bad Toli's not here. He would love this.' I blurted out, 'No, he won't ever be here. He won't ever see any of this.' I started crying. It was like seeing shadows.

The phone rang a few hours later, around midnight. It was Simone Moro. It was a terrible conversation. There's just no way of protecting yourself against that sort of pain. He said there had been an avalanche. They were fixing rope on the ridge between Annapurna South and the summit of Annapurna I when a cornice broke off above them, and shattered into big blocks. Simone was in the lead; the avalanche yanked out his anchor and he was swept down in its wake. He yelled a warning to the other two – he said he saw Anatoli start to run.

Simone said he couldn't search for long; he was injured and had to get down. He said that maybe Toli and Dima (Soubelev) had survived the avalanche. I told him, 'Just send somebody back up there. Don't stop looking until you know for sure.' I got on a plane the next day. I was in Kathmandu eighteen hours later. I went not daring to hope, but still hoping something. I went because I couldn't stay in America and deal with it here again. It was better to be in Nepal – the best times Toli and I had were there. I flew over with a bag of money, to pay for the helicopters and the bills on the expedition.

Simone had already tried to go back up in a helicopter, but the clouds were too low. I went up there twice. There had been so much snow, everything was so white and huge, you couldn't make out any features. When I got out of the helicopter at Base Camp, I was almost up to my waist in snow. What had Toli been thinking? Local people they met in lodges along the way had warned them not to climb in such conditions, but Toli wouldn't listen.

The first time we went up, we dropped some Sherpas at the base camp, and they started trekking to Camp One, about seven hours away. I was hoping that maybe Toli had got back there, that he was injured, waiting for rescue. While they set off, we flew around the basin, then we went straight back to Kathmandu. Four or five boys from Toli's sports club in Almaty had arrived to help look for him. Next morning we took a bigger helicopter to base camp. The Sherpas were there. They had been up to Camp One. Toli wasn't in the tent. We flew the whole search crew up to the high camp, dropped them off and they searched the avalanche site. We didn't find anything.

I took some photographs of the area with a camera I'd borrowed from a Swiss climber in Kathmandu. When I returned it, he looked carefully at me and said, 'What's bothering you?' And I found myself telling him. What did Toli see when he was dying? How long did it take for him to die? Was he crushed? Was he broken? Did it hurt? Until I knew, there was really no way to deliver him. This man told me that he had nearly died once, in a stone fall. When he was dying, he felt himself being pulled through a tunnel towards a beautiful light, and when he reached the light it was all-encompassing, and tranquil, and he was free, and floating. Then he turned around and saw a black hole. He'd been resuscitated with CPR by some other climbers. He realised he had an opportunity to go back through the tunnel, but he was ambivalent. When he decided to live, re-entering his body was extremely painful.

Not being able to say goodbye, that's a big part of the sadness. I went to see an old lama in Kathmandu and made arrangements for him to start praying. There were forty monks in the temple, chanting and singing. I gave them pictures of Toli, and they put them between little statues made of yak butter. After seven days there was a ceremony when the photos were burned, releasing his spirit. The monks' chanting was to tell him he was in the world between life and death, and to orient his spirit to its possibilities. They did the same prayers every seven days, until the forty-ninth day. The gongs, the incense, the chanting – I could hear his name among the monks' invocations. It was soothing for me. It helped me accept that he was really dead.

I didn't want to go home; I could have stayed there for ever. Someone took a picture of me right after I came back. I look so wrecked. I looked like I had died myself.

He wrote his last letter to his wife and children from Death Bivouac, a snow cave three quarters of the way up the North Wall of the Eiger. 'We are hoping to make the top in a few days, but we are being very safe so don't worry. Love you all very very much.'

One of his team climbed down with the letter, and sent it to Marilyn in Leysin. 'Don't play with the gods up there,' she wrote back. 'We give you all our support through this last stretch. And much much much love.'

They had to get the news to her fast. The reporters would already be filing stories. John Harlin, falling to his death from the North Face of the Eiger – it would make headlines in the US. Her phone might already be ringing.

They said, 'There's been an accident.' That was all they needed to say. Otherwise they'd have said, 'John broke his arm,' or 'John smashed his leg.' Minutes after Don and Audrey Whillans told me, it was broadcast on Swiss radio. Then the telegrams started to come in. I called John's parents; I had to tell them that their only child had died. That was so hard. But the hardest part was telling our children, having to look into their eyes. I can remember very much not wanting to do it. They slept with me that night.

On the day of the funeral there was a storm. I remember standing in the graveyard, snow falling thickly around us. They said a woman was crying hysterically, trying to jump into the grave when the coffin was being lowered. No one did that – I was there! John had built up a cult around himself. There were a lot of people interested in him. Whether he really had any affairs – he claimed that he didn't – I feel they were a lot of rumour.

He was a maverick in every way. When we met at Stanford University he was in the Stanford Climbing Club. He was so phenomenally good. He started to do things outside the rules. He just went up cliffs monkey-style, without protection. He was thrown out of the club because of this. It was the same when he trained as a fighter pilot. He did extraordinary things. He dived through telephone wires and sucked them up into his engine – did a lot of damage. He once flew so low to a hill where I was standing I could feel the after-blast of heat on my legs.

With the risk, and the differences between us, it was quite a romance. I knew I'd tangled with a powerhouse. I wanted to go on into graduate studies, and become a professional biologist, so I was rethinking the relationship. Then John came over one night on a surprise visit. That night I got pregnant.

He had wanted to be a dress designer. At Stanford he majored in fine art and dress and costume design – he was the only man to do so. Before that he applied to Balmain, and managed to get an interview with Pierre Balmain himself. He didn't get the job, but he obviously made an impression; Balmain invited him to his country home for the weekend. Liberace was there too. There's this story that John wandered around the garden dressed in nothing but a tiny pair of red shorts. With his astonishing physique, he was certainly noticed. After John died, Balmain wrote me a condolence note and returned a book on climbing that John had left there.

He liked dresses. When we hiked or climbed I had to wear a dress. I have a flying rib cage, so my waist wasn't small enough and he couldn't take that. Aesthetics were very important to him. He insisted I wear a waist cincher the whole time. He wanted me to be the first woman up the Eiger North Wall. I said, 'Wait, let's do a reality check on this. Someone's got to raise the children.' So it wasn't always easy, but you couldn't measure him with the yardstick you'd use for ordinary men. And I had the opportunity to have someone who was interesting. We shared a lot intellectually. I appreciated his strength. He was artistic, and that attracted me very much. He wrote eloquently. When people asked me what my husband did, I would say, jet fighter pilot, alpinist, writer, dress designer.

I knew when I went into the relationship that he climbed at the edge. I didn't have any illusions that it was going to be a long-term marriage. I thought we would separate, or he would die. Ten years was what we had. That tenth year was the first anniversary we celebrated. We went out for dinner by ourselves. I recall he said, 'If I had to do it all over again, I'd have married you.' And he said tenderly that he wanted to stay with me for the rest of his life. That really flattered me. We had been through a lot of ups and downs. We were married young . . . the children were stressful for him.

John hadn't made a will. When I had to list his assets, it was – X number of pairs of skis, sleeping bags, crampons, ice axes . . . and two children. Under Swiss law, I had to apply for custody of the children. It took months to process. By then most of his things were gone. After all these years you can still get me shaking about it. That so-called friends of John's would go down into our basement and take his things. It was heartbreaking. And Dougal Haston, who was climbing with him when he fell, he wrote to me and said I was just John's woman. That because of the things they had shared climbing, he knew him better than I. That letter had me so fired up.

John was thirty when he died. I was thirty-one. It seemed pretty grown-up at the time. Now my son is forty-five and my daughter is forty-three. It's like no time has gone by at all. I've been engaged three times since. It's never worked out. A therapist I went to said I wanted stability, but that I was addicted to excitement for myself. Maybe. I was addicted to the lifestyle I had with John.

'Oh horror! Horror! Horror!' Sarah Richard shuddered. She was building the set for a theatre production of Macbeth. *Through the walls of her studio she could hear the rehearsal. She knew the superstitions: that the play always brought bad luck, that even referring to it by name was best avoided. She tried not to think about that. Not with her boyfriend, Alex MacIntyre, away climbing* Annapurna.

When I first met him, he told me that climbers needed to know that there was someone waiting for them at home, willing them to come back, loving them. Before the first expedition he said, 'Do you know what I want? I want you to fall in love with me before I go away again.' I already had, so his wish was fulfilled. He went on three expeditions while we were together. Makalu, Shishapangma and then Annapurna. When he went away, my life was on hold. I'd always be aware of him. I'd wonder if Alex was cold, or hungry. Sometimes I'd feel guilty about being comfortable. So I started Iyengar yoga; it was Eastern, it was physically tough. And I would try to starve myself when he was gone . . . to feel more a part of what he was doing.

By the time Annapurna came around we were committed to one another. But there was a definite sense of foreboding all the time. Once he said that even if he knew he would die on a trip, he'd still have to go. And he kept saying, 'Don't worry about this trip. This isn't the one to worry about. If you're going to worry about any of them, worry about the next one, K2.' He said it so many times, I told him I was getting worried that he was making such a point of it. I never went to the airport with him. I hated saying goodbye. When he was going to Annapurna, we parted at our cottage in Hayfield. I left him there to go to work. It was really sunny and I kissed him, then went back and kissed him again. I walked away and didn't turn back, and drove off.

When he left, he forgot his passport, then his car broke down on the way to the airport. Waiting for the AA van, he wrote me this letter saying, 'Whatever happens, remember I love you and I'll always love you.' And then at the airport he said to his mother, 'Keep in touch with Sarah.'

On the night of 17 October, I kept waking up, seeing a shadow walk across my vision. It happened all night long. Just something walking. Nepal is five hours ahead of us. He died on 18 October.

On the 21st, the day after my birthday, I was at the Newcastle Playhouse, in the studio with a student, dyeing some costumes black. I was feeling incredibly jumpy. I knew something wasn't right. The phone went, and I thought, This is going to be about Alex. It was his mother. She said, 'Sarah darling, I want you to sit down, I've got some bad news. Alex has been killed.'

I said, 'He can't have been, I love him.'

And she said, 'I know, dear. And he loved you.'

Then I just dissolved. I remember leaning against the wall, sliding down to the floor, sitting there, wailing. There was this black lacy dress hanging in my office, that I'd worn for an art school ball I went to with Alex, just after we met. It was beautiful, from the thirties. I'd just picked it up from the dry cleaners. I was going to wear it the day Alex got home. I couldn't stand seeing it. I threw it away.

Ten days later, a letter came from him. Opening it was unbearable. He wrote that the weather was unseasonable and it was really hard work and he was looking forward to getting back and us having a long hot bath together. It upset me terribly, because I thought, Maybe he was thinking about me at the time. Maybe he wasn't really focused.

When I cleared out our cottage in Hayfield, I wanted to take some photographs, to remember the place. But my camera wouldn't work. After I left the cottage, it worked fine. What's the significance of that? Was someone saying, 'Look, move on. Don't ponder on the past.' But it wasn't that easy.

I still don't know exactly how he died. Hit by a rock, I think, but I never actually asked. It was too brutal and final to be told the details. Maybe if I didn't know he could still be alive in a way.

Years before she met Mick Burke, Beth had seen a film about a British woman who loved a man in the French Resistance. News of the man's death reached the woman on her daughter's second birthday. It was a story Beth never forgot.

When their baby, Sara, arrived, Mick doted on her. Then came the invitation to the 1975 South-West Face of Everest Expedition. It would be his last big trip, he told Beth. He was sorry he would miss Sara's second birthday, but he would be there for all the other birthdays to come.

In 1971, I had gone to Everest with Mick as a sort of base camp nurse. Before we left I remember standing and looking at this amazing mountain, and I had this weird, strong feeling that if Mick climbed it again he wouldn't come back. So I was very nervous about him going to Everest in 1975. One night I tried to have a serious talk with him about it. I said, 'I really don't think you're going to come back.' I suppose I wanted him to promise that he definitely would come back, but that was impossible. Then he hurt his knees on a job in France, and they sent him home. There was a set of steep steps up to our house, and as he limped up them I thought, 'One good push and he'll break his legs, and he can't go to Everest.' But I couldn't do it. I knew he had to go.

When the news came through that Doug Scott and Dougal Haston had got to the summit – the first British climbers to do so – I sent Mick a telegram. I remember thinking, I wonder if he'll ever get this. That weekend I was really restless, I had a ghastly feeling. On the Thursday night, Sara was restless too. She kept getting out of bed, and she was in a strange mood. I said to her, 'What's the matter? Where are you?' The next morning I had this dropping-away sensation in my belly. We had a meal with a vicar, and I don't know why, but I started this discussion about what happens to people when they die.

Three days later, on Sara's second birthday, we were visiting my friend Cilla in Aberdeen. I was laying the table for Sara's party when the phone rang. I picked it up. Somebody said, 'I need to talk with Mrs Racey.' Cilla's husband was in Africa at that time and I thought, I hope there's nothing wrong with Paul. I called her. I was in the kitchen and suddenly I heard her cry, 'No, no!' I charged in saying, 'What's the matter? What's the matter?' She was in pieces. She just handed me the phone. I said, 'It's Beth here. What's wrong?' This guy on the other end had to tell me what he'd been asking her to tell me. He said, 'Mick has lost his life.' For a split second there was relief. I thought, Oh, I won't have to worry about that any more. I said something like, 'All right, thank you,' and put the phone down. Cilla and I just sat there and looked at each other; it didn't seem real. About half an hour later, John Hunt called. He said, 'Beth, has anybody rung you?' I said, 'Oh yes, but I don't believe him, so it's all right.' And he said, 'Beth, I'm afraid it's true.' Then Wendy Bonington rang me up. They'd known for a few hours. They'd planned how I was going to be told.

I thought, If it's on television, it must be true. Mick had been sending film back to the BBC, for the children's programme *Blue Peter*. The programme came on, and it was the first bit of news. Pete Boardman and Pertemba Sherpa were coming down from the summit when they met Mick coming up. They said he was moving slowly, and the weather was deteriorating, but he was determined to carry on. They told him they'd wait for him. After two hours, the storm was getting so bad, they had to go down without him. So that was it – he just walked up into the clouds, and he never came back.

We went on with the birthday party. Cilla had three little boys. I can't really remember it. We just didn't know what we were doing. Nothing was real.

I went through quite a strange phase afterwards. I couldn't bear to answer the phone, and I found it really hard to phone anyone, in case they were out. That felt like another loss. Early every morning, I used to go into the bathroom and throw up. I don't know why, it just kept happening. In the summer I took Sara to Vancouver for three months, and we stayed with a friend there. When we came back, she said, 'Oh Mommy, this is that house where you was always sick.' . . . This little girl standing back and watching – it's dreadful, isn't it? At the time I thought I was being quite okay with her, but seeing pictures of her at that age she looks haunted. She didn't really grasp what was going on, and how do you tell a two-year-old? I'd said, 'He's gone to heaven and he's living amongst the stars and that's a really nice place for him because he liked being high up on mountains.'

I remember thinking, Stay on the tightrope. If I go this way I'll go mad, and if I go the other way I'll go mad. Keep straight on. I remember someone saying, 'At least it's not as bad as divorce. You haven't got the rejection to deal with.' But it's the ultimate rejection – he's not here! That's how it felt to me.

Everest Base Camp. 1996. Satellite phones. The immediate communication meant Sue Thompson was living the drama, every single minute. Despite Bruce Herrod's regular calls and emails, reassuring her that all was well, she worried. She'd been worried since he left. A gut instinct; she didn't like what was going on. Now, after almost two months, she was utterly exhausted by it all.

Bruce was an Antarctic geophysicist by training. He'd spent seven years with the British Antarctic Survey. He had a lot of expedition experience, such as crossing the Patagonia Icecap, but none at extreme high altitude. He'd only really discovered the Himalayas a couple of years before I met him, in 1990. His imagination was captured by the big mountains. He was fascinated by snow and ice. He was one of the few people on this planet who would far rather be struggling at minus 40 or 50 than sitting on a beach.

When we met I had just finished ten years in Japanese investment banking, and I wanted to try new things. I got this bizarre notion to trek up a 6,000-metre peak, so I joined an expedition to Stok Kangri in Ladakh. Bruce was trek leader.

We had this idealistic notion that we could make a living out of writing and photography. We tried it for a while, travelling and climbing together; I wrote the articles and he took the photographs. In 1993 we climbed Aconcagua, nearly 23,000 feet. I got to 21,500 feet, but Bruce made it to the top, and that was the highest mountain he'd done before Everest. I think I'd always assumed he'd climb Everest one day, but I knew it was out of my league. He was invited there in 1996 by a South African expedition, as expedition photographer. After that invitation we discussed nothing else except Everest. It was such a big feature in his life, there was no time to even think what the future would be beyond it.

I went with him to South Africa, to meet the team before they all flew to Nepal. I said to him, 'I want to know who these people are if something goes wrong.' I clashed with the expedition leader from day one. After four days I was so unhappy I nearly went home. But for some reason I stayed, which is a good job, because that's the last time we had together. The expedition was big news in South Africa. Nelson Mandela was the patron. When they got to Everest, the four best climbers on the team had a blow-up with the leader. They questioned him about his own climbing experience, among other things, and they left. It was a big scandal. When Bruce phoned next I said, 'Do you realise what's being said in the press about this expedition?' He said, 'Don't worry about it. Not everything you read is true.' It was like the shutters going down and him saying, 'Don't question me about this. If I'm going to be fully focused, I need your support, not your questioning.' That was very difficult. You felt you were being forced into this situation of support, while your common sense said to you, 'I'd rather he pulled out.'

On 10 May the base camp manager rang me and said something terrible was going on, a big storm, but that Bruce was okay. Over the next few days the whole extent of it unfolded in the press, all the deaths. I had assumed the South African team would just come home. Then Bruce phoned me and announced they had decided to go back up the mountain. I said, 'Without any discussion?' and he said, 'It's not your decision. It's mine.' I knew that whatever I said would probably be futile. I do remember saying to him – one of these classics – 'You will promise, won't you, to turn around by one or two o'clock?' I can't remember whether or not I got a reply to that.

I suppose like everyone involved in these things, you think you can put it right afterwards. The climber knows they've pushed the other person pretty much to the brink in terms of support. But both of you assume that life will resume some sort of normality afterwards. And that there will be extra affection and devotion to say 'Thank you for having supported me.'

On the day they were going for the summit, he radioed base camp at twelve thirty Nepal time. I always thought afterwards that if I'd managed to speak to him then, five hours before he got to the top, I could have said, 'This is absurd, you are going too slowly.' If you could ever go back and rewrite things, that's the point where I might just possibly have pierced the chink in his armour.

My friend John stayed with me all that day. The poor guy – you know how people get locked into these situations with you for the rest of your lives? It was just this chance phone call on the Saturday morning. He was supposed to go to Twickenham for a rugby match. He called and said, 'I was just wondering how things are.' I said, 'I don't know. Bruce is going for the summit. He's out of contact. He's not with the rest of the team. I don't like it.' He asked if I'd like him to come round and I said, 'Yes.' I'm not the sort of person who would normally have done that. He arrived, took one look at me and said, 'I think I'm going to give Twickenham a miss.'

It was nearly twelve thirty here, five fifteen p.m. in Nepal. And no word. I didn't know what to do. John said, 'Leave it a couple of minutes and phone again.' I phoned Base Camp and literally as I got through I heard Bruce's voice over the radio saying, 'Can you patch me through to Sue?' He was on the summit of the mountain.

If I had realised it was going to be absolutely our last conversation on earth, I'd probably have done it slightly differently. I never said 'Congratulations', because I thought, 'Really, really, this has just gone horribly wrong by now.' He sounded absolutely fine. As usual he just wanted to chat. I was thinking, You haven't got the sense of urgency that you need to have by now. I was aware of the effects of altitude. You believe you're thinking clearly, but in fact you're not. I just wanted him to get down, but he was quite happy to keep chatting. He said, 'I've left all the bits and pieces on the summit.' I knew that meant a photograph of me, and a vial of water from a lake near Mount Kailash where we'd gone with some Sherpa friends in 1995. I told him he had to get going, that he had to be really careful. He said, 'Don't worry, I've got too much to look forward to.' I knew something was terribly wrong when he said, 'I love you dearly.' He'd never said that before. And then he said, 'Over and out, Campden Grove. It's been a real pleasure.'

I put the phone down. Then I waited. I phoned again after four or five hours, by which time it was ten at night there. If he was still alive he must have bivouacked. John stayed overnight, and we had two bottles of red wine. I didn't feel a thing – not the effects of alcohol, nothing. And still no word. I must have phoned at three or four in the morning here. So it was seven or eight in the morning in Nepal. Light. There was no word, nothing. That was the Sunday. Two or three hours later they phoned from base camp. They had decided to report him missing to the British Embassy in Kathmandu.

Two days earlier, his mother had phoned me. She was very chatty.

She wanted to know when Bruce was due back because she was going to have a hip operation in a few weeks' time. Then she said, 'Where is he by the way?' He wasn't close to his family; they knew he was on an expedition but that's all he'd told them. They obviously missed all the press coverage. So I was really put on the spot. I thought about just being vague but for some reason I said, 'Well actually he's climbing Everest.' So she had had two days to get used to the idea. But when I called her to say he was missing she said, 'I'm sure he's resting somewhere and he'll be able to come down.' I had to say, 'I wouldn't harbour those hopes if I were you.'

Then the nightmare started. The phone never stopped going. The *Daily Mail* were doorstepping me. You suddenly realise there's this voracious appetite – people want to know. And the whole saga of people saying, 'What can I do to help?' I told them I wasn't bothered about the here and now. It was that unimaginable leap of three months, six months, nine months, a year, and when do you ever get over it?

I had planned to go out and meet him in Nepal. I did end up going . . . but to get his belongings and death certificate.

At first light, Gary Pfisterer looks out of the tent. He sees a threatening sky, the high slopes of Dhaulagiri heavy with snow. Ginette is brewing tea. Sitting close together, they pass a mug back and forth, their breath mingling in the freezing air. He wonders aloud if they should go up at all today. Conditions are marginal. Let's give it a try, she says. We'll push for Camp Three. If the weather doesn't improve, we'll pack up and go home.

She's ready before him. And impatient. This will be her fifth 8,000-metre peak, and there's only a small window of opportunity left. Is it okay if she heads out first? Sure, he says, I'll try and catch you up. Take care.

Moving strongly, she steadily overtakes other climbers on the route. They nod to her as she passes, conserving their energy in the thin air of 6,500 metres. Finally there is just one figure a little way ahead, Dawa Dorje Sherpa, from the French team. Like him she drops down the slope to skirt a crevasse, then heads back up again towards the ridge. Instantly, she realises the danger. Around her feet, the snow cracks like a windscreen hit by a stone, sending tiny fracture lines in all directions. Wind slab. Beneath this top crust, beaten flat and hard by the wind, is powdery, unconsolidated snow. Dangerous conditions, making for the worst kind of avalanche. Just one foot going through can trigger the whole thing off.

*

It was a story-book romance, I guess. We met in 1993 on Everest. We'd both turned up from our respective corners of the world and joined a team. We fell in love on the way in to the mountain, and we summited it holding hands.

She was the second British woman to climb Everest. After that she wanted to complete the Seven Summits, the highest mountain on every continent. I was doing them too, so we completed them together. I'd quit my law practice by then, so I was pretty free.

When we weren't climbing, we travelled back and forth to see each other. She was living in Australia when we met, then she moved back to the UK. Finally she decided to come to the States and get licensed as a doctor here. We got married in 1997. She wanted children, but by the time we were seriously involved I was forty-three; the prospect of teenagers when I was sixty wasn't really an option. And it didn't fit with our lifestyle, so we decided against it. She got a job that allowed her to work as a doctor six months of the year in three-month increments. It was perfect for the climbing season schedule.

We went all over the world climbing. It was a blast to be out there doing this kind of thing with your mate. There aren't that many women climbers at her level, so I felt really lucky to be able to hook up with Ginette. She was a very highly charged particle; she never sat still. Curiously enough, we always expected that I would be the one to go. She was fairly conservative on technical ground, where I was inclined to go for it on steep ice and rock. But up high on the hills Ginette was the more aggressive about achieving success. It meant more to her to get to the top. Something was driving her. She only weighed about 110 pounds but she could carry a load that was at least as much as I could carry. She performed extremely well at higher altitudes. The climbs where I outperformed her were few and far between.

On Kangchenjunga, the year before, I turned back at the pinnacles. I was totally knackered; it was pushing two p.m., I was concerned about getting benighted. We'd already passed the bodies of two Japanese guys who had got caught out on the hill the night before. So they were up there dead and the rest of their team were severely frostbitten. It was a pretty sobering situation. But Ginette carried on. She went for the top alone. She was the first woman to climb the mountain. It seems like all the cutting-edge women climbers eventually do get killed. They are just that much more driven. Where a guy might put in 90 per cent, a woman would try to put in 110 per cent.

Dhaulagiri had received a lot of snow in the autumn of 1999. Prior to the avalanche that killed Ginette, we were involved in other stuff that was moving around on the mountain. Snow fields that started to slough and then stop, things like that. I guess you develop a sort of hardness to it; you get insensitive to the danger after a while. Two of our team had already summited – that season we were the only team to put anyone on top of an 8,000 metre peak in Nepal.

By the time I got going that morning, there were seven climbers ahead of me, strung out for about a hundred metres. Ginette was near the top, right behind a Sherpa from the French team. We were on a ridge route. A crevasse fractured the ridge and we had to drop down lower to get around it. It was while Ginette and the Sherpa were climbing back up to the ridge that the whole slope let go. It all happened very quickly. I can still see it in my mind's eye, the slope just broke into pieces, like a giant jigsaw puzzle. I saw two people tumbling by me and I thought one of them was Ginette, so when the snow stopped moving I was yelling for her. Then these two guys popped out of the snow.

We spent hours on the ridge, futilely poking and prodding. But we weren't even in the right place. Later, when we made radio contact with the French team leader in base camp, he told us he'd seen people being swept down the north face of the mountain in the avalanche debris. It was Ginette and the Sherpa. The two French guys got taken down the line of the ridge to the north and came to the surface. The two people behind them got knocked down and dusted. I was in the back, with nothing.

We couldn't go down below and search – the detritus from the avalanche was too unstable. There was probably a hundred thousand tons of material that went down the mountain. Later that night it all broke loose again. I'm virtually certain she wound up in a crevasse, buried by the debris. There was nothing we could do. We had talked about the possibility of one of us getting killed on a mountain and basically both agreed to be left where we were if that happened. I'm glad we talked about it because it would have been distressing otherwise, not knowing what to try to do.

In base camp I called her parents, so they would find out before the media got hold of the story. That was the only call I made. We just backed off and packed up and went home.

It was a really, really sad time. It was sad for a long time. Different little things would spark the tears. When I came home, dinnertime would roll around and I'd half expect her to come in the back door. People say 'Time heals' and I don't really agree with that. I think you develop mechanisms to work around it, but you don't really ever get over it.

After she died it was important to me to get back out into the mountains. I needed to have a focus, and to assimilate how life was going to be without her. I took a team to K2 in 2000, and in 2003 I'm going back to Kangchenjunga, though not with a great deal of enthusiasm. I've pressed on with the climbing, but it's become a bit mundane now. I think I achieved what I needed to in terms of going back to the high mountains. I'm slowly just moving on, away from the bigger hills.

I felt cheated by Ginette's death. And part of that was anger. I just didn't think it was fair. You see so many people that are unhappy together, people that are at each other's throats and wouldn't give a shit if their spouse was killed. Here we were so happy and so together . . . Ginette was such a good person. She was always so generous, doing good deeds and good things, it just seemed unfair to have fate step in and take her and leave all the others. As well as anger there was frustration and powerlessness to change what had happened. You think, If it had just been different. Ten million things could've happened which would not have placed her up at the front of that line that morning.

Being left behind is lousy. It's not like life's been terrible or anything, it's just not been the same. And never will be again.

6

The Mourning Work

No one would tell me Joe was dead, not at first. Disappeared, is what they said. Missing — from the North East Ridge of Everest, while making a summit attempt with Pete Boardman. Lost without trace, on a knife-edge of ice and snow, at 27,000 feet, almost the highest point on earth. However they phrased it, one thing was certain — Joe Tasker, the man I loved, the man who, foolishly perhaps, I had hoped to grow old with, was never coming home. For months afterwards, I took a bundle of his clothes to bed with me, and slept with them clutched to my body. Recently, Linda Wylie told me she did the same after Anatoli Boukreev was killed in an avalanche on Annapurna. 'Trying to find his smell,' she said. 'It's so animal that part, you can't even believe yourself, howling in a corner. Oh it's so raw. It is the most primeval, god-awful experience.'

I remember watching a ewe in Ireland repeatedly going back to sniff the same patch of heather where she had given birth to a dead lamb, long after the farmer had removed its tiny body. I understand this impulse, just as I understand the greylag goose searching frantically for a lost mate, flying great distances to places where he might be found, uttering what the biologist Konrad Lorenz calls 'a penetrating, long distance call'. Pete Boardman's widow Hilary and I set off on our own long journey, in September 1982, following the footsteps our men had taken six months before, on their way to Everest. We flew from London to Hong Kong, through China and into Tibet, searching for their traces. We stayed in the same hotels they had been in, we crossed the high, dusty plains of Tibet on the back of a rattling, bone-bruising truck, just as they had. We trekked for ten days, across the high passes of the Kharta and Kharma Valleys on the eastern side of the mountain, and on the northern side up the rough twelve-mile trail to the site of their Advance Base Camp at 21,000 feet. We sat in flattened-out areas where their tents had stood, and we collected the bits and pieces of garbage the rest of the team had left behind. To us they were precious relics: an empty whisky bottle, film cartridges, a packet of aspirin, the tattered remains of Bruce Chatwin's *In Patagonia*, a book I had given Joe to read on the trip. Down in the Rongbuk Valley, at the mountain's foot, we left messages and mementos among the stones of Joe and Pete's memorial cairn. Then we planted a garden around it, scrabbling in the dirt with our fingers, transplanting patches of moss, burying poppy seeds, desperately trying to beautify the nearest thing we had to a grave. At thirty years old, I had never before considered the rituals around death, but suddenly I realised their import. I understood the need to commit a body to earth, fire, water or air. I longed for the finality of such a ritual, the positive proof that a shell is gone and the person you loved can never inhabit it again.

No one can teach you how to mourn. Like climbing a mountain, you can try to prepare for it, but it's impossible to know what will happen once you are on its steep slopes. Beverly Raphael, an Australian professor of psychiatry describes mourning as 'the processes whereby the bereaved gradually undoes the psychological bonds that bound him to the deceased'. It begins with the acute stage – shock, disbelief and denial. Then comes the longer, much harder, chronic stage that Freud called the 'mourning work'. William Worden, author of *Grief Counseling and Grief Therapy* claims that there are 'four tasks of mourning' which must be accomplished to avoid what he calls 'abnormal grief'. The tasks are to accept the reality of the loss; to work through the pain of grief; to adjust to an environment in which the deceased is missing; and to emotionally relocate the deceased. Only then, apparently, can one move on with life.

When I went to Everest with Hilary, I hadn't read any of the current theories on grief, and of this I am glad. Our process was an instinctive one, and I would have been appalled to be told then that our intense pilgrimage to the mountain had nudged us only a tiny way along the first of the prescribed stages of mourning work, the acceptance that the men we loved were really gone.

A decade later, I was in Austria, kayaking on the River Danube with my husband Dag. On a windy afternoon, the sky filled with roiling storm clouds, we pulled ashore in Vienna, stored our boats and gear in the safe care of a friendly kayak club, and set off for the city centre. While Dag studied a menu at the marble-topped table of an elegant coffee house, I went outside to a phone booth to call my mother in England. On hearing me, she responded not with her usual delight and relief, but in a voice choked with tears. 'They found a body on Everest,' she blurted out. Shock coursed through me, time slowed, images sharpened. As thunder growled overhead, the clouds opened. I leaned against the glass door of the telephone booth, staring at fat, perfect raindrops bouncing off the shining flagstones of the square. 'It was on the news,' my mother continued haltingly. 'They say it has to be either Joe or Pete, but they don't know which one it is yet.'

I tried to reach Hilary, but got no reply. At the home of Charlie Clarke, the doctor on the 1982 expedition, his wife Ruth picked up the phone. She told me a Russian climber had come across the body on the North East Ridge. He had photographed it, then tracked down Chris Bonington, who was also climbing in the Himalaya, and given him the film. It would be several weeks before Chris got home, and until then no identification could be made.

I walked slowly through the downpour, back towards the coffee house. For the past ten years, Chris Bonington had believed that Joe and Pete fell to their deaths, 12,000 feet down the Kangshung Face. I had always pictured Joe buried in snow, somewhere among the folds of crevasses at the foot of the mountain. Now, I had to rework that image.

A photograph, I told Dag. If it were of Joe, how would he look after lying for a decade close to the summit of Everest? Surely he would be perfectly preserved, like Snow White, forever youthful as I'd grown older? Gently, Dag broke this illusion; he warned me about the ravages of UV radiation, dry winds and extreme cold; he prepared me for the fact that the remains might not be pretty, might not be recognisable at all.

While Pete and Joe lay still on the mountain, life had gone on for Hilary and me. Our trek to 21,000 feet on Everest had been a hard physical endeavour, but it was easy compared to what awaited us at home – facing the routine of daily life again and making some sense out of it all. My first year was one of confusion – I drank heavily, smoked too much pot, drove recklessly. I lurched from day to day, trying to block out the pain, but at the same time I was desperately attempting to regain a feeling of aliveness. Then, to others, it appeared that I started to get better. I moved to an old cottage in the countryside and threw myself into renovations. I began training for a marathon and applying for new teaching jobs. But I knew I was still running from despair, fleeing the terrifying emptiness in my life, frantically trying to fill the gap that Joe had left behind, to fill my lost future.

Hilary took a different path through those years. A skilled climber, she began spending all her spare time in the mountains, pushing herself to exhaustion. She was trying to stop the 'constant chatter' in her mind about what had happened to Peter. No matter how hard and how competitively she climbed, however, those questions still plagued her. At a friend's suggestion, she took up yoga, but she continued to climb, until the day she took a bad fall while leading a route in the Alps. Her belay held, and she got away with just a few bruises, but the accident changed her way of thinking. 'I recognised the fact that I could die if I kept pushing it,' she said. 'From that moment onwards I gave up climbing for twelve years and got totally into yoga. It was as though I'd switched completely from one mode of being, to looking desperately for something else that would satisfy this enormous gap. I became obsessive about yoga, mainly because it allowed me every now and again to have these moments of complete silence when my brain switched off. When I stopped wondering where Pete was and whether or not the next phone call was going to be him.'

Soon, she was meditating for three hours a day, journeying into a space beyond the physical, a space where she felt in contact with Pete. During a session of guided visualisation, her yoga teacher took the class through an imaginary rock wall. For Hilary, it was a distressing experience. 'I just couldn't get through to the other side of that wall. I was totally stuck because we hadn't had any closure on this whole situation. I didn't want closure either, because in a way the spiritual journey I'd started allowed me to be very close to Pete.'

At an international yoga convention, she met the head of the Divine Light Mission, Swami Chidananda. He had a profound effect on Hilary; she began going on retreats that he led, and visiting his centre in India, to be in his presence. She moved into an ashram in Switzerland, and although she continued to work as a teacher, she withdrew from her old life in the mountains. She gave up skiing and running. She rarely saw her friends in the climbing world. She assured me she was happy in her new life, yet beneath her apparent calm lay something deeply unresolved. It was the lack of a body. After several years in the ashram a return to a more mainstream way of life called to her, but she couldn't admit that to herself until Pete was found. 'I had to absolutely know for certain,' she said recently, 'that he was no longer going to come home.'

Conclusive proof of death is a basic human need. How can we know for certain that the person isn't ever coming home if we haven't seen his body, if no one can bear witness to his very last moments? In 1997, the Slovenian mountaineer Tomaz Humar struggled through hurricane-force winds towards the summit of Nuptse, a little behind his fellow climber Janez Jeglic. Coming over the final rise towards the peak, he lost sight of Jeglic. He followed his footprints – until the prints abruptly stopped. Apart from a radio lying in the snow, there was no sign of Jeglic, and Humar could only presume that his friend had been blown off the mountain. He returned to Slovenia bearing Jeglic's wallet and passport, which he had collected from his tent at base camp. 'I give these things to his wife,' he recalled, 'and she say, "Without his passport and the wallet, how can Janez come home now?" I say to her, "There is no chance. Janez is gone." She say, "I know he will come home."'

Two months after the British climber Mick Burke disappeared on Everest in 1975, his wife Beth saw a police car pull up across the street from where she lived. She was convinced they'd come to tell her that Mick had been found alive. For three years after the Canadian climber Dan Culver plummeted into oblivion off the side of K2, his wife Patricia would drive up to the house she once shared with him, and expect to see his truck parked outside. In August 1982, I was waiting to be served in a greengrocers in Manchester, half listening to the five o'clock news on the radio behind the counter. 'A climber who was missing, presumed dead, on Everest has turned up alive and well in Nepal,' said the broadcaster, and for a moment, before the man's name was announced, I had a wild, impossible flash of conviction that it must be Joe.

A month after I stood in that phone booth in Vienna, Chris Bonington returned to England with the roll of film, the evidence of the body on the mountain. He sent the images to Hilary and her mother-in-law, who, by details of clothing, identified the body as Pete's remains. For Hilary, it was an affirmation of her long-held belief that Pete hadn't fallen. If he'd died violently, she had always claimed, she would have sensed it. I too was relieved, for during the weeks of waiting I'd begun to dread what the discovery of Joe's body might unearth in me. But I felt compelled to see the photograph, to understand what death on a mountain looked like.

When Hilary and I next met, she handed me a large brown envelope containing a copy of the black and white photograph, then quietly withdrew. I recalled my husband's gentle warnings in Vienna, about the destructive powers of the elements; I thought I was prepared. But the image I saw twisted my heart so hard I cried out loud: desiccated skin drawn tight over bones, hair bleached bone-white, the head uncovered, the hand lying gloveless in the snow, the posture one of repose, of surrender. As shocking as the ravaged body, however, was the supreme bleakness of the place where it lay. Pete Boardman's shell, leaning against a bank of snow on the North East Ridge of Everest, is fixed in my memory as an image of profound loneliness and desolation. When I cried over it, I cried for Joe too, for the fact that he had perished so far from warmth, from life, from my love. 'This is a desperate place,' he wrote to me from Everest Base Camp, a few weeks before he died, describing the high winds, the bitter cold and the barren, unforgiving landscapes of the mountain. And now I saw, truly, what he meant.

I gave the photograph back to Hilary. Alone, in the meditation room of her Swiss home, she set a match to it. She watched as the image of her husband's body caught fire and curled up in the flames. Then she gathered the ashes, took them to India and placed them in the River Ganges. 'I know Pete's mother still has his picture,' she said. 'I know that Chris [Bonington] made copies of the slide. But it doesn't matter that they still exist. The picture is in my mind, but the actual burning of the picture is also in my mind. It was a very integrative moment when I did that. It meant that he could physically disappear.'

In May 1996, after Bruce Herrod was patched through by phone and radio from the summit of Everest to his girlfriend, Sue Thompson, in London, he was never heard from again. His fate on the mountain remained a mystery for a year. Then Sue received an email from an expedition on Everest, telling her that a climbing team led by Anatoli Boukreev had found a body attached to the fixed ropes at the bottom of the Hillary Step, not far below the summit. There was little doubt that it was Herrod, as he had been the last person to summit the mountain in 1996, and Boukreev's team was the first to get so high since then. 'My first reaction when I got the email saying they'd found him was, Oh, so you can come home now,' said Sue. 'Until you think, No, he's still just as dead as ever.'

She contacted several expeditions at Everest Base Camp, requesting them to look for personal effects on Herrod's body, and bring them back to her. Most important for her was his camera – Herrod was a professional photographer and she knew he would have been recording his journey for as long as he was able. 'You're aware it's the most horrible request to make – can you look through his rucksack, and if his camera's there, can you bring it back? But that became my obsession, my focus of how to bring this thing to a close. I said, "Only at no risk to yourselves," because it sounded as if he was in a very precarious position.'

An expedition led by David Breashears agreed to the task, but almost immediately a series of storms moved in, and for three weeks no one could get close to the summit. When a sudden break in the weather allowed the team to make their bid, Breashears and Ed Viesturs were the lead climbers. They found Herrod's body clipped into the fixed ropes with a figure-of-eight rappel brake. He was hanging upside down, his arms dangling, his mouth open and his skin black. 'Like Captain Ahab,' Breashears later wrote, 'lashed to his white whale.'

Eager to get to the summit while the conditions were fair, Breashears and Viesturs climbed around the body. Not long afterwards, another team member, Pete Athans, arrived at the Hillary Step. 'On the way up, people were going by Bruce and saying, "We'll deal with it on the way down,"' he said. 'But you never know what's going to happen, so I started taking care of it right then.'

After securing Herrod's pack to the fixed lines, he cut the body free and watched it fall down the mountain until it disappeared from sight. It was the highest ever burial service on a mountain that has become a vast graveyard.

Athans returned to Everest Base Camp with Herrod's ice axe and camera bag. A British climber, Jon Tinker, travelled back to London with these precious items, and delivered them to Sue Thompson. Immediately, she headed to a professional laboratory to have the film developed. 'I said to them in the lab, "This camera has been sitting at 29,000 feet for one year at minus 50 degrees, and it belongs to a dead climber who cannot go back and take these shots again." I don't think they believed me.'

They opened the camera. The film inside was marked in Herrod's writing, 'Eve of 24/5/96 South Col.' There were only two exposed frames on the roll. While they were being developed, Sue paced around London, clutching Bruce's ice axe. Back at the lab, she placed the two shots on a light box. It was immediately apparent that they were identical. 'I put the eye glass down and the first thing I saw was the blue of his duvet. I thought, at least they're of him. Then I suddenly saw this perfect shot with the curvature of the earth.' She also saw the memento-strewn tripod on the summit of Everest, and Herrod, leaning over in front of it, smiling jubilantly at the camera. 'I didn't feel as emotional as I thought I would,' Sue admitted. 'It was like, well they're pretty good shots, but where are the rest of them? And more to the point, where are you, Bruce?'

The summit picture did not bring Sue the closure she had hoped for. Still haunting her were the questions of what had happened to Herrod, how he had died, and whether he had suffered. In April 1999, she went out to Everest where, at base camp, she knew she would meet Pete Athans. 'Going to Everest for me would not have had much significance without meeting him. This human link was the key to clearing it up . . . To meet the guy who carried out the burial, who sent Bruce spinning thousands of feet into space, is the ultimate proof that his body has gone and he no longer exists. I knew that when I shook his hand, the hand that had cut the rope, this would be confronting the final truth as far as I was ever going to see it.'

She met Athans when he had just come down through the Khumbu Icefall, after summiting Everest again. Their conversation, she recalls, was neither long nor profound, but she made herself ask him what Herrod's body had looked like. She suspects he was being kind when he assured her that, despite having hung near the top of the world for a year, he was still recognisable. He reported that Herrod had suffered a very bad head wound, and that he thought it likely that he had got his leg caught in old ropes, and flipped back. There were two possibilities for what happened next – either he was knocked out in the fall, or he simply couldn't right himself and dangled from the ropes until he died. 'That's the bit I still don't like to think about,' she said. 'I prefer to assume he hit his head and went unconscious. That means he would have died within about forty or fifty minutes of speaking to me.'

While Sue was on Everest, the world was abuzz with the news that an American team had found the body of George Mallory, who disappeared along with Sandy Irvine on the North East Ridge of Everest in 1924. Treating it like an archaeological artefact, the climbers photographed the body extensively and stripped it of its belongings. Sue dreaded the thought of her lover's remains ever being subjected to a similar fate, but Athans assured her that there would be little left to find; from where he had cast off Herrod, the fall was very long and very hard. 'I got this image of a body in pieces,' said Sue, 'and it's almost like that was the dissolution I needed. I realised it's somehow easier to deal with when you don't think of the body as a dead entity any more. It's somehow dissipated.'

Setting a photograph alight, imagining a body broken into a thousand pieces, watching a coffin being lowered into the earth. These acts are a way of finding acceptance that someone is truly gone. For both Sue Thompson and Hilary Boardman, this 'integrative moment' was a turning point. They could finally move away from a preoccupation with death and begin a journey back into their own lives. 'When his body was found, and cut free, it was the final cut, in every sense of the word. I crossed a sort of barrier,' said Sue. 'After that had happened, I found life got a lot easier.'

Easier, but the shadow that lingers over deaths in the high mountains was still present. Bruce Herrod chose to go to the summit of Everest alone, late in the day, when the rest of his team were already on their way down. Mick Burke, the cameraman on the first successful all-British expedition to Everest in 1975, was close to the summit when his climbing partners advised him that he was too tired and conditions were too sketchy for him to carry on. Disregarding them, he plodded on upwards, never to return. Joe Tasker and Pete Boardman were fully aware that their strength was sapped by weeks already spent high on Everest. They knew that if anything went wrong with their summit attempt, there was no chance of being rescued, as their already tiny team had been depleted by illness. Nonetheless, the two men set off from Advance Base Camp for the North East Ridge, early on 15 May. Monitored through a telescope by Chris Bonington and Adrian Gordon, they climbed for two days, on challenging terrain, without supplementary oxygen, into the 'Death Zone' of 8,000 metres and above. As light faded on 17 May, they moved out of sight, behind a rock pinnacle on the ridge. They never reappeared. What befell them remains a mystery; Joe's body has never been found, and no one has gone looking for the diary that Hilary is convinced lies in Pete's clothing, that will tell the story of his last hours. What is certain, however, is that they didn't say to each other in good enough time, 'This is crazy. We're way beyond our limits. Let's turn back. Let's return to the women who love us.'

I used to claim I felt no anger over Joe's death. I used to say, 'At least he died doing what he loved best.' As if that somehow made it all right, both for him and for me. Mick Burke's widow, Beth, told me that she, too, had never felt any anger about Mick dying. Then she remembered how, just after the news came through, a friend had sent her a beautiful bouquet of flowers. She'd taken those flowers and kicked them around the house.

My friend Ruth Seifert always used to insist that, at some level, I had to be angry. 'Joe and Pete, all the climbers, they pursued a passion which was above their responsibility and love for their family, and which took precedence. So there's an anger about that, it's like a mistress, really. The anger has to come out somewhere.'

Six months after Joe died I began venturing into relationships once more. In hindsight, I simply wasn't ready to love again, my emotional wounds were too raw, but I couldn't stand the void that loomed before me; I wanted to be reassured that happiness was possible, that my life wasn't over. One man stood in the wings, ready to offer affection and security, but I constantly rejected him, gravitating instead to people who were wary of commitment and who, inevitably, fled in the face of my neediness. Time and time again, over the course of the next two years, I set myself up to be hurt, until my sense of self-worth was in shreds.

Eventually, my friend Julie Saunders drove down from Wales to see me. She knew about grief; her boyfriend, the climber Al Harris, had been killed in a car crash a few years before. We went for dinner in a pub, and halfway through the meal she told me she was tired of hearing my tales of romantic woe. 'Why,' she asked, 'are you stuck in this pattern?' I started blaming the men, but she wouldn't have it; the problem, she insisted, was with me. She wondered if I could hear myself talking about Joe all the time, how I made him out as the ultimate man for whom I could never find a match. 'But he wasn't that perfect, was he?' she said, holding my gaze.

'No,' I admitted, 'he wasn't.' The mountains were his biggest passion, and I had to fit in where and when I could. He had claimed that he made no demands on me, and therefore, by default, I could ask little of him – no commitment, no promises, and precious little shared time. I suppose that in the long run it was more honest than making plans for babies, a house and growing old together, but it left me feeling hopelessly insecure.

Shortly before his last expedition, I began to suspect there was another woman in Joe's life. He was due to spend a week in London at a time that exactly coincided with my school's half-term break, but made excuses as to why I couldn't accompany him. He didn't call me during his week away, and when he returned I asked him outright if he was involved with someone else. He reacted with furious denial. He told me I was stifling him with my jealousy and threatening our relationship. And yet he was determined that we mend the rift quickly, carrying me up to bed and making love to me with an un-characteristically insistent passion. Reassuring myself that I'd been hasty in my presumptions, I stored my fears away, not wanting to spoil the little time we had together before he left.

Joe never returned from Everest, but his trunk of personal belongings did. A red trunk, heartbreakingly familiar from the weeks it had stood in the middle of his living room floor, with climbing clothes and equipment spilling out. In the last-minute rush before he left, I'd helped him pack it. Now, pushing up the lid felt like opening a coffin, facing the reality of something unacceptable. One by one, I took out all the belongings I knew so well – the fleece jackets, the sweaters, the sheepskin boots, the silk scarves, the socks, the contact lens solution bottles, the books . . .

At the bottom of the trunk, I found the letters from home. In his methodical fashion he had arranged them in separate bundles, held together by rubber bands, according to the person who had sent them and in the order they had been received. There was a bundle from me. And there was a bundle from a woman in London. Sitting on my bedroom floor, surrounded by Joe's things, I read her letters to him. In the first one she recalled the night, during his week in the city, when he'd taken her out for dinner, accompanied her back to her flat, and suggested they sleep together. She apologised now for refusing him. She told him it was partly because of her concern that he had a girlfriend, despite his reassurance that she was 'nothing serious'. She was regretful of her decision, she wrote. Since he'd left she had realised her feelings for him, and reassured him that she would wait for him, and wouldn't refuse him again.

There were lots more letters from her, detailing her daily life in London, her weekends in the country. The fact that eventually the letters became questioning, wondering why he was writing less and less often, was little consolation. I read them all, carefully, just once, then took them downstairs, laid them in my kitchen sink and set fire to them. I remember standing there a long time, hunched over the small pile of ashes, weeping angry, bitter tears. It was hard enough to bear that he had heaped infidelity and lies on top of the separations, the stress and the fears that I already faced in our relationship. But what ripped me apart was the knowledge that, had he lived and come home, I might still have lost him.

I didn't speak of these letters for two years, until, in a country pub, I was confronted by my friend's unwavering honesty. *He wasn't that perfect, was he?* As the story tumbled out, I experienced a huge upwelling of anger towards Joe, for what he'd put me through, for what he'd expected of me, for what he'd left me with. Julie, however, had little sympathy. 'He probably had lots of affairs you didn't know about,' she said. 'What does it matter now?'

I turned my fury on her – how could she be so insensitive? But she was relentless. 'He might have come home and got rid of the other woman. Or he might have dumped you for her. Most likely he would have carried on with her behind your back, and strung you both along. Who will ever know? It's immaterial now. He's frozen on a mountain. You're warm and alive. Get over it, girl, you owe it to yourself.'

I railed at her until the pub closed, trying to make her see the pain I was in, trying to win her sympathy. Back at my house, we drank whisky until the early hours, while I cried and screamed and poured out two years of anger, and while she sat unwavering in her counsel. Get over it, she kept telling me. Move on. LIVE.

Around four in the morning we both fell asleep on the living room floor, too exhausted, too drunk to go upstairs to bed. When I woke some hours later, my head was pounding dangerously, and yet at the same time I felt light, clear, released. My friend had lanced a boil in my psyche, and allowed the anger to finally emerge, and start seeping away.

In *The Mourner's Dance: What We Do When People Die*, Katherine Ashenburg records her daughter saying, after her fiancé's sudden death, 'Time doesn't heal. Grieving does.' Thomas Attig, the author of *How We Grieve*, describes grieving as happening not in stages but through the completion of a number of tasks which help us relearn the world without the deceased person, while still keeping that person's memory as part of our lives. Such tasks, of course, take time. The ancient Greeks had two concepts of time: *chronos* is chronological time, measured by the movement of stars across the sky and the earth around the sun; *kairos*, which comes from a word meaning circumstances or opportunity, is a measure of significant moments, when conditions are right for crucial actions. According to the authors of *Bio-Spirituality*, Peter Campbell and Edwin McMahen, it is during kairotic time that 'personal lives move forward'.

In April 1990, my father lay dying of cancer in a bedroom of the house where I had grown up. Six days before, I'd flown to England from Canada and since then had been keeping vigil at his side. My mother, a nurse, knew all the signs of approaching death – the cold feet, the fingers scrabbling at sheets, the sudden bloom of health in the skin. Those were days of high intensity; gusts of March wind shook the bedroom window and I would look outside and register every tiny detail of the buds trembling at the tips of branches. On the final morning, when my father's breathing changed, when the raw gasps began, I saw a sudden flash of panic in his eyes. Yet even as I searched for words to reassure him, the fear passed and he withdrew into a state of utter focus. A bubble of self-absorption formed around him: he was unreachable then, as if he knew that this was something no one in the world could help him with, that he was about to pass into a territory beyond all of our imaginations. For those few seconds, he was a man *in extremis*, in the throes of death, and yet he was totally alive, totally in the moment. And then, in an instant, his face fell in on itself, his skin drained of all colour and he was gone.

Nothing had prepared me for the suddenness, the certainty, of that change from life to death. It was impossible to absorb at first, but the rituals of Irish Catholicism gave me some time. My mother brought in a bowl of warm water, soap, and towels. We bathed my father's body. We dressed him in fresh clothes. Gently, we inserted his false teeth. We placed coins on his eyelids and propped a book under his chin so that rigor mortis would set his face in an expression of repose. Then we sat around his body, talking and drinking tea, for several hours. Finally my mother stood up and opened a window. The time had come for his soul to leave his body, she explained, and we had to allow it an easy passage. These were intimate, tender acts, which even in those early hours of shock soothed and brought solace and some peace of mind.

At his funeral, a Requiem Mass concelebrated by three priests, I was determined to be composed, but the chanted prayers, the incense, the candles, the trilling bells as the Eucharist was held aloft – all the weighty rituals so familiar from my childhood – tore down my defences. Throughout the long and solemn service, I wept uncontrollably, for my father, and also for Joe. His death had been abstract; the only real evidence of it had been his absence from my life. Now, I'd seen the fact of death. I'd touched it, sat with it, recognised it as a journey both profound and inevitable. Finally, I could imagine Joe's last moments, and lay him to rest on his mountain grave.

Two years after Mick Burke disappeared on Everest, his closest friend Dougal Haston perished in an avalanche in the Swiss Alps. Beth Burke attended the funeral, which was held in the village of Leysin, where she had first met her husband. 'I remember standing in this cemetery surrounded by mountains,' she said. 'It was so beautiful, and there was a body. It was tangible. I thought, This is my funeral for Mick.'

Five years later, out of the blue, she had the sensation of actually letting go of Mick. 'I suddenly thought that all my memories were mine for ever. I wouldn't lose any of them, no matter what happened. It just felt better, more complete.'

Such are the moments of *kairos*, as life moves forward. But when you think you have reached acceptance, when you are sure it's all sorted out and neatly in its place, your subconscious tells you otherwise. Just after I started writing this book, Joe visited me in my dreams for the first time in years. He was alive, he looked exactly as he did the last time I saw him, at Heathrow Airport, when he left for Everest in 1982. He was sorry for all the upset he had caused me. He wanted us to be together again. But in my dream, as in real life, I was happily married, and horribly torn by this collision of the past and the present. I awoke, in great distress, in the arms of my husband, unable to admit to him the struggle I had just surfaced from.

After her husband died in a fall from the North Face of the Eiger, Marilyn Harlin refused to see his body. 'I did not want to remember him as torn and dismembered,' she said. Judging by Chris Bonington's description of finding John Harlin lying at the base of the wall 'grotesque, distorted by the appalling impact of his 4,000-foot fall but still horribly recognisable . . .' it was probably a wise decision. But the widow of a fighter pilot warned Marilyn that not seeing the body meant she would be haunted by dreams. 'She was right,' said Marilyn. 'My dreams went this way. His death was a hoax. John had gone off to Algeria and this was his way of escaping his family commitment – which on the one hand he really had. Then I met him on a tram going up skiing and I said, "How could you do that to the children?" As if I accepted that he could do it to me. It was his right, his choice, and I could take it or leave it. But he shouldn't have done it to the children. In these dreams I'd always meet him on trams or trains – then gradually they happened less and less frequently.'

After Hilary Nunn's husband Paul was killed by a falling sérac on Haramosh II in 1995, it took her four years to accept that he wasn't coming home. Even now, she dreams about him turning up. 'He'll explain where he's been and I'll say, "Now you really are here, aren't you? I'm not dreaming, am I?" Because in my dream somehow I know it's not right. But he'll laugh and say, "No, no, you're not dreaming, Hilary." And then I wake up. It makes you feel pretty bad. You think you're in control and things are going the way you choose them to go. Subconsciously there must be something still there that's not sorted out.'

Each year since 1996, Sue Thompson has got rid of more of Bruce Herrod's possessions. Just after the most recent clear-out, she had a dream that he'd come home. 'I was in my flat and someone had laid out a huge table for dinner for twelve with candles and all the rest of it, and he walked through the door with another woman. I said, "What the hell are you doing here? Where have you been?" And he said something completely absurd like he'd been working near Nottingham. I said, "Why didn't you come and clear out your own stuff? Why leave me to do it?"'

Their relationship had been strong and secure, with no hint of infidelity, yet this was the second time she'd dreamt of him coming home with another woman. 'I suspect the woman is almost a symbol for the mountain,' she said. 'That the mountain took over as his other love.'

'You and Joe were only together for a relatively short time, weren't you?' observed eighty-nine-year-old Dr Charlie Houston, a veteran of the 1953 American expedition to K2. Here we go, I thought – in the past, many people had commented that Hilary's grief must have been much worse than mine, as Joe and I weren't married and had been together for less than three years. But I underestimated Houston's insight. 'How devastating for you to lose him when the passion was still so very strong,' he continued, 'before you'd reached a level of serenity with each other where you could sit together without touching. When the fire is burning so brightly, and then suddenly goes out, the darkness must be truly terrible.'

A love affair cut short in its infancy brings a special sort of pain, that of a future lost. Eighteen months was all Sarah Richard had with Alex MacIntyre, before he was killed on Annapurna by a stone fall. 'I'd met this man, and we'd fallen head over heels in love,' she said. 'We were talking about having a child. It was the first stage of a life together, it was on the road to happening. It was all completely shattered.'

The only clarity Sarah had was the need to make a new life for herself, one that bore no resemblance to her projected life with MacIntyre. She moved to another city, and a new job. But the changes did nothing to ease her grief. 'The first two years after Alex died seemed interminable,' she recalls. 'I was completely and utterly depressed. Those depressions were like a black whirlwind above your head that sucked down and came into your being. They seeped through you like a grey cloud. I could see it coming, see it and sense it. Then I'd be inside it and I'd think God, it's come. Everything would feel grey and look grey, have no taste, no colour.'

Her longing for the child they'd planned continued, and in 1989, seven years after his death, her first son was born. She named him Jack Alex. Another son followed two years later. She found great joy in her children, but depression still dogged her. 'Years later I went to a doctor about something else. Suddenly I broke down and started talking about Alex. He asked how long it was since Alex had died. It was fourteen years. He said, "I think it's time you had some counselling about this." He arranged for me to take group therapy. After three sessions someone said, "Sarah's the only one who hasn't said much about herself." I just lost it, I cried and cried. It felt like all the tension that had built up over the years finally came out.'

Sarah is separated from the father of her children. 'In the back of my mind there's always this perfect Alex,' she said. 'Our relationship was so lovely. I can't ever imagine that ever happening again.'

Weeks after Joe died, I visited Chris Bonington at his home in the Lake District. We walked up to High Pike with his dogs, and he listened to me with kind patience as I talked endlessly, repetitively, about Joe. Standing on the top of the hill, watching cloud shadows slide over the rolling green fells beneath us, Chris suddenly said to me, 'I know you can't imagine it now, but one day you will fall in love again, and be happy.'

I remember feeling angry with him, as if he underestimated the depth of my grief, as if being happy again would be a betrayal of my feelings for the man I had lost. Forming a new and healthy emotional attachment, many of the grief experts say, is a sign that the mourning work is over. When Chris Bonington's prediction came to pass, however, I was still spiralling around my grief, and the man I met became an integral part of that journey.

Halfway through a one-year teaching exchange to Canada, I met

Dag at a t'ai chi class. It was in early February 1986, and he had also been in the country for six months, doing research for his PhD at the University of Munich. When I first saw him, a door in my heart that had long since shut tight suddenly swung open. Stepping through it, I went into emotional freefall. At first, Dag held back, wary of my intensity and the hard shell I had built around myself. One Friday night, I called in to see him on my way home from work, just as the first snowflakes began drifting down from a leaden sky. We sat on the floor of his tiny apartment, drinking wine and talking. The snow was falling thickly when I began to tell him about Joe. Since arriving in Canada, this was the first time that I had shared the full story with anyone. I talked for hours, about how we met, our times together, his expeditions, his death, my journey to Everest. Dag listened intently, saying little. Eventually, and without shame, he cried – for Joe's loss, for my sorrow, for the hurt and vulnerable person I had finally let him see beneath my bravado. When the story came to an end, the snow was drifting around my car and piling up on his balcony. We spent a tender night together, barely touching, but sharing deep intimacies. It would be another year before we intertwined our futures, but that night sealed something between us. When people ask Dag if he feels in the shadow of the legendary mountaineer Joe Tasker, he smiles and says no, that it was Joe who brought us together.

There are no rules, no guidelines, for when love should come again after loss in the mountains. For Hilary Boardman, it was thirteen years. Burning the photograph of her dead husband was a turning point. She left the ashram after that, took up climbing and skiing again, and, after so long alone and self-sufficient, began feeling lonely for male companionship. 'David and I just kept coming across each other,' she said, of her old friend and teaching colleague David Rhodes. Romance grew gently between them, and in 1998 they were married.

For others it happens more quickly. A few months after Alex Lowe died on Shishapangma, his widow Jenny became romantically involved with Conrad Anker, her husband's best friend and the only survivor of the avalanche that killed him. Since then they have married, and together with Jenny's three sons are doing their grieving work together. There is a shrine to Alex in their house, photographs of him hang on the walls, and his name comes into their conversation daily. Conrad is a wise man, who instinctively understands about mourning. In the spring of 2002, he persuaded Jenny Lowe to travel with him to the Himalaya, her first visit to the place where so many of Alex's obsessions lay. Flying into Kathmandu, she had a perfect view of Shishapangma rising from billowing white clouds, and saw the face where Alex is buried. And in early 2003, along with her three sons, she accompanied Conrad to Antarctica, one of Alex's favourite places in the world to climb.

My own experience of grief has not been in stages, or in tasks completed. Rather, it has been like a spiral, continuously circling around the defining event of Joe's death. At first the spiral was so tight I could see nothing beyond it. Now, it is made up of huge arcs, only faintly perceived on the far horizon. Within that spiral there have been the moments of kairotic time. Sitting at 21,000 feet on Everest staring at the North East Ridge. Holding my father's hand as he slipped from life. Standing in a phone booth in Vienna watching the rain fall. Pulling a photograph from an envelope. Meeting a man's eyes across a room. Each of those moments, and many more, have in some way brought me back again to the cause of my grief, and in doing so allowed me to distance myself from it a little more. No doubt there are more such moments still to come. Sometimes I'm asked how I found closure after Joe disappeared on Everest. I never know how to answer, where to start. 'What is closure, anyway?' my husband said recently. 'Life is like a house, you inhabit its rooms and walk around between them. When you shut the doors, it's only for a time, you don't lock them for ever behind you.'

7

Badges of Honour

d Webster stands with two other climbers at 27,000 feet on the South
East Ridge of Everest. It's five a.m. The temperature is minus 29
degrees Fahrenheit. He's gasping for breath; at this altitude the air holds
scarcely a third as much oxygen as at sea level. This is a brutal place, where
nothing grows and no one can survive for long. The few humans who venture
here know without question they have no margin for error, that the tiniest
mistake can grow with devastating swiftness into a problem of immense
proportions.

The first gleam of light seeps into the sky, chasing away the stars. A sea of
peaks appear: Cholatse, Tawache, Ama Dablam, Lhotse, bathed in an eerie
golden glow. A perfect photograph. Before taking the camera from its bag, Ed
removes his bulky down overmitts. The inner gloves he wears are thin enough
for his fingers to focus the lens, for the air to penetrate to his skin, and for him
to sense the temperature of the camera, which later he will remember as 'like a
lump of dry ice'.

While he brackets the first shot, Ed's nerves send alarm signals to his brain,
reporting on the extreme cold attacking his body through his fingers. The
response is rapid, and uncompromising – to prevent the cold reaching further into
his body, his extremities must be sacrificed. Like the captain of the damaged
Titanic sealing off the lower sections of the hull, Ed's brain orders the blood

vessels at the tips of his fingers to close. *The flow of warm blood is reduced to a trickle. The frigid metal of the camera quickly sucks the last remnants of warmth from his fingertips; the superficial layer of Ed's skin freezes. Fiddling with lenses and dials, he's aware of a numbness, but the scene before him is breathtaking, and dominates his thoughts. He spends two minutes taking eight photographs; meanwhile, microscopic ice crystals form in the tissues beneath his skin, steadily expanding in the cells, and rupturing them.*

Unaware of the damage, Ed climbs upwards for hours, to 28,700 feet. Just below the South Summit, exhausted and beset by hallucinations, he turns back. Finally, after retracing his steps to the South Col, he removes his gloves and examines his fingers. They are pale grey, the texture of wood. Ed knows he has superficial frostbite — a gentle name for a serious condition. He knows he should only rewarm his frozen fingers when all chances of refreezing them have passed. But he's at 25,900 feet, without oxygen, and hypoxia is blurring his judgement. Although Base Camp is 8,000 feet away, down Everest's most challenging and deadly face, he feels confident that the worst is behind him. He leans over to a pot steaming on a camp stove, and lowers his fingers into the hot water.

The Kangshung Face. Seracs as big as houses, precipitous rock buttresses, overhanging ledges of blue-green ice, steep gullies down which huge avalanches roar. Until a few years ago no one dared climb here. Ed and his friends have put a new route up this 12,000 foot face, without the help of porters or supplementary oxygen. Their achievement is great, but it can't be enjoyed until they're safely down.

To reduce extra weight on this final retreat from the mountain, they jettison their tents. In error, they also leave their rope behind. Ed's down gloves weigh a mere six ounces, but he decides they are too heavy to take with him. He sets off wearing woollen mittens. The three-day descent is a spiralling nightmare. They struggle through thigh-deep snow and white-out conditions. They have no food. During a fall they lose two ice axes. Ed takes the lead, holding the remaining axe in his left hand. On his wrist is a steel Rolex watch. As the axe and watch steadily conduct cold to his hand, more alarm signals are sent, more blood vessels close, and ice crystals begin to form in the deeper tissues. Serum, the liquid compound of Ed's blood, starts leaking out of the injured cells lining his veins, causing his hands to swell and further restricting the blood flow.

On the third day, as darkness falls, they reach a 3,000-foot rock buttress, down which they must rappel on fixed ropes. The little blood still flowing in Ed's fingers has thickened and turned to sludge. He fumbles ineffectively with the frozen ropes, cursing aloud at his awkwardness. So far on this retreat, his main concern has been survival. Now, he begins to seriously worry about the state of his stiff, cold hands.

During the rappelling, Ed's mittens repeatedly fill with snow, and the friction of the rope shreds the frostbite blisters on his fingers. When he reaches advance base camp, his fingers are purple, swollen and solid. Quite literally, they have turned into blocks of ice. Dread creeps over him as he realises that the damage to the tissue of his fingers is severe, that gangrene is possible, and that amputations are all but inevitable.

Until I met Ed Webster, I'd never thought of frostbite as a particularly big deal. Joe Tasker had always shrugged off my questions about it. 'It's something you try to avoid,' he'd say. Or he'd recount the story of how Dick Renshaw got frostbite during their descent from Dunagiri. Dick had removed his gloves to hammer in an ice peg and tie some ropes together. Later, he was sitting in his sleeping bag eating a piece of chocolate when he realised he had finished the piece and was nibbling on the ends of his own fingers, which were now as dark, hard and frozen as the chocolate had been. 'They were a strange sight,' Joe would say, 'not purply-black like a bruise, but utterly black, a blackness deep as the bone. It looked like he had alien growths on the ends of his fingers.' Dick lost the last few millimetres of bone on three fingers, a fact I barely noticed. But with Ed Webster, the results of his frostbite were a very different matter.

We met at the 1999 Banff Mountain Film Festival, where I took part in a seminar on the consequences of risk-taking in the mountains. After the event, I was signing books when I noticed a handsome, fit-looking man with a shock of grey-streaked hair striding across the room towards me. At first I was struck by his piercingly blue eyes, and the intensity of his gaze. Then, as he introduced himself, he took one of my hands between both of his, and I felt the foreshortened fingers. He spread his hands on the table, and leaned over so that our faces were close. He talked of his admiration for Joe Tasker, and of how my book about our relationship had affected him. But I barely heard his words – I was focused on his hands, staring at them in shock. From the wrist to the knuckles they were big, strong and capable. Climber's hands. From the knuckles down, they were mutilated, with half of one thumb gone, and eight fingers missing their last joint. When I looked up again, Ed was smiling kindly.

'You're interested in the consequences of climbing?' he asked. 'Here they are.'

Whenever Joe Tasker set off on one of his frequent Himalayan expeditions, I used to think that this was what wartime must have been like for my mother and grandmother. I felt like a war bride, left at home for long and uncertain periods, waiting for news and praying that it would be good. Back then it was the strain of the long separations, and the possibility of Joe dying in the mountains, that kept me awake at night. I never considered the other possibilities, that he might return disabled or disfigured. Or that for Joe, too, there were parallels with the experience of war. Now, talking to Ed Webster, I thought of some of the combative language of mountaineering: 'battling against the mountain', 'siege tactics', 'mounting an assault', 'fighting the elements'. I thought of the old man who came to talk at my school one Remembrance Day. He had fought in the trenches during the First World War, and told us tales of men drowning in mud, having their limbs or their eyes shot away, losing their minds. Of fleeing from attack, abandoning people who were injured beyond help, and letting them die alone. It was the worst of times, he said, yet it gave him his most profound experiences, his closest friendships, and his strongest emotions. I remembered my grandfather, how he would sit by the fire at the end of his life, singing the songs of that war. 'Goodbye Dolly, I must leave you, though it breaks my heart to go . . .' It was the time that obsessed men of his generation, inhabiting their dreams up to the day they died.

With Ed Webster on that historic climb up the Kangshung Face was the British mountaineer Stephen Venables. When his team mates became exhausted, he pressed on alone to the top, then spent a night in the open on the South Summit, kept company by an imaginary crowd of people, including the long-dead explorer Eric Shipton. He returned with frostbitten feet, and later lost four toes. Stephen admits he had always been curious about taking himself to the absolute limit of experience. 'Although you don't deliberately seek an epic, you know that one day something like that might happen. When it did happen on Everest it was harder and more prolonged and draining than anything I had ever done, but also more exhilarating than anything I had ever done. It was like a watershed. It was something I was probably never going to repeat. So in a sense I'd lost something. Lost that potential to experience anything so extraordinarily cathartic again. I sometimes feel quite nostalgic that that great moment has gone.'

The world of high-altitude mountaineering is a place where the line between safety and disaster is finely drawn. Accidents are commonplace, the fatality rate is high. Experienced mountaineers know about pain and suffering. Many of them have seen friends swept away in avalanches. They've walked past corpses frozen on the side of a high mountain, they've buried broken bodies in crevasses. Some have had bad falls or frostbite; some have had their lives changed irrevocably by injuries. And yet they claim that such things are a necessary component of what makes mountaineering worthwhile.

'Without risk to life and limb,' said Yvon Chouinard, a legendary US climber, 'there's no adventure.'

According to Ruth Seifert, this acceptance of physical risk is a totally abstract concept. Neither soldiers nor climbers, she says, ever really believe that disaster will strike them personally. 'No one would ever go to war if they thought they were going to get killed or horribly injured. It's the same for mountaineers – they know terrible things happen to other people, but they think those people have been unlucky or made some mistakes. They say, "Oh, I'm a careful person, I've survived lots of other expeditions, I'm going to be all right." They're convinced there's no risk for them.'

When Beck Weathers set off to climb Everest in the spring of 1996, he didn't expect to die. Nor did he expect to sustain severe frostbite, leading to massive disfigurement and disability. The doctors who first assisted him, after his astonishing return from the dead on Everest in 1996, said that his was the most extreme case of frostbite they'd ever seen. And no wonder: he had spent ten hours standing at 27,600 feet, waiting in vain for the return of his guide, then lain on the mountainside for an entire night and much of the next day in a blizzard, without shelter, fully exposed to the wind and sub-zero temperatures. After miraculously managing to rouse himself and find his way back to camp, he was left alone in a tent that was torn open by the wind, and so spent a second night at the mercy of the elements.

'I saw this guy with his arm held up and frozen in place,' said Pete Athans, who with Todd Burleson was the first to see Beck stagger into camp. 'Everything up to his elbow was white like ivory or alabaster. His jacket was completely open and he was covered with snow. It was surreal.'

'This man had no face,' Burleson later told a TV interviewer. 'It was completely black, solid black, like he had a crust over him.'

Helped by Todd Burleson, Pete Athans and members of the IMAX crew, Beck made it down the mountain as far as the edge of the Khumbu Icefall at 20,000 feet. A brave helicopter pilot risked his own life to fly up to that altitude twice, and collect Beck and another injured climber, Makalu Gau. He ferried Beck to Kathmandu where his brother, Dan, an accident and emergency doctor, had arrived from Dallas to help care for him. Dan recalled that Beck 'smelled like a burns patient', and that his right hand looked as though it had been stuck into a hot fire, and left there a while.

When soldiers return from a war disabled or disfigured, usually they can find some vindication for their suffering. They were fighting for a just cause, or they joined up out of a sense of duty to their country. But if they cannot name a reason for such sacrifice – as happened in the Vietnam War – they have no hook on which to hang their grief, and are often left with feelings of abandonment, anger and bitterness. Climbing, however, is never done in the name of justice, nor is it a necessary act. Mountaineers put their lives and limbs on the line, and suffer the deprivations of high altitude, for purely selfish reasons – sometimes in the hope of fame and sponsorship, but mostly just for the deep satisfaction that scaling a peak brings them. So, when disaster strikes, where do they hang their grief?

'If I'd got the frostbite while I was fighting for my life, I think it would have been easier to accept,' admits Ed Webster. 'But it wasn't a do-or-die situation, it was something that, with hindsight, was so preventable. I took my gloves off to take some photographs – I mean, how stupid is that? My initial feelings about it were of pure shame. I thought I'd be ridiculed by every other climber in the world. And tied into those feelings was a profound hatred of Everest. I was totally freaked out – my God, as a climber you panic when you have a little muscle injury, and here suddenly I faced losing all my fingertips. I couldn't believe it had happened. I felt like I hated this mountain. I couldn't even look at Everest when we were leaving.'

Unlike Ed Webster, who quickly understood the consequences of his frostbite, Beck Weathers went into denial. He convinced himself that, at worst, he would lose only parts of his fingers, and still be left with workable hands. But the progress of frostbite is so graphic that its reality cannot be denied for long. To ascertain what tissue will die off irrevocably, and what can be saved, doctors usually delay surgery for as long as possible, leaving the patient to watch as whole parts of his body slowly decay. In Beck Weathers' case, his hands 'turned to stone', shrank, and mummified.

To Ed Webster, it seemed his body was betraying him, trying to rid itself of its now useless parts. Being in public during this time was excruciatingly embarrassing.

'I'd be at a restaurant or a dinner party, trying to eat with these blackened claws, and dribbling food and wine all over the place. My friends would be politely looking the other way, but I'd be floating around somewhere up by the ceiling, staring down at myself and saying, "Ed, don't worry, this isn't *really* happening to you."'

For Brummie Stokes and Bronco Lane, the long wait for their bodies to demarcate dead from living flesh took on a particularly nightmarish quality. During a British Army expedition to Everest in 1976, the two men spent a night in the open on the South East Ridge. 'We had no sleeping bags with us, no tents, stoves or radios,' Bronco recalled. 'On the way up we'd stashed a bottle of oxygen at 28,000 feet. We reached the summit at three p.m., and started down just after four. The weather was deteriorating, blowing snow had covered our foot prints.'

It was dark by the time they found their stashed oxygen. They dug a platform, sat on their rucksacks and prepared for a long, cold night. But when Brummie tried to attach the new bottle of oxygen to his mask, it wouldn't fit. Bronco started fiddling with it; he took off his outer mitts and spent an hour on the problem. 'I was wearing my liner gloves, but basically it was flesh on metal.' He credits their survival to the fact he succeeded. But there was a cost – when they came down from the mountain, Bronco's right hand was frozen. And both he and Brummie had severely frostbitten feet.

It was three months before their doctors decided to go ahead with the necessary surgeries; unfortunately, these months coincided with a summer when Britain had record-breaking high temperatures. Before long Brummie's toes started to smell terribly, but worse was to come.

'After the first month, I noticed that tiny maggots were eating at the dead tissue in between the frostbite that had gone hard and the healthy flesh on my foot,' he wrote in *Soldiers and Sherpas*. 'A gap was appearing between the two that began to expose the bones of my now-dead toes.'

He tried picking out the maggots, until he realised that they were helping to get rid of the decaying flesh. Like Maurice Herzog, whose toes also became home to maggots when he was returning to France from Annapurna in 1950, he decided to leave the creatures to get on with their gruesome task. In Herzog's case, by the time he reached Paris, 'these maggots had grown huge and there was quite half a pound of them'.

Bronco Lane wasn't quite so relaxed about the uninvited guests. One Sunday afternoon, after a big lunch at his mother-in-law's house, he was sunning himself in the garden. He removed the dressings on his feet to air the blackened stumps, then dozed off. Twenty minutes later, his wife Jan woke him up. 'You want to cover up those toes,' she told him. 'There are flies about.'

The following morning, Bronco felt a tingling sensation in one of his feet. 'I knew something wasn't right. I waited until my wife had gone to work, then I took off the dressings. One on toe, between the dead and living flesh at the metatarsal head, there were these maggots, eyeing me up. I got a cocktail stick and flicked them out.'

Bronco Lane lost his toes, and the thumb and top halves of his fingers on his right hand. Brummie Stokes lost all his toes and part of each foot. Ed Webster's seven operations left him with only one finger and thumb fully intact. Beck Weathers' right hand was amputated above the wrist, and what could be salvaged from his left hand was fashioned into a kind of cloven paw. His nose was removed and a new one, cobbled together from grafts of skin, tissue and cartilage, was grown on his forehead. All the men were then left to come to terms with their disabilities – a part of the mountaineering story they had not been prepared for.

'You can't hide the fact that all your fingertips have been amputated,' said Ed Webster. 'One of the most awful feelings at first was being in the check-out line in the grocery store and having to hand over the money to the clerk. Some high-school girl would take the money, and I'd think, God she's going to look at my hands, she's going to look at these hot dogs my fingers have turned into. Ninety per cent of the time, nobody seemed to notice. But sometimes the check-out girl would go,

"Wow, if you don't mind me asking, what happened to you?" Occasionally I would say, "Well, actually, I was frostbitten on Mount Everest," and usually she'd go, "Uh huh, no kidding. Well, nice to meet you." So I invented these silly stories about what happened. My favourite ones were, "Actually, I'm a very bad carpenter, and I had this little problem with my saw." Or, "You won't believe this, but I got attacked by a shark." When I really wanted to gross them out, I'd say, "You know, there are times I get so nervous I start biting my fingernails and I just can't stop.'"

Humour also helped others deal with their situation. 'The frostbite was a good career move,' Brummie Stokes joked recently. 'Now I can model children's shoes for Mothercare.'

The doctor who amputated several of Kurt Diemberger's fingers after his return from K2 in 1986 presented him with one of the digits in a plastic container. 'At first I thought, What should I do with it?' Kurt recalled. 'My friend Herbert Tichy, who made the first ascent of Cho Oyu, he kept one of the fingers he lost to that climb. He told me he uses it when he is negotiating book contracts. When the publisher doesn't want to give him a good deal, he puts the finger on the table and says, "Look, that's the *Einstatz* – the stakes."' Despite this advice, Kurt did nothing with his finger until a museum in Salzburg asked him to donate something to their Exhibition of Mountain Climbing. Now the finger is in a glass case, alongside a picture of him in hospital, awaiting his operation. 'When the school classes are coming in, they are saying, 'Where's the finger?' It's a real warning about the dangers of mountaineering, and all the risks we take. Those people who go into winter climbing – I am absolutely sure if they see this finger they may think twice about uncertain weather, they may check their decision.'

In 2000, Bronco Lane self-published *Military Mountaineering*, a history of British services mountaineering since 1945. His first book signings were not a great success, so he decided he needed a way to attract more public attention. For years, his amputated digits had been stored in the medical inspection room of an army hospital in Hereford. He claimed them back, and at future signings set a plastic hand with five black finger tips next to his pile of books. 'They helped me break even on the costs of publication,' he said. Bronco, who is now a long distance cyclist, used to travel to his readings by bike. 'I'd be terrified of getting knocked over and having the police find the fingers in my pannier. Eventually I thought, 'I've got to find a new home for these.'

A solution came when The National Army Museum in Chelsea asked him if he would donate some personal items for an exhibit. 'I think they were expecting a woolly hat and an ice axe,' he said. Instead, they received ten blackened toes and the top halves of five fingers. 'They were an unusual gift,' said Jo Woolley, a spokeswoman for the museum. 'But our aim is to tell the story of the ordinary soldier past and present and what he or she has been through, so we value objects that have a story behind them.' The toes were not in good enough condition to be displayed, but the fingers were mounted on a wooden hand-shaped plinth, and encased in formaldehyde. Plans are underway to move the digits to the National Mountaineering Exhibition in Cumbria's Rhegged Discovery Centre. Bronco, who considers himself 'only an amateur mountaineer', is greatly pleased by this prospect. 'It's where the great and good climbers are commemorated,' he said proudly. 'And my fingers will be there among them.'

After losing his hands, Beck Weathers had no choice but to give up mountaineering. For those climbers whose injuries are not quite as severe, however, their rehabilitation is often linked to a return to high places.

When Brummie Stokes was undergoing his amputations, his mother travelled halfway down the country to visit him. 'I could see the strain in [her] face,' he later wrote, 'and tried to put her mind at rest by telling her that everything would be all right and that before she knew it, I would be back climbing again. She attacked me verbally, as only mothers can, and told me that I must on no account climb again, that I should take up a more sedate hobby.' He paid no heed to his mother's advice. Determined to become the first British climber to summit Everest from both sides, he made three subsequent attempts on its North East Ridge. During expeditions in 1986 and 1988, he suffered a total of six bouts of cerebral oedema. He returned in 1994, and broke his neck in an avalanche on the North Face.

Ruth Seifert believes that such determination has as much to do with feelings of competition as a love of climbing. 'There's this battle that goes on with the serious mountaineers, that if they fail to climb a mountain, or if they've lost fingers or toes or been hurt in some other way, they've got to come out the winners. *They've* got to be on top, and not the mountain. They've lost the fight, and something has stopped them doing what they want, and so they go back. They get into loggerheads with the climbing – they say, I'm going to get the better of this, no matter what.'

Ed Webster agrees with her. 'In a way it was uncanny – I had even more willpower, even more drive to climb after I recovered from my frostbite injuries. As far as I knew, no other climber had lost eight fingertips and had still gone back and become as good a rock climber as they had been before. I wanted to prove I could do that. It took a while, but I did. Between 1991 and 1995 I climbed almost non-stop. There was one year – 1993 – when I went on three expeditions in a row. In the spring I went to Bhutan and tried a seven-thousand-metre peak, then I went to climb in Arctic Norway for the whole summer, and in the fall I went back to Nepal and I climbed Cholatse. I was away from Colorado for eight and a half months. Now I can barely comprehend it. But that shows how manic I was to prove that I was still a climber after I had done this stupid thing getting frostbitten, up high on Everest. I felt it was so unfair, I wanted to throw it back in the face of God.'

But it's more than just a competitive spirit that drives them back up the mountains. 'For the serious mountaineer, to lose your ability to climb is to lose your entire sense of self,' said Ed Webster. 'It strips you bare.' He speaks from double experience. Some years after the amputations of his fingers, when he was climbing strongly again, he began suffering from inexplicable neurological problems, including severe twitching in his leg muscles. Although no conclusive diagnosis has ever been made, he thinks such symptoms might be linked to the fact that he spent four nights in the 'Death Zone' above 26,000 feet, without supplementary oxygen, during his Kangshung Face climb. Whatever the reason for them, these problems signalled the end of his days as a climber.

'When I've tried to go on a long hike or a climb, I feel awful afterwards. My legs feel worse; the back of my head starts to ache; I'm light-headed; I get yawning attacks. I feel really sad about it . . . You end up being caught in this awful position, of loving climbing almost more than anything else in your life, but knowing it has also brought you these horrific agonies. So you're having these terrible things happen to you, and yet part of you is longing for the mountains, longing to see the light play over them, and part of your heart is saying, "Oh, couldn't I just be up there again?" It's a terrible dilemma that serious climbers face.'

On a clear afternoon in 1986, three climbers approached the summit of El Pico de Orizaba, the highest mountain in Mexico. Fifty feet from their goal, one man slipped, pulling the others off. Gary Guller and his friends, one of whom 'was like a brother', went into an uncontrolled slide down a 50 degree slope. During their 1,500 feet fall, Gary broke his neck in two places and his left arm was paralyzed. His friends suffered severe internal injuries. 'After we came to a stop, we tried to stand up,' said Gary. 'Then we realized how badly messed up we were.' They lay on the ice for three days before rescuers arrived. During that time, his closest friend died. 'On the second night, we held each other,' Gary recalled. 'I said, "This isn't going to get any better. Let's just go to sleep." I woke up, but he didn't.'

Back in the States, Gary's surgeons repaired his broken neck, but his arm was beyond saving. Finally, he made the decision to have it amputated above the elbow. After a few years of intense physiotherapy, 'and some serious rethinking', he started climbing again. First in Canada and Scotland. Eventually, in the Andes and the Himalayas. Now he runs an adventure travel company, and leads guided climbs. He's summited Aconcagua, attempted Lhotse, and reached 7,600 metres on Everest. In March 2003 he's returning to Everest, for another try at the summit. 'Being in the high mountains gives me a sense of freedom,' he said. 'I couldn't give that up.'

In writing about the search for the North-West Passage, Christopher Isherwood said that sometimes extreme adventure is chosen because, despite the dangers and hardships, it is easier to face than the trials of domestic life. According to the British mountaineer Joe Simpson, the fears climbers face in the mountains are archetypal ones, of falling from heights or suffocating in an avalanche. Such fears evoke a 'fight or flight' response with a definite end result – survival or death. Against these he sets 'uncontrolled fears', about money, children, career, success, love – the patina of daily concerns that can never be fully resolved and which never go away.

When I mentioned these theories to Chris Bonington, he smiled knowingly. 'The big questions are simple questions, aren't they? It's the little questions that are hard: struggling with the next chapter of your book, sorting out your income tax, trying to make the fridge work, getting the car fixed, dealing with your children being expelled from school or wanting to borrow money from you so they can do something you don't really approve of – those sort of things are much more difficult questions than trying to climb a mountain, or facing life and death. Life and death are simple.'

Joe Tasker and Pete Boardman faced the ultimate big, simple question in 1982, when they disappeared on the North East Ridge of Everest. A decade later, Pete's body was discovered lying in a snow bank on the ridge, but what happened to Joe is still pure conjecture. One possibility was that a cornice – a wind-blown overhanging mass of snow – gave way beneath him and he fell 12,000 feet down the Kangshung Face. *Twelve thousand feet.* Immediately after his death, the terror of such a fall haunted me. My mind could not accept the reality of Joe plummeting through so much space, or the violence and pain of his landing. But mountaineering friends who had survived long and near-fatal falls assured me it would not have been the horrifying end I imagined. They described their own experiences, and said they'd felt no pain or fear, just resignation, mild curiosity about what would happen next, and then surprise to find themselves alive. For years, I had an image of Joe free-falling peacefully through space, bypassing the overhangs, ledges, gullies and séracs of the Kangshung Face, picking up so much speed that he was unconscious before the terrible impact happened. Only much later did I begin to wonder if – for what I'm sure were the kindest of reasons – some of my old friends had been bending the truth.

'I am still appalled by the violence of it,' writes Peter Potterfield, a Seattle-based climber, about a fall off Chimney Rock in the Cascade Mountains of Washington. After failing on a move and losing his grip on the wall, he remembers anticipating the jerk when the rope would catch him. But the belay failed and he continued to tumble down the mountain, his body smashing against the rock face. 'My sensations were of cannon-loud explosions as my helmet crashed against the rock, and sledgehammer blows as impact after impact jarred and tossed my body.' He heard his bones breaking and registered pain that was 'spectacular'.

Joe Simpson was more reassuring – as unpleasant experiences go, he said, falling is not so bad. 'The avalanche I was in, that was frightening.

It was like being badly beaten up by a group of very big men. I was being smashed to pieces and when I was getting suffocated it was very scary. But falling – it was never this Hollywood idea of howling and screaming to your death.' His first fall, on a Scottish mountain, resulted in several broken ribs, a fractured fibula, torn neck muscles and a damaged bladder. But this was only a warm-up for other, far more dramatic accidents. In the French Alps, a ledge he was bivouacking on collapsed, and for the next twelve hours, until rescue came, he and a friend dangled from an insecurely fastened hand-rail rope, against a vertical rock wall, with 2,000 feet of space beneath them. In the Peruvian Andes, he broke his leg in a fall, then plunged into a crevasse when his climbing partner was forced to cut the rope between them. Surviving that ordeal left him with psychological and physical wounds that took over two years to heal. In 1991, he returned to the Himalaya, and promptly suffered a 500-foot fall on Mount Pachermo. He lay all night in the open at 20,000 feet with a badly broken ankle and gaping head wounds. Once again, he survived. His accidents have left him with facial scars, an awkward gait and arthritis in his knee and ankle, but he regrets none of them.

'I consider myself privileged to have had such moments in my life. They've shown me things about myself and my friends that I would never have otherwise seen.'

Gary Guller, with one arm, climbs to 7,600 metres on Everest, Brummie Stokes endures worms eating parts of his body, Joe Simpson crawls from the bowels of the earth, Beck Weathers rises from the dead. Only an injury of the most debilitating kind will dent the determination of serious mountaineers. Their disablements and disfigurements are the battle scars of the warrior, the marks of the hero, the trophies of the victor. In Ed Webster's book, *Snow in the Kingdom*, there is a photograph of Reinhold Messner, who has lost toes to frostbite, examining with great interest Ed's damaged hands after his ordeal on the Kangshung face. 'The only positive thing about frostbite is that it's proof you've had some remarkable experiences,' said Ed. 'And the fact that I got these wounds on Everest has made it easier to deal with psychologically. No one wants to get badly frostbitten, but to mountaineers, it's a badge of honour.'

8

Masters of Denial

*H*alfway up a high mountain wall, at the southernmost tip of South America, he hacks out a place to sit in the snow. He's too tired to make a ledge so he can lie down. Too tired to eat. His world is wind and cold, the misery of a blizzard, hours of stormy darkness stretching interminably ahead. Huddled inside his bivouac bag, he takes refuge in memory. Curled up with his wife in the warmth and peace of their bed. Their daughter singing happy nonsense in her cot. Other memories crowd in, unwelcome but impossible to fight back. His wife's tearful face, her choked voice. 'If you love us so much, why are you leaving again?' His friends, shaking their heads over pints of beer in the pub. 'Patagonia in winter, Andy? Are you crackers, mate?' The local people he met on his way to Cerro Torre, warning him of this year's record snowfalls and low temperatures.

Tendrils of sleep curl around his brain, but bring no respite. He dreams of frozen babies, of his daughter climbing on to his face, suffocating him. He wakes in panic; his head is almost buried in snow. Frantically scrabbling at the cowl of his bivouac bag, he pushes off its heavy load. Unnerved, he slides one hand inside his jacket to feel his treasured talismans: the laminated photos of his wife Mandy and his daughter Ella that he takes on every climb. As his fingers find the squares of plastic, a desperate longing overwhelms him. To hear his small *daughter's voice again, to hold his wife. Why am I here? he thinks. What am I doing this for?*

The two desires tear at Andy Kirkpatrick, endlessly. At home, all he thinks about is his next climb. On the climb, he wants it to be over, so that he can go home. He's never satisfied in either place. It's a curse. Like being madly in love with two people at the same time, unable to choose between them, but terrified of letting either one go.

Mandy hates him climbing. Always has. He'd got into it after they met, when he was nineteen and she was twenty-one. After he'd taken the tests she'd insisted on, tests to find out why he'd always failed at school. 'A classic case of dyslexia,' the doctor said. But the spatial tests, the puzzles, in those he scored brilliantly. If he could find a career which put such skills to use, the doctor told him, he was bound to succeed. What he found was ice climbing. Gigantic spatial puzzles on frozen waterfalls and the faces of winterbound mountains. Solving them gave him a satisfaction and sense of personal accomplishment that had eluded him throughout his school years. And brought him an alluring level of public recognition.

He put off having a family for as long as he could. The thought of fatherhood scared him. Too much responsibility – and what about his climbing career? But Mandy handed him an ultimatum: a baby or a divorce. He could never have anticipated the joy Ella would bring into his life. Or how much he would miss her, when he was away in the mountains.

Andy Kirkpatrick returned from Patagonia to Sheffield full of love for his family, realising anew just how much he had at home. Some months later, when he was itching to leave again, Mandy found a lump in one of her breasts. Her mother had died of breast cancer when Mandy was five years old. She remembered her bewilderment at losing a parent. She knew she had a high probability of developing the disease. Waiting for the results of the biopsy was terrifying. 'I kept thinking how terrible it would be for Ella if I died,' she said. 'I just wanted to live, to survive, to be there for her.' The lump was benign, but since then fear of the disease has hung over Mandy, like a cloud. 'There's nothing I can do apart from getting screened and having regular check-ups. But Andy's putting a cloud over his life, over all our lives, of his own free will. He voluntarily goes into risky situations . . . It's horrific to me. I would never, ever do that. How could I?'

Shortly after the breast cancer scare, Mandy became pregnant again. Andy, whose career as a professional climber was just starting to take off, responded with panic. 'I was coming up to thirty and I was about to have a second kid. I felt like I had one hand tied behind my back. None of my climbing friends are married. They are totally free. They can do what they want. I was this climber that people thought did all these incredible things, but in fact I was at home most of the time watching *The Simpsons*.'

To vent his frustration, he decided to do a solo ascent of the Reticent Wall in the Yosemite Valley, considered one of the three hardest big-wall routes in the world, and impossibly dangerous. Mandy, he recalled, 'went from really worrying about me to really hating me'. The night before he left they had a huge argument about his climbing. 'Bloody well go to America,' she shouted at him, 'and make up your mind what you're going to do.' She made him sleep downstairs on the settee. Early next morning he left without saying goodbye to his pregnant wife or his daughter.

Andy was on the Reticent Wall, alone, for twelve days. 'The climb was close to committing suicide in a way, because the chances of an accident were pretty high,' he admitted. 'There were two mornings where I remember lying in my bivvy sac and looking up at where I had to go, and I wasn't sure I'd be alive at the end of the day.'

Everything he needed to survive on the wall had to be hauled up behind him in large heavy bags. The tension on the ropes pulled the knots so tight, only the blows of a hammer would loosen them. As the days progressed, Andy began to see this process as a metaphor: his life was a tangled knot, slowly being picked open by the rigours of the climb. 'I inflicted on myself a huge amount of pain and fear. I was so scared on some pitches I was literally blacking out. I'd be hanging on by "sky hooks" to these tiny flakes that could break off at any second. But I wasn't thinking about where I was. I was thinking about my life at home and sorting it out. As I climbed, slowly I began to feel better. I was thinking, Yes, you are trapped. You have got a boring life. But you've been able to come here and do this really hard route. The second to last day I remember waking up, looking out over the Sierras and thinking, Oh, I'd love to bring my kids here. I could take them hiking and not go climbing ever again.'

In September 2001, barely three months after his success on the Reticent Wall, his son Euan was born. Early in 2002, Andy attempted a winter ascent of the North Face of the Dru, a 4,000-metre wall in the Alps, where he spent eleven days surviving what he later called the 'most challenging climbing and weather conditions' he'd ever experienced.

When Andy Kirkpatrick was six years old, his own parents had divorced. For the rest of his childhood he rarely saw his father, who was away with the RAF for long periods. 'I don't know how my father can have missed so much,' he said. 'The other day someone told me they'd never seen a kid love their father as much as my daughter loves me. We have such an amazing time together. She's the funniest, most interesting person I know.'

Ella and her baby brother Euan, says Andy, are the centre of his life. When he's at home, he doesn't go to gym or the local crags, like other climbers; he spends as much time as possible with the children. Mandy works four days a week as a special projects manager for a health education charity. For three of those days she's employed a nanny, whether Andy is there or not. 'He shares the care of the children when he's here,' she said, 'but when he goes away it's just too disruptive.' He's gone for about three months of the year, in Patagonia or the Alps, tackling difficult routes in lightweight, alpine style. Often he climbs in winter, in conditions most mountaineers go to great pains to avoid. His reputation has grown so fast because he is known to try extremely hard objectives, with a minimum of training. 'My ambition,' he admits, 'often outstrips my ability.'

And if he dies climbing? His biggest regret would be that his children are too small to have any real memories of him. Otherwise, he's sure they would survive the loss. 'Coming from a single-parent family, I feel you don't need a father figure, as long as you've got a good mother who loves you. And Mandy is a good mother, so I think it wouldn't be so bad if I wasn't around.'

Mandy Kirkpatrick worries that as her husband becomes more famous, he will be tempted to go for increasingly hard climbing objectives. She fears he will be drawn to the Himalaya. On completing the first winter ascent of Aguja in Patagonia in 2000, Andy said, 'That's probably the least rewarding trip I've been on . . . Nothing happened . . . If you're not putting your life at risk, then what's the point of being alive?' Mandy's worries, it would seem, are well founded. She fantasises about having a normal life, one in which the family could take holidays together, and she wouldn't have to spend months of each year worrying about her husband's safety. She understands how much of Andy's self-esteem is wrapped up in his climbing, and the writing career that is its offshoot. She knows that he's not going to stop. She's struck a bargain with him – if he makes life worthwhile for her while he's at home, she will try to cope with the rest. But it's a tenuous deal. 'Every eighteen months or so we have a crisis. We sit down and discuss whether or not we want to stay together. Up to now we've said yes. We are real soul mates. We love each other, we're very compatible, and Andy's a fantastic father. But it's so difficult, this climbing thing. If I could have Andy without the climbing, it would be perfect. He often says to me, "You'd be much happier with a regular bloke." And I think, Well, I would. If we ever did split up, I would never go out with another climber, ever in a million years, never. I wouldn't touch one with a bargepole.'

Without a family, Andy would be away climbing much more of the year; he believes he has made huge compromises. And he doesn't see the climbing as affecting his children, or his relationship with them. Not yet. In January 2003, he left home to climb in the Alps. 'Ella's four now,' he said, 'and at the airport she started crying. It's the first time that's happened. I thought, "My number's up soon." When there is a competition between my kids and climbing, I will stop. Which is terrible for my wife, because I wouldn't stop for her.'

In his essay 'Moments of Doubt', the American author David Roberts reflects on one year of his climbing career, when he was in his early twenties. He went on three major climbs, took some extraordinary risks, watched three people die and almost lost his own life in a fall. Despite all that, he writes, 'nowhere else on Earth, not even in the harbors of reciprocal love, have I felt pure happiness take hold of me and shake me like a puppy . . .'

Pure happiness. The price of reciprocal love may be negotiable with an adult, but what of the trusting, unconditional love of a child? Early on in her relationship with Eric Simonson, his wife Erin posed some direct questions about the issue of climbing and children. The couple met in the autumn of 1997 on an expedition to Kilimanjaro organised by Eric's company, International Mountain Guides. Erin was a client; Eric was the trip leader. By then, he had already been on some twenty Himalayan expeditions and had climbed Everest twice, once from the north and once from the south side. Would he climb Everest again, Erin asked, if he had a family? If children were involved, he told her, he would take a long, hard look at the proposition of high-altitude climbing. 'What his answer told me,' said Erin, 'was that he felt he wouldn't have the same sense of responsibility to a wife that he would have to children.'

After the Kilimanjaro trip, Eric was in the States for a month, then spent December in Antarctica. He was on Kilimanjaro again for all of January 1998. After a few weeks at home, he left in March for Everest. And on it went. 'In that first year of our relationship I think he was home maybe two months out of twelve,' said Erin. 'And it was all climbing.'

In 1999 Eric led the expedition that discovered the body of George Mallory, high on the slopes of Everest. The following year, in late March, Erin gave birth to a daughter, Audrey. Eric chose not to go to Everest that season, and soon he was taking the 'long, hard look' he had talked about on Kilimanjaro.

'I used to feel like I came home from trips with my little bag of experience fuller than when I had left,' he said, in the autumn of 2001. 'That whatever I brought back with me overcompensated for something I might have missed; it was a net gain. But when I came home from Everest this spring I really felt like I had missed something. And honest to God, I don't think I'd ever had that feeling before. I had been gone for three months, during which time Audrey went from being twelve months to fifteen months old. This was a key period of her development: she had barely been walking when I left, and now she was running all over. She hadn't been talking at all and now she was starting to talk. It was a really significant period in her life, and I totally missed it. I can look at the videotapes and the pictures but I realised for the first time there was a tangible price tag. You can't rewind the tape on a kid, you're either there or you're not.'

His climbing and guiding work continues to take him away from home several months of each year, but he has made a conscious effort to reduce the time he spends at high altitude. These days, his role on expeditions is largely a managerial one, from base camp. In 2002 he led an expedition to the south side of Everest; he climbed up through the Khumbu Icefall, but went no higher on the mountain. Eight members of his team summited without him. In 2003 he is going to the north side of Everest, but only as leader of a trekking group. Becoming a father in his forties, he said, has made this transition easier – unlike Jim Wickwire or Andy Kirkpatrick, he was no longer a young man burning with ambitions when parenthood loomed.

'But let's put this into perspective,' said Erin, who helps manage his business. 'Some great climbers have been killed on Mount Rainier and Eric will continue to climb there. He's already climbed it successfully 270 times, but that doesn't mean he's out of the woods. I know and he knows he can get killed on that mountain if he's not paying attention. He's still willing to take that risk, even as a father.'

The conflict between parenthood and climbing comes into sharp relief during the lead-up to an expedition. The routines of family life – meals together, bath times, stories before bed – are fractured by the constant phone calls, the endless 'to do' lists, the stress of last minute packing. A frenetic momentum builds up, disrupting the entire household.

'The preparation puts us all on edge,' admitted Ed Viesturs, shortly before leaving for Annapurna in the spring of 2002. 'My wife is like, "Okay I just want you to be gone now."' After a year of planning, Ed admitted he is relieved when it's time to finally board the plane and get the expedition rolling. He goes through his now familiar routine of departure: driving to SeaTac airport in Seattle with his wife Paula and their two children; unloading his gear on the sidewalk outside the Departures building, and saying goodbye there. How hard are those final goodbyes for his children?

'They get teary-eyed. Ella's still tiny enough that she just thinks I'm saying goodbye for the day or whatever. Later she keeps asking where Daddy is. But Gilbert knows that I'm going for a while and he gets rather sad. Letting go of his hug is really hard.'

Climbers commonly describe being able to 'compartmentalise' their emotions when they leave on an expedition, turning their focus with ease away from home and towards the mountain. 'When you step on the plane, it's like, "Okay, here we go,"' said Ed. 'You're finally doing the thing you've been planning for so long. You're in expedition mode, you have a different way of thinking.'

On Annapurna, Ed Viesturs awakened each morning at base camp to an alarm clock with a digital recording of Gilbert's voice saying, 'Hi, Daddy, its time to get up.' At all times on the mountain he carried his 'juju bag' of good luck charms: a print of a Tibetan mandala; a postcard Paula sent him during his first expedition after they met; a playing card. And the tiny medical bands his son and daughter wore in the hospital just after they were born.

Juju. Mementos to defend against loneliness. Charms to ward off disaster. Tangible evidence to fight the charge of selfishness: 'Part of you is here with me; I'm climbing this mountain for all of us.' When Tomaz Humar leaves home to tackle difficult mountain faces, alpine-style, he always takes a tiny shoe that his son, now eleven, wore as a baby. 'My children know I take this with me,' he said. 'You know what they always say to me? Bring the shoe back, Daddy.'

In the bedroom of a twelve-year-old girl in Owestry is a collection of teddy bears with a stellar climbing record. Whenever the Seattle-born Steve Sustad left home on an expedition, his daughter Katie gave him a teddy bear to take with him, swapping it for the teddy from his previous trip. 'She never said a word about me going away,' Steve recalled, 'but I know she had an inkling something wasn't quite right.' Those teddy bears were important talismans for him. When he jettisoned all extra equipment for a final summit push, that did not include the bear; Teddy always went to the top of the mountain with him.

In the mid 1990s he attempted the south face of Aconcagua, solo. In one day he got three-quarters of the way up the face. Then a storm moved in, dumping huge amounts of snow on the steep slopes above him. His retreat took several days. The avalanche danger was extreme; he knew that when one swept down the mountain, as it inevitably would, he lay in its path. By the third day, he was breaking trail through snow that was almost up to his head. After struggling for hours – and covering barely 300 metres – he found a sheltered spot at the edge of a sérac, and dug a snow hole. He had crawled inside and was sorting out his gear when he heard a huge roar. His icy world shook violently. The roof of the snow cave fell in. For a few seconds he thought he was being buried by an avalanche, but then the air cleared. He was sitting on a ledge. Above him was the sky. Below, thousands of feet of air.

The sérac had carved right through the middle of the cave, and fallen down the mountain, taking all Steve's gear with it. He had no ropes, no equipment to climb the near-vertical ice cliffs that lay between him and the bottom of the mountain. His first thought was to jump off the ledge – a better option than waiting around to die slowly. Then he saw the lid of his rucksack, which he had removed just before the sérac broke in half, lying close by. Inside was a stove, two spare ice picks and, 'most importantly', Katie's teddy bear. He decided to fight for his life.

'With the picks I thought that I might be able to downclimb the ice. It was more likely I'd die trying, but it was at least a chance. I had no emotions at all, other than annoyance. I just rationally worked out what needed to be done.'

He got frostbitten feet on the way down, but he made it. So did the teddy bear – it came home to Katie in his pocket.

Why would anyone so committed to climbing have children in the first place? Like Andy Kirkpatrick, Steve Sustad originally agreed for the sake of his wife, to 'put something in the kitty for her'. Many partners of climbers, he believes, press for a child 'to preserve a shard of their spouse' in case they die in the mountains. And many climbers, like him, then discover that 'having a child is positive and life-enhancing, whereas climbing can be so bleak'.

For some climbers, it's a deep need from the start. 'You must know who you belong to, and who to come back to,' said Tomaz Humar. 'I cannot live without the mountains, but it's also true I cannot live without my family. I am in the middle, wired to both.'

In 1941 Barbara Washburn left a three-and-a-half-month-old baby to join her husband Brad on the first ascent of Mount Hayes, Alaska, and was gone for almost eight weeks. 'I endured a great deal of soul-searching,' she wrote in her biography, 'but finally decided I should attempt to share Brad's life as much as possible. If I was going to adhere to that philosophy for the lifetime of our marriage, I knew it would mean making some difficult choices along the way. Whether to leave Dottie behind for an Alaskan expedition would be the first one.' Several years later, when she had three children aged six years, four years and nine months, she became the first woman to climb Mount McKinley, in Alaska, an expedition that took her away for fifteen weeks.

In 1996, shortly before being blown to her death off the side of K2, the British mountaineer Alison Hargreaves, who was the mother of two small children, wrote from base camp, 'It eats away at me – wanting the children and wanting K2. I feel like I'm being pulled in two.' It's a feeling Cherie Bremer-Kamp can empathise with. 'I think women who climb and leave their kids at home are complex characters,' she said. 'They do it because they have to, not because it's a real choice. It was hard for me to leave my kids. It was like being drawn between different desires.' During the 1970s and 1980s, Cherie was an active Himalayan mountaineer, and a member of the 1978 American K2 expedition. Like several of the men on that team, she was a parent. She discovered she was pregnant with her first child in 1971, when she was working in Kathmandu, as a midwife in a mission hospital. She was also preparing to climb Dhaulagiri. Suddenly, the consequences of climbing at altitude were writ large. The effects of hypoxia worried her, and she was concerned she might miscarry the child. 'Then I thought about the pregnant women with bad hearts I had taken care of whose babies were fine. I told myself I wasn't going to be very high that long. That I would descend at any sign of impaired oxygenation. I bargained with it. I really wanted to climb and I really wanted to have kids. I thought I could do it all. Now I'm a grandmother, I look back and think, Crazy woman!'

When she was preparing to set off for K2 in 1978, her son Daniel was four years old. He had heard that the mountain was the second highest in the world, and very steep. Solemnly, he counselled his mother to carry a parachute at all times, in case she fell and her rope broke.

During a seminar held at the 1999 Banff Mountain Film Festival, the American alpinist Kitty Calhoun talked guardedly about what it was like to be a mountaineer and a mother. She explained that she and her ex-husband shared the care of their son Grady, who at the time was almost four years old. On average, she said, she spent ten days a month with him. Becoming a mother hadn't affected her climbing, 'Except that I have more reasons to live now.' She talked about how hard it was for any parent to balance work, which in her case was climbing, and family. She used an argument common among climbing parents of both genders – that when she was with Grady, she was focused only on him, and therefore they had more 'quality time' together than they would if she worked at a regular job. Several times she stressed that the situation wasn't easy for her, but only once did she touch on how it was for

Grady. 'Last summer we were hiking and he said, "Mummy lives in my heart" . . . He knows that if I'm not with him I'm still thinking about him and that I love him. He's starting to develop an understanding of what it means to have a relationship with a person but not physically be with them all the time.'

Aware that her divorce already separated her from Grady, Kitty had considered the impact of her climbing on her child; not all her peers have done as much. At the time of his famed West Ridge of Everest expedition in 1963, Tom Hornbein had five children aged two, four, six, eight and ten. He was away from home for five months. Years later he admitted he never talked to his wife or children about how they dealt with such a long separation. And he's far from being the only climber with little to offer on how those they leave behind cope in their absence.

'If you're a mother with a young baby, you're pretty busy,' said Stephen Venables, a father of two. 'You don't have a lot of time to hang around worrying.'

'I think the people at home probably get used to it,' said Kurt Diemberger, a veteran Austrian mountaineer and the father of two daughters. 'The climber keeps coming back, so you create a certain philosophy in your mind. You are a fatalist. One day he might not come back, but by then you will have a formula to be able to live without that person.'

Andy Kirkpatrick was defensive. 'If I were an armed first–response cop, would it be any different?'

Doug Scott was brutally honest. 'If you're worrying about how they are coping at home, you shouldn't be climbing at all. It takes your mind off it. You've got to be totally focused in the mountains and not worrying about that side of things.'

'My wife is a steel lady,' said Tomaz Humar, who was away on Ama Dablam when his second child was born. 'If I were in her skin, this is impossible for me. Mission Impossible. Waiting for some guy coming and going, coming and going. What kind of life is this?'

Paradoxically, mountaineers often claim that in times of great crisis it is thoughts – and sometimes visions – of their families that keep them alive. While struggling down K2 after spending a night in the open at 27,750 feet, the repetition of a mantra made up of his wife and children's names kept Jim Wickwire going. During Tomaz Humar's desperate descent of Nuptse, after his friend Janez Jeglic had been blown off the summit, he believes his small son 'visited' him twice, urging him to come home. And when Cherie Bremer-Kamp's husband Chris Chandler died on the high slopes of Kangchenjunga in 1986, it was only the sense of her children standing close by that stopped her lying down next to Chandler's body and waiting for the mountain to take her life.

'Climbers are masters of denial,' said the Polish mountaineer Wanda Rutkiewicz. Can this be turned around to ask, what would they be denying themselves if they stopped climbing, and how would this affect their loved ones? During a climbing conference in England, in the autumn of 2001, Chris Bonington said, 'At the end of the day, climbing probably is irresponsible. But we're better parents because we're doing things that fulfil us.' It's a common argument: climbing is my calling; if you take that away my spirit will die, I won't be a complete person and my children will suffer.

'I think had I not followed my heart I would have been a terrible mum,' said Cherie Bremer-Kamp. 'And what I got from the mountains, I've been able to give back to the kids in different ways. Obviously it's been hard for them. But they've grown from it, grown strong in character. Life is never a bed of roses, is it?'

What do the children say? The eldest daughter of Jim Wickwire was eleven years old in 1975, when her father was preparing for his first Himalayan expedition, to K2. To Annie and her four siblings, it seemed like fun. They played in Jim's tents when he put them up in the garden to test them. They went along to the warehouse where the expedition food was being sorted, and helped to label freeze-dried goods and pack them into boxes. Just before he left, he took each of his children out separately for a special treat. Annie chose to see the movie *Saturday Night Fever* and have dinner afterwards. It was a time she never forgot.

It was the summer holiday while he was on K2; Annie played with her friends and her mother kept life running as usual. When he came back there was a huge, exciting fuss. After that he kept going away on expeditions, year after year. Usually, he missed her birthday, in late June. He promised her he'd be thinking of her on the day, and that he'd send her a postcard. He kept reminding her that as she was the eldest child, when he was gone she had to help her mother and look out for her brothers and sisters. But he wasn't just going away for a weekend, or a week, like he sometimes did for his law job. He was going away for months at a time. 'I felt a lot of responsibility at an early age,' she said. 'It was heavy, like a weight.'

His subsequent homecomings weren't always so exciting. When she was thirteen, he returned from Alaska upset because he'd seen two of his friends fall to their deaths. Annie attended the memorial service with him and her mother. There were other memorials, too, for friends of her parents who died on various climbs. They gave her an early understanding of the harsher realities of her father's passion. 'There was that uncertainty . . . It made me feel fearful and a little unprotected, knowing that anything could happen to him at any time.'

When she was fourteen Jim went on another expedition to K2, and returned sick and shrunken from the effects of frostbite, pneumonia, pleurisy and pulmonary emboli. For a time he couldn't make it up the stairs, so their mother brought his bed down into the living room and the whole family had to tiptoe around so as not to disturb him. When Annie was fifteen, she started to rebel, 'I was pretty wild. Staying out all night, experimenting with drugs . . . and inappropriate relationships with men.' Looking back, she sees it as a way of trying to connect with her father, to get his attention. 'I was acting out my anger at him for not being around to be my role model guide, or to say, "Hey, I really care about you." If he had decided not to go on an expedition because of something that was happening to me, that would have been a message that he really cared. But it didn't seem to matter what was going on at home, he had to climb.'

In 1981, when she was seventeen, her father came back from Alaska devastated, because he had not been able to rescue Chris Kerrebrock from a crevasse. The following year, he left for Everest, an expedition on which Marty Hoey died. A few months after his return Annie went on a visit to Florida. When she got there she called up her parents and told them she wasn't coming home. She stayed away, largely estranged from her family, for four years. 'It was hard on my parents,' she said. 'On my mother, especially. From an early age she had had a lot of responsibility; first being the oldest of thirteen children and then having a husband who just gets to go away and do what he wants. And then her daughter does the same.'

It wasn't until she was twenty-seven, and working in a hotel close to her father's law office in Seattle, that the rifts with her family began to heal properly. Every morning she and Jim travelled to work together. They started talking, building bridges of understanding. The publication of Jim's book *Addicted to Danger* was a watershed in this process. For the first time Annie realised just how much climbing had meant to her father. 'All along, subtly, I'd thought, If he really cared about us, he wouldn't go. So it was good to know it was something he just couldn't do without. That it gave him a piece of himself he needed to keep going and living. Where one draws the line as to whether that is healthy or unhealthy is up to that person and the people around them. But I'm glad he wasn't addicted to something like drinking or drugs. That would have been much worse for me.'

A few years ago she married, and gave birth to twins. Her father is devoted to his granddaughters. Some of his climbing friends joke that finally Jim Wickwire got around to finding out what it's like to hold a baby. 'It's true,' said Annie. 'When they were small and he was changing their diapers he'd say, "I never used to do this for you."'

And her reaction to him deciding to return to Everest, at the age of sixty-three? 'I know it would mean a lot to him to climb the mountain. I hope he gets to the summit, and gets that monkey off his back, so that we don't have to go through it again.'

Chris Bonington's younger son, Rupert, now in his early thirties, remembers a father who was 'gone a lot' when he was small. In his teens, with his father still frequently away from home on long expeditions, both he and his brother Dan, two years his elder, went through a rebellious stage. 'We were nightmares,' said Rupert. 'I look back, and I think, my poor mum. I can remember us being in a car, my mum slamming on the brakes, stopping in the middle of the road, screaming hysterically and punching the steering wheel. I brought that on because of the way I was behaving generally. A lot of that would have been because of our situation, with Dad being gone and Mum having to cope with us on her own. How different it would have been if Dad had had a normal job, I don't know. We might have been just the same. There were plenty of other bad kids around.'

According to Dan, both boys longed for an 'ordinary' lifestyle. 'Kids haven't got a choice. We didn't ask for our dad to climb. We loved him to death but we wanted a bigger share of him. Even when he was home he was always off giving lectures and going to meetings. We wanted him to do ordinary stuff with us. We wished he was a farmer or a fireman, something normal. We chose our mates from people who came from the most normal working class backgrounds. We worked hard on our Cumbrian accents. We got into mod gangs, scooter gangs. We wanted to fit in somewhere and be like everyone else.'

Dan was keenly aware of the shadow his famous father cast over him. When Chris appeared in an advertisement for Bovril, Dan was mercilessly teased at school, and referred to as 'Bovril Boy', both by fellow students and by one of his teachers. 'People would always say, "Are you going to be a climber when you grow up?" It was all about Dad, never about me. I resented it. So I worked hard at infamy instead of fame. My brother and I found the worst kids around, and because we had inherited Dad's leadership qualities we got them organized into all sorts of escapades. It was Dad's adventurous spirit, I suppose, but in a destructive direction.'

Thieving, late night car chases and running illicit poker clubs resulted in the boys being expelled from two different schools, and, at times, getting into trouble with the law. Dan was always remorseful about how his behaviour affected his mother. 'But I wasn't worried about Dad, because he'd upset us.'

They remember their mother's tears whenever news came that someone had died in the mountains. 'Normally Dad wasn't there,' said Rupert. 'He was gone on an expedition. Whenever anybody died, we always had the thing of, "We don't want Dad to go away again." But it soon passed because that was just what our dad did.'

For Dan, the effects were more long-term. 'From when I was very small until my early teens, it felt like someone was dying in a climbing accident every year. Someone who had been around to our house and played with us, and we'd sat on their knees. One person I can remember vividly is Mick Burke. He used to spend ages playing with us when he came for expedition meetings. We thought he was brilliant. Mick's death really made an impact. I was seven. After that I used to dread hearing news from the expeditions. When someone I knew had died I was so upset, but I was also glad that it wasn't my dad, and then I felt really guilty about that. We'd go to the memorial services and I'd meet people like you or Hilary Boardman and I'd just feel awful.'

After Joe Tasker and Pete Boardman died on Everest, Dan, then in his early teens, wrote me a condolence letter. After signing his name, he added a postscript: 'PS I hope this stops Dad climbing.' It didn't, but Chris promised his wife that he would never return to Everest. A promise he broke. 'How many times did my dad come back and promise that because my mum was hysterical and scared?' said Rupert. 'Then she'd catch him sneakily planning the next trip. When you're that driven, you can't actually allow for compromise. You might have moments of it, but there's always an agenda that you're going to get what you want.'

After this period of what Dan calls 'the Everest lies', both boys' behaviour deteriorated. 'Everything started to change for me and Rupert then. It was like, if Dad can do what he wants and get away with it, so can we.'

Dan's troubles, and his conflicted feelings, lasted into his early twenties. At a time when he was at his 'lowest ebb', his father suggested they climb Mt. Kilimanjaro together. It was an experience that transformed Dan's life. ' I was going pretty strong on the mountain. Me and Dad were at the front. Dad said, let's wait for the others. But I really wanted to go on to the top alone and get a sense of what Dad experienced when he climbed. So I reached the summit by myself. I was looking across Africa, through the clouds, down to the blue of the glacier. The beauty, the sense of the vastness of nature, it was awesome. It was like the power of the mountain exploded up through me . . . Suddenly I realized what had been driving Dad all those years. And for the first time, I wasn't bitter about what I'd been through when I was growing up. I became incredibly emotional. I cried and cried. I released so much. I cried for my childhood, for my Mum, for everyone we'd lost.'

Five hundred metres below him, Chris was also in tears. Understanding that Dan needed time to himself on the summit, he asked the rest of the group to wait. Finally, he joined a son who had 'a new respect' for his father. 'That experience began the process of us sorting out our relationship,' said Dan. 'And it was the start of me getting my head back together. It helped me in all areas of my life; my whole behaviour changed. It's such a shame that as a child you can't understand the world through the adult's eyes. You have to look back in retrospect.'

The Bonington boys speak glowingly of their father. They say they appreciate the role model he's given them by following his heart and living life to the fullest. Both are married, and happy. Rupert lives close to his parents; he has his own company, BNM Interactive, and designs and manages websites, including his father's. In 2002 his wife Ann gave birth to a baby daughter. Dan has moved to Australia, the home of his wife, Jude. He's a personal trainer, also with his own company, Trekfit. 'Motivating people is the key to my work,' he said, 'and I got that skill from my dad. Looking back, there are parts of my childhood I wish I could change, like not losing Mick and Nick and Pete and Joe. But I've got this fantastic example of being able to chase dreams; I realize what human beings are capable of if they are willing to push on through. I'm really proud of Dad. He's still passionate about life, with a child-like exuberance. Sometimes I have clients in their forties or fifties who say, Oh I'm too old for this or that. When that happens, I tell them that my dad is sixty-eight and has just come back from rock climbing in Morocco. I say, "So I'm sure you can manage three more bench presses."'

But when he reads in the newspapers about a climbing accident, the old hurt comes flooding back. 'I get so upset for the family. For the wife, having to worry all those years and then . . . it's the awful sense of certainty that it's going to happen one day.'

Neither Annie Wickwire or the Bonington boys tried to follow in the footsteps of their famous fathers, but many children of mountaineers do. Peter Whittaker is the son and nephew of one of America's most famous climbing teams – the identical twins Lou and Jim Whittaker. In May 1963, Jim Whittaker, Peter's uncle, became the first American to stand on the summit of Mount Everest. 'There was a big fanfare around that,' recalled Peter, who was five years old at the time. 'We lived in Seattle and I remember a lot of people in suits, who appeared to be dignitaries of some kind.'

While Peter was growing up, most of his father's climbing was in their 'backyard', Mount Rainier, where Lou Whittaker established the guiding company Rainier Mountaineering Inc. Peter started skiing and hiking on the mountain when he was six. His father's company had a camp on Rainier at 10,000 feet. Getting there involved four or five hours of climbing, and crossing a number of snowfields en route. By the time Peter was eleven, he had been up to 'Camp Rainier' numerous times. During his summer holidays he was a 'cabin boy' there, helping the cooks prepare meals for the groups coming through.

When he was twelve years old, as part of a group led by his father, he became the youngest person to summit Mount Rainier. He can't recall now whether it was principally his desire to climb the mountain, or his father's. He hated the experience. He was inadequately dressed in long johns and jeans. Bad weather moved in while they were climbing. He got thoroughly wet, and his jeans froze solid. 'I was very miserable and uncomfortable. I can remember being in tears on the summit. I'm amazed I continued climbing, because it wasn't a great experience for me that first time.'

He never planned to follow his father into a career as a mountain guide. It was just there; it was convenient; and he loved being in the mountains. By the time he was sixteen, he was being paid to lead groups up Mount Rainier. At seventeen, he was in an avalanche with one of those groups. 'I had a bad feeling about the conditions. But my father was the lead guide. I called to him, "I don't like this. How is it looking up there?" Dad took three more steps and the whole slope ripped. The avalanche took us down 600 vertical feet. My father dislocated his shoulder and I broke my ankle. One of my rope team broke an ankle, too. We could all have died, easily.'

On Father's Day 1981, Peter, then twenty-two years old, was one of several guides leading a group of twenty-four amateur climbers up the mountain. They started at 5,400 feet from the Paradise Inn and climbed to 10,000 feet to spend the night at Camp Muir. At around four the next morning, they set out along the south-east face of the mountain, towards the peak. An hour and a half later, three climbers decided they didn't have the stamina to carry on. A guide accompanied them back to Camp Muir. At 11,000 feet, one of the men roped to Peter told him he was having difficulties keeping up. He said he didn't think he could make it to the summit. Peter told him that, because of the conditions, it was unlikely any of the group would be going to the top. He encouraged the man to carry on – the sun was soon to rise, the morning would be beautiful. The man agreed.

The guides stopped the group for a rest. They chose a place protected from the danger of falling ice. While everyone relaxed, Peter and two other guides climbed a further 300 yards, to assess the conditions higher up the mountain. Suddenly, they heard a thunderous crack. A thousand feet above them, a chunk of the Ingraham Glacier had sheared off. Peter's first thought was, 'Icefall – our people are tucked in. They're out of its range.' Then he realised the size of the fall. He started screaming at the group to run. It took a few seconds for them to register he was yelling at them. Several more seconds for them to react. Too late. A torrent of ice blocks, 'as big as Volkswagen buses', smashed down. A massive wave of snow. A huge air blast.

Then silence.

Peter and the other guides scrambled across the icefall debris. 'It was 150 yards wide, and in places over forty feet deep. It was hard blue glacial ice, huge blocks of it.' There were thirteen shocked people for them to gather up and sit down. Eleven people to search for. 'We were looking for ropes, hats, packs, anything. There was nothing. We realised this wasn't a rescue. It was a recovery of bodies.'

Not even that. The icefall had fanned out and caught the group in their protected spot. Eleven were swept down the mountain about 100 feet, into a seventy-foot crevasse, and buried under tons of ice and snow. One guide and ten clients. They remain buried on Mount Rainier, victims of the worst accident to date in North American mountaineering history.

Peter had to rally the survivors and get them down the mountain. Even then, the ordeal wasn't over. When finally they reached the safety of the Paradise Inn, they were met by a scrum of press, and a group of distraught relatives. 'They all knew there had been this big accident, but no one knew who was dead and who was alive. My dad was there, and he put his arms around me. Then this woman came up. I remembered her from the beginning of the trip. I knew her husband had just been killed. She said, "Did he make it?" I froze. At twenty-two, I'd already done a lot of things, but I'd never had to look someone in the eyes and tell them that a person they loved was dead. My dad stepped in and saved me from having to do it. He knew by my expression what the answer was. He grabbed the woman and took her outside. I just went and hid.'

When his father came back into the Inn, he took Peter to one side. 'He said, "You know, Peter, if you don't want to be a mountain guide any more, that's okay; don't do it because of me." I told him I appreciated that. I took some time off and rafted the Colorado River with another guide who had also been on the trip. I decided I'd loved Rainier, and I wanted to carry on.' An independent board of enquiry exonerated Peter and the other guides from any charges of negligence. Within weeks, he was leading groups up the mountain again, past the crevasse that was now a mass grave.

And his climbing ambitions broadened. Three years later he was on Everest, as part of an expedition led by his father, attempting to become the first American to summit the mountain from its north side. He came close to achieving that goal, until, without warning, Lou Whittaker pulled him off the summit team. In front of the rest of the team, some of whom already knew of Lou's decision. In front of a cameraman who was filming the climb. 'There was a meeting at Base Camp,' Peter recalled. 'I knew there was going to be a merging of the first team and the second team. Steve Marts had the camera rolling and when my father announced that I was not going to be on the summit team any more, that I was going to be in a support role instead, Steve zoomed in on me. Man, I was completely blown away. You can see it on my face. It was devastating.'

Peter's new role was to ferry loads of gear to the high camp, for the people who would go for the summit. After carrying the final load, he stormed down to Advance Base Camp alone, without waiting for the others in the support team. His emotions were in uproar. At twenty-five, he was the youngest member of the expedition. After two and a half months on the mountain he was strong, fit, acclimatised and ready for the summit. Now, the expedition was over for him. As he approached Base Camp, he saw Lou walking up to meet him. 'I got this lump in my throat. I was trying to be cool. There we were, mountaineers, mountain guides, insecure males with tremendous egos, all that wrapped into one. The Whittaker family, we're macho, we don't wear our emotions on our sleeves. I saw my father and all these emotions were welling up. When he was fifty feet away I just burst into tears. He came up and gave me a big hug. He held me and said what a great job I'd done . . . It was one of the more emotional moments for me and my father.'

Beyond this, they never discussed Lou Whittaker's decision, and the matter lay unresolved between them for almost twenty years. Until, in 2002, Lou admitted to his son that he had been worried for his safety. Peter's route to the summit would have taken him into the same couloir from where the young American climber Marty Hoey had fallen to her death, two years earlier, during Lou's expedition. This, he explained, had been preying on his mind. 'It was a good thing to hear finally,' said Peter. 'To realise he was afraid for me, and was trying to protect me.'

Peter is now a father himself, of a five-year-old boy and a four-year-old girl. He looks askance at people in his community who encourage their children to climb at an early age – like the friends who had tiny crampons custom-made for their five-year-old and took him up Mount Rainier to win the title of the mountain's youngest ever summiteer. 'I think that's way too ambitious,' said Peter. 'If my children had no desire to climb, it wouldn't bother me a bit. Mountains are wonderful and I hope they come to like them. But I'll only expose them to mountains in a way that is comfortable for them, so they can make their own decisions.'

When Peter was about nine or ten, his parents' marriage began to deteriorate, and by the time he was twelve, they were divorced. It was a terrible upheaval for Peter, and one he is determined his own children won't go through. Currently he has no ambitions to summit Everest, and two years ago he closed down his international guiding company, which was taking him away to mountains in South America and Africa. He could no longer bear to be away from his wife and children for weeks at a time, and he was concerned about the risk factor. He continues to climb in the Pacific Northwest. And mostly on Rainier. 'The exposure on Rainier is somewhat limited,' he said. 'Yes, there are icefalls, there are avalanches. But I use my experience to educate my clients and protect them. I have strategies to reduce the risks. Obviously I can't eliminate it, but I've achieved a balance I feel is reasonable.'

Rainier. Where he saw a group of people buried in an icefall. Where he's rescued many, and retrieved bodies when rescue is no longer possible. He's climbed the mountain 205 times. In 2002, seven times he led a group past the crevasse where eleven former clients lie entombed.

A year after the disaster, a group of the victims' friends and relatives gathered at the Henry M. Jackson Visitors' Center on Mount Rainier for a memorial service. They unveiled a plaque with the names of the eleven lost climbers. They dedicated to the centre a photograph taken by twenty-seven-year-old Jonathan Laitone, an hour before he died in the icefall. It's a haunting shot: the top of Little Tahoma a dark presence in the background. Snow, ice, white clouds. On the horizon, a long, thin, red line. The sunrise that Peter Whittaker promised to the man who wanted to turn back.

Katie Sustad's teddy bear collection is now complete. Her father Steve claims he has given up mountaineering for good. In 2002 he had planned to go to Shishapangma to try a winter ascent of the south face, alpine style. 'But I couldn't face the idea of yet again spending months in a freezing miserable tent in order to get three days' climbing. It was then I realised the fire within was extinguished.'

He has no regrets about the years spent in the mountains. For him it was 'a wonderful journey' and he's come out the other end happy and contented. But he admits the journey cost him his marriage to Katie's mother. 'She is a wonderful person and fantastic mother who quite rightly wouldn't take second place to my obsession. I broke her heart and deserve a place in hell for that. She deserved better.'

He claims his twelve-year-old daughter laughs about his eccentricities. 'Dad, you're not normal,' she wrote on his most recent Father's Day card. Despite his many absences when she was younger, she is a relaxed and happy child, for which Sustad gives all credit to his ex-wife. 'I have a daughter who is as perfect as any parent could hope for. To my shame there was no balance between family and climbing. How could there be? A parent gambling one's life away for an intangible prize is inexcusable by any civilised measure. And yet . . . I would do it all over again.'

9

Voices II: An Absence of Light

*C*onrad *Anker explained it to them as best he could. How they ran from the avalanche in different directions. How snow moves in unpredictable ways. How it all happened so fast. How when it was over, Alex Lowe was simply gone.*

A father, dead. Buried on a distant mountain under tons of ice and snow. Impossible to comprehend. Ten-year-old Max and eight-year-old Sam kept thinking he might come home. And three-year-old Isaac? A friend of the family saw him playing in the sandpit at preschool. He was burying toy people, and digging them up. Burying them and digging them up. Again and again.

Tara Mortenson understood what Isaac was doing, when she saw him in the sandpit. She too had lost a father, albeit much later in life. Barry Bishop was a member of the first US team to climb Everest in 1963. Ironically, it wasn't climbing that killed him, but a lapse of concentration when he was driving his car. Tara was thirty years old at the time but, like Isaac, she needed to recreate the details of the accident in her imagination, time and time again. 'It was like a video playing in my head,' she said. 'That was part of internalising what had happened, to make sense of it.'

How do children make sense of parents disappearing from their lives?

When Tserin Cheesmond was three and a half years old she told her mother, Gillian, 'Daddy's died.' They were driving into the Rockies to go camping. Dave Cheesmond was away climbing in Alaska. Her mother reassured her: Daddy was fine; he'd be home soon; he hadn't been killed. 'Yes, he has,' insisted Tserin. 'He's been killed in an avalanche.' She knew about avalanches. The previous summer, she'd been hiking with her parents on a glacier when they saw an avalanche in the distance, and her father explained what it was, how it formed. A few days after Tserin's death announcement, news came that Dave Cheesmond had gone missing on Mount Logan in Alaska along with the US climber Catherine Freer, while they were attempting the Hummingbird Ridge, alpine style. Tserin can't remember the conversation in the car, or the avalanche, or her father. Her memories start a few years later. Memories of going home in tears because the children in her Grade Five class teased her that her father had faked his death, and run away from her and her mother. The envious feelings towards her cousin, who was her 'daddy's little princess'. She felt she missed out on that. She wrote a poem about it. Her father wrote poems, too – she keeps them in a scrapbook. He liked loud music and so does she. She listens to the music of his era; she dresses in the style of the 1980s punk rockers. Now nineteen years old, she's tall and rangy like him; she has the same physical grace, the same boundless energy, the same desire to live on the edge.

She doesn't mind that she has no memory of him. 'It's the way it's always been. I've accepted it. I have friends who won't talk about their fathers because they left their mothers, and they had horrible divorces. But I never hear anything bad about my dad. I've only ever heard good things about him.'

When Tserin was twelve, her mother Gillian arranged a 'leaving ceremony' in their local church. Gillian had remarried by then, and had another child. She was having recurring dreams about Dave coming home; she decided she needed a spiritual goodbye. She stood with Tserin at the altar. They read one of Dave's poems, then sang 'Morning Has Broken', a song from his youth. Gillian took off the ring she'd worn since her wedding to Dave; after it was blessed, she gave it to her daughter.

Tserin says she didn't need that spiritual goodbye; her mother did. The ceremony didn't make her feel any different. But not long afterwards, her father's body was discovered on Mount Logan. Some people flying by the Hummingbird Ridge took a photograph of the remains, frozen into the ice. A photograph, says Tserin, that looks like 'a snowsuit, standing in the snow'. The discovery shook her deeply. 'Mum told me, and at first I thought, Well, okay. Then I went to school. I started crying there, and I couldn't stop. Suddenly there was this body, and it was like him dying all over again. It was like another death.'

She's not sure about how, or if, his death has affected her as an adult. 'I think I've only started to figure it out now,' she said. 'I'm useless at relationships. I'm in and out of them. I tend to get annoyed and bored with boyfriends and dump them. Whether that's got anything to do with my dad, I don't know. But I like exciting people.'

Sara Burke also has trouble with relationships. 'I tend to assume that they are going to end, so it's better not to get too involved in the first place. I find it hard to trust people.' Sara's father, Mick Burke, was last seen near the summit of Everest in 1975. The news of his death reached her mother on Sara's second birthday. Sara has no memory of him, and only shadowy recollections of the time right after the tragedy – of her mother, Beth, crying.

Beth's friend, the psychiatrist Ruth Seifert, visited the family shortly after Mick's death. Both women have daughters the same age, and the two little girls were playing together. 'Sara had a toy phone and was pretending to talk to her father,' Ruth recalled. 'My daughter Becky said, "You can't phone your daddy. He's dead on the mountain." "No he's not," said Sara. They started arguing about it. It was dreadful. Poor little Sara. She lost the argument.'

The fact that she can't remember the man she calls 'Dad' is something Sara Burke sees as 'a silver lining'. Because she never knew him, she has nothing to miss. And yet, at the age of thirty, she finds it hard to talk about him without breaking into tears. She rarely tells new friends about him. She never discusses him with her mother, for fear they might both get upset. And she tries not to question how his death affected her, fearing it will cause more pain than it will cure. 'I keep it neatly filed away at the back of my mind,' she said. 'There's a part of me that thinks it was better he went to Everest instead of staying at home with us because it was his duty. Then there's another part of me that thinks, Damn you! He knew the dangers, and he took the risk anyway. I do feel angry with him. But to go too closely into that means examining whether he loved climbing more than he loved us. And that's not somewhere I'm prepared to go yet.'

She has a few things to remember him by. The letter he wrote to her the night she was born. A gold badge from the children's programme *Blue Peter*, that he was filming for on Everest. One of his rucksacks, that she took on a school hiking trip. A woollen sweater she wore on a skiing trip. His watch. Big and heavy, it is 'like a presence' on her wrist.

'Dad was just unlucky,' she said. 'He got lost one day. At least he died doing the hardest thing he could possibly do. And it really matters to me to think he did get to the summit of Everest before he died. Otherwise, what would have been the point?'

It doesn't matter to Andréa Cilento that her father never finished his dream climb, the Eiger Direct. Or that the route now bears his name. What matters to her is that, since she was eight years old, she never had the father she needed and wanted 'to help me figure things out'.

Her father was the American climber John Harlin II. When Andréa was five, the family moved to Leysin in Switzerland. Both her parents had jobs at the American School there, and in the surrounding Alps her father could pursue his passion for mountaineering. By the time she was eight, he had given up his regular job. He was establishing an International School of Mountaineering in Leysin. And he was focusing on his dream of forging a direct route up the formidable North Wall of the Eiger.

Now in her forties, all it takes for Andréa to be flooded with happy memories of her father is the smell of wet woollen socks. 'He was mostly away climbing. But when I walked through the door from school and smelt dirty wet wool, I always knew he was back. I'd go, "Daddy's home!" A lot of Andréa's memories centre on her father's absences. Her longing for him. The letters he wrote to her. What she hated most about his being away climbing were the journeys her family took, to visit his base camps. With her brother John, two years her senior, and her mother Marilyn, she would ski and trek up hills and across glaciers. 'You know when your hands freeze and then they thaw, that burning sensation? I hated that. I was always the youngest, the littlest, and a girl to boot. I was never able to keep up.'

Just before they left on one trip, Andréa heard about some bodies that had washed out of a glacier, into a nearby river. The remains were of climbers thought to have fallen into a crevasse some years before. 'So I'm six or seven, we're hiking across crevasses on snow bridges, and what I know is that if I fall into a crevasse I will eventually come out in the river down by the town. That terrified me. I couldn't move. My mother and brother got frustrated with me. They went on, and I stayed behind and waited for them. I remember sitting on the slope for what seemed like hours waiting for them to come back.'

Being reunited with her father made everything worthwhile. 'He would dance with me and talk about things,' she said. 'He was so nice to me. I was Daddy's little girl, very special.'

Andréa felt her mother was jealous of the attention her father gave her. In turn, she resented the closeness between her mother and brother. Marilyn Harlin admits that she had an 'easier flow of communication' with her son than with her daughter. 'John and I had the same way of looking at things. But Andréa and I were in a different orbit. My husband and I had said that if the marriage had broken down, Andréa would go with her father and young John would go with me.'

Andréa's brother John remembers an incident that illustrated these different orbits, and the understanding between father and daughter. 'One time, when my sister was five or six, she came home from school very late. She'd walked home on her own, which is hard for people to imagine these days, but we did that, we walked for a least a mile. My mother and father were worried, and when they asked her why she was so late she said it was because she had been kidnapped, and it had taken her a while to escape. Dad said, "That's not true." She said, "Yes it is." She held to her story. Finally Dad said, "Go to your room until you tell me the truth." My mother was saying, "John, how can you be doing this to her? She's just been kidnapped!" Andréa came down from her room at one point and he said, "Are you going to tell the truth now?" She stuck to her story and he sent her back. Eventually she admitted that she'd made the whole thing up. Mom asked my dad how he had known. He said, "When I first accused her of lying she didn't break down in tears; she just kept to her story. I would have done exactly the same thing." And my mother said, "When she's a teenager, you'll have to figure her out."'

In the winter of 1966, John Harlin left home to make his attempt on the North Wall of the Eiger. He was gone for weeks. Andréa wrote him a letter, asking him to 'Come home soon.' He wrote back, promising he would return before long, and asking how her ballet lessons were going.

On both sides of the Atlantic, the Eiger expedition was big news. In late March, a British reporter, Peter Gillman, was on a hotel balcony at the bottom of the mountain, scanning the north face through a telescope. He was searching for John Harlin and his climbing partner, Dougal Haston. Suddenly he saw a speck of red, falling. A human figure. 'It was stretched out,' he wrote in *Eiger Direct*, 'and was turning over slowly, gently, with awful finality.'

John Harlin's children were playing with two friends in a neighbour's chalet when their mother walked in and broke the news to them. Andréa remembers her saying, 'What's the worst thing that could happen to this family?' After that, mostly she remembers her own anger. 'I was furious because he was supposed to come home and be my daddy. I was so mad, I wasn't even sad. I had to fake crying. I kept that anger for so long.'

But she couldn't be angry with the man she loved. So she turned that anger on her mother. There were terrible tantrums. A climbing friend of her father's, Gary Hemming, visited them shortly after the funeral, and when Andréa acted up, he spanked her. 'I remember thinking, "You're not my father."'

Soon after getting the news about her husband's death, Marilyn Harlin decided to return to the States, and resume her studies. She sent Andréa on ahead of her.

'It was not long after the funeral,' Andréa recalled. 'I travelled there with my father's parents, who I knew, and I went to stay with my mother's parents, who I didn't know, on the Olympic Peninsula. I was on my own with them for months. I didn't have my brother, my dog, my cat, my friends. I looked at my mom's picture and cried and cried and cried. I was only eight. I didn't understand what she'd gone through, what it meant for her to have just lost a husband. I just knew that she'd sent me away and kept my brother.'

Andréa built up a fantasy around her father's absence. He hadn't died. He'd faked his death. It was perfectly plausible. Who had seen his body? Her mother hadn't. Neither had she. All she'd seen at the funeral was a closed casket. He hadn't been inside it. He wasn't buried in the earth. He'd run away to start a new life. Eventually he would come back. He would let Andréa know where he was. It would be their secret, and she could go and visit him.

She held on to that fantasy for seven years. 'It wasn't until I was a junior in high school that I let go of it,' she said. 'I remember having a very defining moment. Standing there at school one day and thinking, No, he's not ever going to come back. He's dead.'

When she started dating, she avoided risk-takers, or anyone interested in outdoor pursuits. She went for 'skinny city boys'. All through high school, she dated a boy called Jerry. What really drew her to him was his family. 'His father was a blue-collar guy who drove a bulldozer. He loved his family and did everything for them. He came home every night and every weekend. That was so important to me. I was always welcome in their house. I wasn't really dating Jerry, I was dating his family. I think I was looking for a father.'

Eventually she married an Italian-American man, from a big family. Now they have a family of their own. In her house, among the framed photographs of her children, are shots of her father, and also of his near-double, her brother John. He too is a climber. And the father of a small child. Andréa shakes her head at the thought.

'When climbers die I hear lots of people saying, "Oh well, it's okay, they died doing what they love best." I don't think that at all. You should make sacrifices when you have children, because they need you. People say also, "If climbers didn't do what they love to do they would die inside." Well excuse me, but there are other people involved in life and you're not an island, especially when you have a family. I can only go by how I felt growing up in that situation. I felt abandoned. I felt like I was less important to my father than that mountain. I still feel that way. So many times I wished I had a father. I still do. If he came back today I'd yell at him, "Where were you all my life?"'

Was she less important than the mountain? Certainly John Harlin loved his children, but he resented the demands of fatherhood. In a letter to his wife in 1960, when Andréa was two and John four, he wrote, 'With [the kids] I have a trapped feeling, and I lose interest in myself, you, even life . . . away, I become a romantic . . . just a different person. This person is more me, and it's the way I want to be.'

In adulthood, John Harlin's son says he 'completely understands' why his father felt that way. 'He had us too early. I wasn't planned. My father was twenty years old when he conceived me. He had great driving ambitions. Your twenties are when you should be most able to focus on such things, and not be concerned with supporting a family. I was twice my father's age when finally I had a child. But I was still frustrated by not having climbed what I felt I should have by then.'

When John junior was six years old, his father took him on his first multi-pitch climb, in the Calanques of southern France. But it was skiing, rather than climbing, that beckoned to the boy, and by the time he was eight years old he had surpassed his father in the sport. His father didn't like it. John Harlin's competitiveness was legendary, and it encompassed his son's accomplishments. While Andréa was his 'playmate', a little friend he could have fun with, young John was his reflection – and just as he was hard on himself, he made near impossible demands on his son. John's memories of him are like 'flashbacks'; among them, two stand out. 'I was nine years old, and I'd just come back from taking part in an international ski race in Italy. I'd fallen twice during the race. My father knew about the first fall from my grandparents, who had taken me to the race. I told him about the second fall. He was visibly upset and disappointed. It was obvious that he thought I'd let him down.'

The second memory was of the time his father saw him fighting with a bully in the school yard. The fact that the bully was on top of John was unforgivable. 'I remember being in the back of our VW van on the way home, and him being furious about it. I was so ashamed.'

The following year, he did much better in the ski race. He was going to tell his father all about it, when he got home from the Eiger. But that never happened. John remembers his mother coming into the room where he was playing with Andréa and their friends. 'She said Dad had fallen off the mountain. That he was dead. I was sitting there, dazed. I couldn't speak. Everyone else was crying. I thought, How could he do that? How could he fall off? I wanted to know the details right away. I needed to know them in order to cope with it. I wanted to hear that he hadn't made a mistake.'

The details were harsh. A fixed rope he was rappelling on broke, and he fell 4,000 feet down the face. His climbing partner, Dougal Haston, later admitted to Marilyn Harlin that he'd noticed the rope was frayed, but thought it would hold.

John remembers the funeral. Snow falling. Sombre people in dark clothes. Being in a car, following the hearse up to the graveyard. 'The German climbing team had made this wreath that said "Goodbye John." We seemed to follow it for ever.'

The move back to the States was far less traumatic for John than for his sister. He describes it as 'a new life'. His mother was doing a PhD at the University of Washington, and one of her friends there, a man called Ken, took John under his wing. Together, they went to the Arctic three summers in a row. When he was thirteen they climbed the highest peak in the Brooks Range. They went on month-long wilderness hikes and river trips. John's favourite book was Farley Mowat's *Never Cry Wolf*. 'There was a wolf family in the book. The parents were the alpha male and female, and another wolf, Uncle Albert, helped to raise the pups. I used to call Ken my Uncle Albert.'

By the time John was approaching his twenties, he had grand climbing ambitions, which included the Harlin Direct on the Eiger. Then, when he was twenty-one, he saw a man fall to his death. He'd gone to the Canadian Rockies to do some climbing with a friend, who called off at the last minute. Instead, he teamed up with Chuck Hospidales, whom he'd met in Jasper. What Chuck lacked in experience as a climber, he made up for in enthusiasm, and John was sure he had found a new best friend. They decided to climb the Wishbone Arête on Mount Robson. John led. Right from the start, Chuck was nervous, wondering if the route was too much for him, but with John's encouragement, they made it to the summit. Their descent took them beneath the Hourglass Couloir, a huge hanging glacier. Darkness was coming. John pushed ahead, scouting out their route. Behind him, Chuck was moving much more slowly. They weren't roped up.

'I got to the bottom of a ten-foot section of vertical rock and was waiting for him. The worst of the climb was over. Once Chuck reached me, we just had to walk along the ledge to a snow couloir that would lead us down the glacier, and back to the hut. Chuck started coming down the cliff. I yelled up, "Do you feel the handhold right there?" He just said, "No, I don't." And then he peeled off. I grabbed at his clothing, but I couldn't hold on. He bounced off the ledge I was standing on, and carried on falling. I saw the sparks of his crampons each time they struck rock.'

John scrambled down after his friend. He found him over 500 feet below. He was blue. 'I was convinced he was dead. In hindsight, I should have checked for vital signs more closely. But I was in such a state. I just ran across the glacier. Once I fell into a crevasse; my feet were dangling free in the hole. I popped out and kept running and running down to the hut. I spent the night there. I didn't sleep, I wrote and wrote in the logbook, for hours.'

In the morning he got to a phone and called the police. The RCMP flew up and retrieved Chuck's body. The authorities contacted Chuck's parents. John never spoke to them, something he's always regretted. But he did call his mother. And her reaction to the accident shook him to the core. 'It wasn't about Chuck's death so much; it was about the possibility of mine. Her voice, the emotion in it. I suddenly understood what I meant to her, and how serious the consequences would be if I died. I felt I didn't have a right to put her through that. I realised that she might well not survive my own death.'

Because of his mother, he 'radically modified' his climbing ambitions. But he didn't eliminate them. He vowed to be safer, and to carefully choose his objectives. He still hopes to climb the Eiger. Now that he has a daughter, however, more than ever he tries to balance work, family and climbing. He makes compromises. He questions his motives for climbing. In 1999, he arranged to go to the Alps, where his father had died, to do some of the alpine climbing he'd vowed not to do. First, he had a holiday in Europe with his wife Adele and their daughter Sienna. 'It was Sienna's first time to Europe and it was a magical experience. She was three years old; you could just hear the neurons crackling and sizzling and connecting in her brain. I had an intense bonding experience with her. And that made it the worst possible time for me to head off on a climbing trip.'

He said goodbye to his family in a Swiss train station. As he walked away, he started crying uncontrollably. Adele and Sienna's train hadn't left yet; he ran back on to it in tears and started hugging his daughter. 'Adele was saying, "What's wrong? What's going on?" I just had to make that connection again. I felt like I was potentially saying goodbye. It was so horrible. Leaving Sienna, what I strongly felt, more than the idea of hurting her if I died, was the thought that I wouldn't be able to see her grow up. And that's what I most wanted.'

Would his father have let feelings about his children get in the way of his ambitions? Three decades after John Harlin fell from the Eiger, he still casts a shadow over his son. 'I'm always feeling that I'm nothing as a climber. I have regrets about the things that I could have done. I tend to look up to the people who are climbing at a level I wish I'd reached. I feel a failure in comparison to them.'

His close friend Mark Jenkins, also a family man, is a climber with a high threshold for risk. John admires him enormously; he measures himself against him, and feels he comes up lacking. He craves his praise. In 1995 they were climbing Mount Waddington in Canada. John was leading a demanding pitch. Below him, Mark was having difficulties. He yelled up, 'John, you're a hard man!' John was thrilled. 'I know it's not true,' he wrote later, 'but still a warm shock of emotion beats in my heart . . . This isn't vanity, though I'm hardly immune to that weakness. No. This is a boy hearing his father's praise. Did I really do well?'

'I used to wonder if I was climbing because of Dad,' said Nick Estcourt's son Tom. 'If I was trying to prove something. Then, after Dave died, I stopped climbing for three years. When I eventually started again, it made me realise I was climbing because I really loved it. It's a wonderful thing to do. It goes on in beautiful surroundings. It's evocative and inspiring. It makes me so happy. Dave and Nick dying made me unhappy. But I wouldn't have had them doing anything else.'

Until he was seven years old, Tom Estcourt had a father, Nick, who was a famous British mountaineer. To Tom he was a 'a special, fairy-tale man', much better than his schoolfriends' parents, whom he considered to be 'fat and boring'. His memories of his father are 'like snapshots which have been looked at over and over again, fingered and re-remembered continually'.

The best memories are of Nick's return from his Himalayan expeditions. There was always a great buzz of excitement when the family picked him up from the airport. He brought exotic presents for Tom and his two siblings – clothes sewn with tiny mirrors, bags with tassels, a toy cannon. Once, a Sherpa who had been on Nick's expedition came back to Britain with him for a visit. The Sherpa stayed at their house and they all spent a day at the zoo. The worst memories are of his father leaving for his three-month-long expeditions. 'I was always sad. I remember being in the car, when we were driving away from Manchester airport one time after he'd left. I was singing, "Don't cry, don't cry, there's a silver lining in the sky." That was the expedition to K2, when he died.'

While his father was away on K2, Tom woke up one morning, and decided he didn't want to go to school that day. He hatched a plan. 'I thought, I'll tell Mum I'm not feeling well. I'll say it in a kind of grown-up way and she'll believe me.'

His mother wasn't in her bedroom. On his way downstairs, he met his nine-year-old brother Matthew coming up. Matthew was crying. He said, 'Dad's dead.' Tom found his mother in the sitting room. She was crying too, sitting on a beanbag chair in the corner. He didn't have to make up a story – school was off for that day.

'My Auntie Sue, Nick's sister, arrived, and she took us kids on a picnic. She gave us loads of fizzy drinks and sweets. We had a great time, but that was confusing, because it was also a bad day. After that I used to worry that it was only because my dad had died that people were being nice to me and giving me presents. I remember worrying all the time about the positives and negatives of your father dying. It's stayed with me ever since. Worrying about whether you're a good person or a bad person because you like attention.'

Nick died in an avalanche. His body was never found. As a child Tom remembers having a few nightmares, and worrying about other people in his family dying, but otherwise he feels he wasn't traumatised by the loss. The second death, the death of his stepfather, was far, far worse.

After Nick Estcourt died, his friend and business partner Dave Pearce became a strong support for the family. Some years later, he married Nick's widow, Carolyn. 'He wasn't really a surrogate father,' said Tom. 'He was just a lovely, fantastic man, and such a wonderful friend of my mum's.'

He was also a well known rock climber. Dave Pearce didn't want to risk putting Carolyn through the same suffering she'd experienced when Nick died, so he cut back on the frequency of his climbing. But he still continued, and when Tom was in his early twenties, the two men started climbing together.

Tom had taken up climbing in his sixth form at school. At university he became really interested in the sport, and spent two summers in the Alps. Dave was just one of a number of climbing partners, but he always loved going out with him. 'He had a fire in his eyes when he was climbing. When he got to the crags he was so excited. He would always do something that was much too hard. He was trying to tone it down for Mum's sake, but he still had really big ambitions. There was a real bad-boy streak in him. I'm sure that's why Mum loved him so much.'

One weekend in 1998, they met in Wales to go climbing on sea cliffs. Tom drove up from London, where he was working as an accident and emergency doctor. Dave set off from Bowdon, in Cheshire. When he left, Carolyn's last words to him were, 'Make sure you look after Tom.'

Tom can't bear to talk in detail about what happened. 'It was just too awful. A silly abseiling accident. It could have happened to anyone. It was incredibly traumatic.' Dave was standing on a ledge. While he was briefly untied from the rope, a handhold gave way and he fell into the sea. He hit rocks on the way down. Tom tried to resuscitate him, but it was too late.

'Dave's death was the ultimate tragedy. Unbelievably world-destroying. Nick's death was part of my childhood. Because I was so young I didn't know it was bad. But my love for Dave was much more developed and mature. I went slightly crazy for a while after his death. I'm still not over it. I think about him every day.'

For a few weeks after Dave's death, Tom couldn't work. He lost all his self-confidence. For a year and a half he didn't sleep properly. And for over three years he couldn't climb. 'About two years after Dave died I went to Stanage, a crag in Derbyshire. I felt shaky and weird on the rock. It was too soon. But recently I've started back again, and it feels absolutely right.'

The blow of her second husband's death is something Tom's mother has never fully recovered from. Three years later, she struggles with efforts to make sense of her days. Tom worries about her, and dreads causing her more pain.

'I'm very anxious and nervous now when I'm climbing, because I've got such a lot of baggage that I'm dragging up there with me. It's not just a rack and a couple of ice axes, it's also all my personal history. It holds me back from doing really dangerous stuff.'

And how does his mother feel? 'I think she's quite pleased that I'm climbing again. She probably likes the fact that I'm getting back to normal. She knows I love climbing. It's become part of who I am. I can't seem to get it out of me.'

10

The Lingering Shadow

*C*amp Three on the unclimbed East Face of Everest. 1983. Several climbers huddle in a tent around their two-way radio, waiting for the daily call from base camp. Yesterday's call brought intriguing news. Word had come that the trekking group on their way to the mountain included a lone woman, who joined the trek at the last minute. On hearing this, the climbers at base camp had all trooped off to take baths.

Up at Camp Three, an update on this situation is more eagerly anticipated than the latest weather report. The radio wheezes with static. Finally, a voice. 'Carlos? There's a woman just coming into camp and she's looking for you.' All eyes turn on Carlos Buhler. He shakes his head, bewildered. It doesn't make sense. 'Hey, Carlos!' the radio demands. 'You'd better get down here, man. It's your mother.'

The fifty-seven-year-old mother of American climber Carlos Buhler was not the trekking type. And Tibet certainly wasn't on her 'must visit' list. But Carlos's latest expedition – to Everest, the biggest mountain in the world – concerned her more than all others. The past thirteen years, since Carlos had started climbing mountains in South America and the Himalayas, had been Julie Dougherty's 'dark age' of worry. Each time her son left, she was terrified it would be the last she ever saw of him. It was her husband Bill's idea that she go to Everest base camp. 'She seemed incredulous at first,' he recalled. 'There was hardly enough time for her to get a visa, the shots and the gear she needed.'

An astonished Carlos rappelled down the fixed ropes to meet his mother. 'I had no more expectation of her turning up at base camp than of winning the lottery,' he admitted. At first, he felt confused by her presence. 'It was my sixth trip to the Himalayas, but I was in this insecure zone, the young pup of a group of high-powered top climbers, with the East Face of Everest, the last unclimbed face of the mountain, looming above us. Then, suddenly, I was in this comfort zone you feel around your mother. We were sitting together on a flat boulder, talking, I had my head in her lap and she was stroking my hair. There was an enormous oddity to it all. I felt like a kid whose mother is walking him to the school bus. Except the bus was Everest.'

Once he got used to the oddity of the situation, he enjoyed having her around. Which is just as well, because Julie had determined that, rather than fretting about him at home, she would accompany Carlos to base camp on all his future climbs.

Over the next thirteen years, she trekked to Makalu, Ama Dablam, Cho Oyu, Dhaulagiri, the Ogre, and, three times, to K2. She never stayed too long at base camp. She didn't want to disturb Carlos's focus, to distract him in any way. She preferred not to know the details of the climb he was doing until it was over and he was safely down. And she couldn't care less whether he got to the top or not. Having a living, breathing, healthy son was what constituted success.

She grew to love the trekking, the mountain life and the local people. She learned all about the dangers of high-altitude mountaineering. She became friendly with several climbers who later died, or simply disappeared. In 1994, for the second time she trekked up to K2's Baltoro Glacier, through terrain that is challenging by anyone's standards. The Polish climber Voytek Kurtyka was along with her and Carlos. 'It depresses me watching you, Julie,' Voytek teased her. 'It makes me realise I have to spend another thirty years doing this.'

Two years later, when she was seventy-one, she trekked up to K2's North Ridge Base Camp. On the way she suffered from back pain; her back had been bothering her for several months, and she had been treating it with massage, sure that it was caused by a sprain. Three months later, when she was at home in the States, Carlos called her to say he'd climbed K2 at last. The bad news was that his climbing partner, Igor Benkin, had died on the mountain. Julie had her own bad news. She didn't have a sprained back. She had pancreatic cancer. Her doctors said she had about eight months to live.

Carlos helped to nurse her during the last months of her life, and laid her body to rest. Climbing friends sent condolences; they told him how much they had liked Julie, how they had envied him having a mother who understood and accepted what he did. But perhaps it wasn't acceptance that had sent Julie Dougherty out to remote base camps. Perhaps she was compelled to go, afraid that a mountain would claim her son for its own.

'All the climbing literature in the world cannot persuade a mother that there is a good reason to risk your life for the sake of climbing,' wrote the American mountaineer Greg Child. 'Mothers create life; mountains threaten to take life away. You might convince a spouse or a friend that there is spiritual merit within the hazardous framework of climbing, or that mountaineering is a treacherous pilgrimage to some inner fulfillment, but mothers know the truth: climbing is dangerous . . .'

In 1997, Greg Child attended the memorial service of a friend who had been killed by a falling ice block while climbing in Alaska. It was a disturbing event. Neither the dead man's wife nor his parents had approved of his climbing. 'His wife was almost hostile to people. His mother was going around asking people if they were climbers. She was saying, "I just don't understand you. How can do you this?" Her anger was palpable. It was such an awkward and negative goodbye. Everyone who had climbed with him brought a few slides of the routes we did. While we were showing these, his mother was crying. Afterwards she was saying, "Climbing took him away. How can you sit there and celebrate it with these pictures?"

A mother's rage, in the face of the unacceptable: the death of her child, the violation of the natural order of life. Worse still, no body to grieve over, no proof of that death. In 1991, Wanda Rutkiewicz, a Polish mountaineer, disappeared close to the summit of Kangchenjunga. Her mother refused to believe the news. 'I know that she is alive,' she said. 'But in a better place, where she is happy.' She told Carlos Carsolio, the last person to see Wanda, at 8,300 metres on

Kangchenjunga, that she thought Wanda had made it down the mountain and was living in a monastery.

Rage. Denial. Both reactions are hard to face. But no easier, perhaps, is quiet, dignified sorrow. Greg Child witnessed such sorrow in 1983, when he visited the parents of the British mountaineer Pete Thexton. Over the previous decade, Robina and Clive Thexton had grown accustomed to their son's passion for climbing. He'd started at school. At university, where he trained to be a doctor, he joined the mountaineering club. Hard alpine climbs led to Himalayan expeditions. 'There was always a background anxiety while he was away,' said Robina. 'The words "climbing accident" jumped out of the morning paper until we had read the names.'

I met Robina and Clive at Heathrow Airport in 1980, when Pete Thexton was leaving on a winter expedition to Everest, along with Joe Tasker. Two years later, when Joe returned to the mountain to attempt the North East Ridge, they followed his expedition in the press. When they heard of his disappearance, along with Pete Boardman, they immediately phoned their son in Sheffield. 'He wouldn't talk about it,' said Robina. 'He changed the subject to mundane matters. He obviously needed to block it out.'

The expedition that Pete Thexton joined in 1983 was an ambitious venture: to do the first ascent of Lobsang Spire, and then attempt two 8,000-metre mountains, Broad Peak and K2, alpine style. Greg Child and Pete met for the first time when the expedition members assembled in Islamabad. They liked each other instantly, and bonded as climbing partners. After successfully climbing Lobsang Spire with Doug Scott, the two men teamed up to climb Broad Peak together. In a sixty-hour push from base camp, they climbed from 15,500 feet up into the 'death zone' above 26,000 feet. Half an hour from the top of the mountain, Greg developed a vicious headache, and became semi-conscious for several minutes. Both he and Pete feared these were symptoms of an altitude-induced brain dysfunction. They turned back. As soon as they began to lose altitude, Greg's condition improved. But at 25,590 feet, it was Pete's turn to falter. His breathing became severely restricted, his lips turned blue. Both men recognised the signs of the other type of deadly high-altitude sickness – pulmonary oedema, when the lungs fill with fluid. Greg spent hours assisting Pete down the slopes, sometimes dragging him, sometimes lowering him on ropes. Their struggle went on into the night, and it was two a.m. before they reached their high camp, where two other climbers were waiting for them. The plan was to rest a while, then continue down the mountain at dawn. After a couple of hours, Pete woke and asked for something to drink. Before he could sip from the offered cup, he died. Greg tried frantically to revive him. But Pete could not be called back. He lay in his sleeping bag, where he would lie for ever, 'with an expression of sublime rest on his face'.

A day after Greg Child descended from Broad Peak, he started on the long walk out from Base Camp, hurrying through the wild valleys of the Karakorum to where he could, at last, make a phone call. He called the wife of his team member Doug Scott, who knew the Thextons, and asked her to break the news.

'Jan rang us early in the morning, while we were still in bed,' recalled Robina Thexton. Instantly numbed by shock, they decided to go on with their day, as they had previously planned. Robina went to the family planning clinic where she worked as a doctor. She made no mention of the tragedy until the end of the afternoon. Before leaving, she said to her nurse and secretary, 'I'm going to tell you something. Then I'm going to rush away.' Her husband had attended the school play performance of their youngest daughter. They didn't break the news to Vicky, who idolised her big brother, until she cycled home from school. 'And that,' said Robina, 'was the hardest telling of all.'

When Greg Child flew into Heathrow airport from Islamabad, Jan Scott picked him up and drove him to the Thextons' house. They wanted him to be honest, she told him. They wanted all the details. It was a warm summer's afternoon. Robina, Clive and two of Pete's siblings were waiting for Greg in their garden, sitting in the shade of a tree. There was no anger directed at him. 'Pete knew the risks,' said Robina. 'It wasn't anyone else's negligence which precipitated his altitude sickness.'

They organised a big memorial service at their local church. Vicky's school choir sang hymns; members of the congregation put on an afternoon tea. The church was full; scores of Pete's climbing friends attended, and some of them spoke from the altar.

Each year, on Pete's birthday, in his memory the Thextons donate a special flower arrangement to their church. They talk about him often. And they maintain a friendship with Greg Child, regularly exchanging letters, sharing memories of Pete. 'The nineteen years since he died fall away when we start thinking and talking about him,' said Robina. 'It's as if it were yesterday . . . I know there is a scar on my heart, and the pain returns at odd moments – like when listening to Handel's *Messiah* and the chorus starts, "Unto us a son is born" . . .'

In his study of bereaved parents, the sociologist Ronald Knapp identified the existence of what he calls 'a lingering shadow grief'. It is a chronic sorrow, he writes, that parents, and mothers especially, bear for the rest of their lives. 'It is characterized by a dull ache in the background of one's feelings that remains fairly constant but under certain circumstances comes bubbling to the surface . . .'

My former housemate, the mountaineer Alex MacIntyre, recognised this intuitively. 'It's not the girlfriends I feel sorry for when someone dies climbing,' he used to say. 'They'll find someone else. It's the mothers I feel sorry for.'

While Alex was still alive, I met his mother a couple of times. A tiny woman with a broad Scottish accent, like Alex she was dauntingly feisty and argumentative. She'd been widowed a few years before, then developed breast cancer, but seemed fiercely determined not to be beaten down by these blows. I was rather frightened of her; Alex obviously adored her.

When Alex died on Annapurna, in the autumn of 1982, I got to know Jean MacIntyre a little better. Along with her daughter, Libby, and Alex's girlfriend, Sarah, she stayed at my house before the memorial service. I drove them all to the church. Afterwards, there was a reception in a pub. On the way home, I accidentally jumped a red light and got stopped by the police. Jean got out of the car. Gazing up at the policeman, who towered above her, she told him firmly that we were on our way back from her only son's funeral. 'This poor girl driving was his friend and she's very upset,' she said. 'It's been a terribly sad day for us all. I hope you'll not make it worse.' The policeman waved me on.

Nineteen years later I went to see her again. Both of us had aged. But not Alex. He gazed out from photographs around her house. One, hanging on a wall, was particularly striking. A blown-up image of him standing up to his thighs in the ocean, dressed in tight denim jeans, a shirt open to the waist. Grinning sexily at the camera, black ringlets tumbling over his eyes. I smiled back at him, flooded by memories of his brimming confidence, his crackling, acerbic wit, and the untidiness that he turned into a fashion statement. 'I had forgotten just how gorgeous he was,' I told Jean.

She turned away. 'Is it tea you'd like, dear, or coffee?'

I spent two nights with Jean. I'd come hoping to talk to her about Alex, about her loss, but it was a subject she could hardly bare to broach. Her pain was still close to the surface, practically raw. 'It's a living nightmare,' is all she would say. 'You never get over it. It's like a big part of you is ripped out.'

When my eldest brother Mick left on an expedition to cross the Patagonian icecap in 1977, my mother was beside herself with worry. Out of all contact with her son for six weeks, she couldn't sleep, she became depressed and was frequently in tears. She kept thinking of him and his two companions out in a vast wilderness of snow, so alone. An *ice cap* – she imagined it as steep and slippery, something from which he could easily fall to his death. I assured her this wasn't the case, and tried to convince her that what he was doing wasn't really so dangerous.

The following year he was back in Patagonia, hoping to climb Torre Egger. On a warm day, as he was walking across the Cerro Torre glacier, a snow bridge gave way beneath him and he plunged into a crevasse. Seventy feet down, the crevasse narrowed to a crack. He was jammed, upside down, staring into the icy depths. All the team's ropes were in the rucksack on his back. Lightly dressed, he soon began to freeze. 'I knew I was going to die,' he said later. 'I'd accepted it.' One of his team members, Don Whillans, refused to accept it. He ran back across the glacier for half a mile, to the snow cave they had left earlier that day. He found slings, and some spare lengths of rope. Returning to the crevasse, he climbed down, freed Mick and helped him jumar to the surface.

The story hit the press in England. 'Climber Rescued from Tomb of Ice!' yelled one headline After that, nothing could convince my mother that climbing wasn't an insanely dangerous pastime.

Some climbers try to shield their parents completely from worrying while they are on the mountain. Joe Simpson told me about a friend of his who, when he was going off to climb the North Face of the Eiger, assured his parents he would only be hill walking. 'He thought he was making it easy for them. I said, "Yeah, until you get splattered on the Eiger – how devastating would that be?"'

Bewildered relatives, suddenly immersed in the world of climbing, often discover a world they never really knew. Sometimes this sudden collision brings comfort. After Joe Tasker disappeared on Everest, his family seemed to become more involved in his life than most of them had been since he was a child. Joe was the eldest son of a large, close-knit, devoutly Catholic family. At thirteen, he left home to join a Jesuit seminary. After seven years he gave up on the priesthood, and went to university. By then, climbing was becoming a huge part of his life; after he graduated, it took over. He did his best to keep in contact with his family. Before and after expeditions he always visited his parents. He wrote to them regularly from the mountains. Various of his siblings usually turned up at Heathrow airport to see him off on expeditions, or to welcome him back. They accepted his mad schedule and seemed not to resent that his visits home were infrequent, and usually fleeting. He was the star of the family, the one who had risen, quite literally, to unprecedented heights.

When Joe and Pete died, family and friends discussed ways of keeping their memory alive. Joe's mother suggested a literary prize. The Boardman Tasker Prize for Mountain Literature has since become a prestigious, much coveted award, presented annually at a ceremony in London. The Tasker family attend in numbers. This is the day when they meet with the people who were part of Joe's life, and who are now a part of theirs. A day when his star still shines down brightly on them. Joe's special day.

For some parents, the sudden immersion in the climbing world can be a revelation. The American alpinist Seth Shaw had largely shielded his father from his world. He didn't share much about his climbs. He ignored his father's requests for a reading list of climbing books and he introduced him to only a couple of his climbing friends. Possibly this was to save him worry, but he was also aware of how much his father wished he would pursue a different lifestyle.

Tom Shaw was a physician who juggled demanding clinical work with teaching and research. He had persuaded his son to go to business school. After a term, Seth left, saying he didn't want to end up on the same treadmill he'd seen his father on all his life. He worked for two summers in Alaska, falling in love with its mountains, glaciers and wildlife. Later he studied meteorology, and became an avalanche forecaster. He chose to work seasonally so that he could optimise his climbing time. Tom was dismayed. 'After he discovered Alaska, he changed; his priorities and life became so different to everyone else's in the family. I tried to persuade him to at least get into some business related to climbing. I suggested photography, writing, a guiding or outfitting business. I offered to go in on it with him. He always rejected that. He wouldn't even talk to me about it. Seth was a minimalist. He lived on almost nothing. I caught him many times walking around, far away from his home in Utah, with only a buck in his pocket.'

The little Tom did learn about his son's climbing adventures in Alaska was increasingly worrying. Trapped by a two-week blizzard in the Cathedral Spire Group, his food supplies gone. Climbing on Middle Triple Peak, when an earthquake hit. Digging through an unstable cornice to get to the summit of Mount Hunter. 'I finally understood the chances of his dying were high. When a person has an irreversible disease and is going downhill, you have to be ready for the worst to happen. I realised I had to do the same with Seth.'

Tom had already lost a child. When Seth was seven, his eighteen-month-old sister Laura had died of an 'overwhelming infection'. As a doctor, Tom was plagued by thoughts that he should have been able to save her. 'I have lived with the horror of losing Laura, and my self doubts, for thirty-three years,' he said. Even now, he is angry about it. Knowing this, Seth would not have wanted his father to endure the fear of losing another child.

On May 25, 2000, Seth Shaw was taking a photograph of a climbing partner on Ruth Glacier, Alaska, when a falling sérac buried him under tons of ice. His surviving sister broke the news to their father, by phone. Tom's response was pure rage. An impulse to sweep everything off all the tables in his house. A rage so impotent it died before he could even act on it.

Days after that phone call, a memorial service for Seth was held in Salt Lake City and Alta. Friends came from all over the US. They told stories about Seth, laughed over his quirks, described his daring climbs, his quiet understatement, his love of mountain environments. Tom was enamoured of the climbers, and thrilled by facets of his son's life that were unfolding before him. Until then he had thought climbing was selfish. Suddenly, he saw it as Seth's calling – what life had given him to do. 'I had been bothered with the way Seth lived. But at the memorial service, I saw he had a good life, a pure life, with more days of happiness and fulfilment in his thirty-eight years than most of us will experience during far longer lifetimes. I realised that his life was not lived in vain. It had great meaning to him, and to many others.'

Tom also realised that Seth had always followed his heart, something he himself had never done. When Seth died, Tom had been preparing to take on a new position in medicine. Instantly, he determined to make a change. Forsaking his new position, he took full retirement and followed something that had called to him for years – to become a writer. He began to record his son's life; now, there is a book in progress. When that is done, he has ideas for a novel. There are stories about his travels and his father he wants to write. It's work that greatly fulfils him; work that Seth's death made possible. 'Going against convention and living in a unique way, like Seth did, is a brave thing. Since his accident it's been easier for me to go on this route. My attitude towards myself and what I need to accomplish in the remainder of my life has changed dramatically.' What's missing, he admits sadly, is the chance to share these new insights with his son. 'Now I take great pride in what Seth did in the mountains and how he did it. My deep regret is that I didn't experience that pride in time to tell him.'

Were there any surprises for Alex Lowe's parents at his memorial service? In May 2002, I travelled from Canada to see the Lowes, and ask them. Conrad Anker, now married to Alex's widow Jenny, had suggested the visit. 'I think it's only fair they get a chance to tell their side of the story,' he said. 'I think they would appreciate it.'

During my journey to their home, deep in the Blue Smoky Mountains of North Carolina, I thought of what had befallen Alex, piecing together the various accounts of his accident. He and Conrad Anker had gone to Shishapangma, in Tibet, on an expedition led by Andrew Maclean, with a film crew that included Dave Bridges and Michael Brown. The plan was that Alex and Conrad would climb the 26,291-foot mountain, and then ski down it. On the morning of 5 October they left their advance base camp along with Dave Bridges to hike along the glacier and check out their route. The terrain they were crossing was easy and they were in high spirits, pumped with the strong coffee Alex had brewed for breakfast. After an hour they reached the top of a small crest. They could see Andrew Maclean, walking about a quarter of a mile away. He had left just before them, and gone a different route. They waved to each other. Separating them was a heavily crevassed section of the glacier; Alex and the others decided to pick their way through it to join Andrew. They were walking close together, in single file, when Conrad heard Alex cry out, 'Holy shit! Look at that avalanche!' Andrew Maclean had seen it, too. 'It started thousands of feet above them,' he said. 'An entire monsoon's worth of snow that released in a huge, huge slide. I saw the initial fracture, and how it grew and propagated. I went from thinking, These guys had better get going, to, This is really bad, to, when they were just little teeny ants running in the path of this huge slide, They're not going to make it.' Andrew dived behind some rocks, and held on. 'There was this huge force, like a bomb blast. I thought it was the end. The hollow I was in filled up with snow.' It wasn't the end. Not for Andrew Maclean. The avalanche had blown over him. He struggled to his feet, and looked around for the others. The heavily crevassed glacier had been transformed into a smooth snow slope. And where previously there had been three men running for their lives, now there was one, stumbling and staggering. 'Initially I thought it was Alex. I ran up to him. It was Conrad. He was in bad shape. His pupils were different sizes, there was blood all over him.'

What Conrad remembers of the avalanche is the sensation of a huge train bearing down. Alex and Dave ran down the glacier. Conrad ran to the side. At the last moment, he threw himself to the ground. The main body of the avalanche bypassed him, but its blast dragged him twenty metres along the snow. It knocked him out, gashed his head in four different places, broke two of his ribs and dislocated his shoulder. Then let him go. He came around clutching his watch, which had been yanked off his wrist. Looking at the watch, at crucial seconds ticking by, he searched for some sign of his friends. 'There was nothing. It was as if they had disappeared, or a higher being had taken them off the planet.'

The team searched all day for Alex Lowe and Dave Bridges. The avalanche had been so huge, the deposition of snow and ice so deep, it was a hopeless task. But they kept trying, until darkness forced them to give up.

Andrew broke the news of Alex Lowe's death to the outside world. His first call was to Alex's wife, Jenny. 'We were on the satellite phone.

There was a really bad connection. I got a hold of her and then it broke up. I called her back. She knew – why else would I be calling her in the middle of the night, instead of Alex? I didn't know what to say. I told her that there had been an avalanche and we thought Alex and David were gone. She said, "Are you sure?" I said, "We're going to continue searching for him. We haven't given up hope. But it's not looking good at this point."'

That night, there was a heavy snowfall on the south side of Shishapangma. By morning, the avalanche danger was too great for anyone to risk going up on to the glacier again.

'When you have a child,' said Jim Lowe, 'you're dealt a card. You can't stop that child doing what he wants to do. Climbing was Alex's personality. We couldn't have prevented it, even if we'd known that at age forty he would be killed.'

Jim Lowe is a big man, strongly built, with a restless energy. A retired professor of entomology and plant pathology, he now spends part of each year leading nature treks in the Blue Smoky Mountains. While we talked about Alex, he cradled his dog, Maggie, on his lap, and frequently broke into tears. Dottie, once an elementary school teacher, has wide, alert eyes, and dresses immaculately. A deeply religious woman, she obviously gains great strength from her Christian faith. She never lost her composure. Like a bow, she might bend and bend under pressure, but it would take a great deal to break her.

Alex gave her much cause to worry, right from the first months of his life. Shortly after he was born, he developed pyloric stenosis. Jim was in the army at Fort Dietrich, Maryland. The doctors there transferred the baby to the army hospital in Washington DC, where he underwent emergency surgery on his stomach. Six months later, there was a polio epidemic; after the first two of three vaccine injections, Alex developed symptoms similar to polio, and was again put in isolation. 'Both times, we couldn't hold him or pick him up,' said Dottie. 'We could only look at him through a glass window. I'd see that his diaper was soaking, and I'd just want to get my hands on him, but I couldn't. I've often wondered if those two bouts of being isolated, and not being held, made him as frenetic as he was.'

At school, his hyperactivity soon got him into trouble. He couldn't sit still in class. When Dottie went to pick him up after school she'd find him rolling on the ground, fighting. He kept catching his clothes on barbed-wire fences and tearing them to bits. He wore shoes out at a fantastic rate. Always in too much of hurry to bother with the laces, he just shoved his feet into them, flattening the backs. And he had little time for affection. 'He was a hard child to cuddle,' Jim recalled. 'He'd push you away. That really kind of stayed with him through life. He was never easy to be close to. Even his brothers felt like they didn't know him too well.'

As soon as he was able, he was climbing. On to the mantelpiece in their living room. Up the tall spruce tree outside their church. 'We'd come out and there would be no Alex,' said Dottie. 'Then we'd look up and he'd be in the very tippy-top of the tree, on branches that were just barely able to hold him up. He was full steam ahead; the devil take the hindmost. That's the way he always was.'

Jim rock climbed in his younger years, and did some instructing. As a family, they hiked and backpacked, so were often in a mountain environment. 'The three boys really took to it, but Alex most of all. By the time he was in high school he was playing hookey to go climbing. There was an army base nearby, and in its training facility there was a rappelling tower, with boards up one side. It had a great big sign that said "KEEP OFF, ONLY AUTHORISED PERSONNEL". But that didn't stop Alex and his friends. We found out he was spending quite a bit of time over there.'

In senior high school, Alex decided he wanted to be a professional mountain guide. By the time he was a freshman at the University of Montana, he was doing some serious climbing. Then the first of his friends died in a climbing accident on Black Ice Couloir in the Grand Tetons. Alex was a pallbearer at the funeral for Marvin MacDonald. 'I can still see him in a borrowed coat, at the church,' said Dottie. 'He looked dazed. It really hit him hard.'

What concerned Jim was how Alex got to and from the mountains. Hitch-hiking, or driving a beat-up old Volkswagen from Montana to Canada and back. He didn't worry so much about the climbing. But Dottie did. 'At one point I used to have these terrible dreams. One night I dreamt that Alex was climbing with some people who were on drugs. He had a fall and was plummeting through the air. I woke up and I thought, I can't go on like this. I decided there was only one thing to do. I thought, God is there. He can protect Alex and be with him, whatever happens. So I just handed him over to the Lord. I guess my faith really took over. After that it was much easier.'

Alex resisted becoming a family man, for a long time. 'His wife Jenny had always wanted to be a mother,' said Dottie. 'We kept telling him, 'Alex, children are just so important to your life and we hope that you will rethink this.' So they had Max. Then along came Sam. The third one, Isaac, was a real surprise, and a shock to Alex. He looks exactly like him. It's uncanny. He's a carbon copy of Alex, too, in his behaviour. We were having dinner with a friend of Jennifer's, and Isaac was in his baby chair. Suddenly he was writhing up and out of it like an octopus. I thought the chair was going to turn over backwards. But he had such good balance, he knew exactly what he was doing.'

They recognised the conflict Alex felt about his family and his climbing. They knew his concern about being an absent father. They understood that climbing was a deep compulsion with him.

'In some ways Alex was not an easy person to be around,' Jim conceded. 'He had boundless energy and drive. He was impatient with the boys and I think that really bothered him. He was the same way with the rest of us. He just didn't have the time. He was always in his office preparing for the next trip, always on the telephone. So even when he was at home he was not present.'

During the last few years of his life, Jim and Dottie saw little of Alex. He sent postcards from all over the world, but even when he was working as a representative for The North Face, and would sometimes drive though Missoula, the town they lived in then, he would rarely stop to see them. His brother, Andy, would hear from fellow citizens in his town that they'd seen the famous Alex Lowe driving through. His youngest brother, Ted, always felt Alex ignored him and underrated him as a climber.

'His brothers loved him very much,' said Dottie. 'They were proud of him and wanted to be part of his life. But he was a man for everybody, for others. He had a charismatic personality that people just really responded to. So in many ways he was not ours. That was difficult, but I understood it was just the way he was.'

He belonged to everyone he met. In many ways he was not ours. Dottie's words at the family's memorial service for Alex.

Jim had had a premonition of his death. Nothing spectacular, just a strong feeling that Alex was having difficulties. 'I was tense and cocked . . . And then suddenly, there it was. Our son Ted called to tell us. Jennifer had called him . . . It was like, this is the time. It was almost a relief.'

He was alone when the call came. Dottie was out, attending a meeting of her Bible group. When she returned, she picked up the mail in the hallway. She carried the letters to the living room and started sorting through them. Jim said, 'Come and sit down a minute. Leave the mail.' She sat down. 'The worst has happened,' he told her.

The first memorial service was held at a ranch about forty miles outside of Bosman, Montana, where Alex had lived with Jenny and the boys. It was a typical climber's memorial. Slides about expeditions. Photographs of him climbing. Eulogies by famous climbers. His brothers played guitars and sang. 'Who will tend the homeplace when I am far away . . .' His parents both got up to say something. Jim couldn't make it through his speech.

Andrew Maclean was at the service, but Dottie and Jim didn't speak to him. They were angry that Alex had gone to Shishapangma. They thought it was a foolish trip. Skiing down a mountain – it was a lark, not the kind of mountaineering that Alex was devoted to. 'We felt resentful that it was a North Face show and a kind of trivial trip,' said Jim. 'We were all feeling to varying degrees that Andrew Maclean, the organiser, was one of these up-and-coming hotshots, bumping and pushing Alex.' Some months later, when they saw the film that Michael Brown made of the trip, their anger dissipated. 'I realised how thrilled Alex was to be in the mountains with some of his closest friends,' said Dottie. 'I thought, Well I'm really glad that he had such a happy time . . . There was no conflict, they were a bunch of boys having a good time together.'

Also at the service was Conrad Anker. Jim wanted to ask him about the accident, but Conrad was withdrawn. 'He was beat up, his scalp was shaved because of his head injuries. He had all these cuts and bruises. He was in no shape to socialise. We tried to talk, but he could not contain himself not to cry. I cried the whole time too.'

Conrad's decision to marry Jennifer puzzled Dottie at first. 'I kept thinking about this handsome, world-travelling mountain climber, taking on a widow and three boys. Was there something wrong with him? But he loves them. He's devoted to the boys. He chooses to stay and do homework with them instead of going climbing. It's remarkable.'

Both she and Jim see Conrad as a blessing. 'He fulfils such a place in Jennifer's life,' said Jim. 'And these boys, they have a real man, a father. I make jokes about it because Jennifer's my daughter-in-law, so I can't figure out if Conrad is my son or son-in-law or what. But that's okay.'

Conrad writes to Dottie and Jim frequently. When his work brings him through their part of the country, he contacts them. In October 2001, he came to Charlotte, North Carolina, to present an IMAX film at a children's discovery centre. He asked Jim and Dottie if they'd like to drive over. 'He arranged for us to stay in the same place as him, this darling little inn,' said Dottie. 'We just had the best time. There was a cocktail party and dinner, and then the showing in this IMAX theatre. We got to spend the whole weekend with him.'

They don't make what seems an obvious comparison to Alex. Perhaps they don't need to. Just as they accepted Alex's need to climb, and the death that climbing brought him, so they can accept the man who has stepped into his shoes.

Dottie misses Alex every day. But she has a calm feeling about her exuberant and hyperactive son. 'He will never grow old, never have to slow down because of arthritis. He will always be at the peak of his form and that was important for him. I'm thankful that he's in the Lord's hands. And that he knows a peace such as he never knew in his life.'

For a year or so after he died, on full-moon nights she found herself talking to him. 'I would go outside and say, "Alex, can you see the brilliance of the moon through all that snow and ice?" I would picture him lying under all that ice, looking up at the sky and seeing the moon. It isn't the sunlight; it's the moonlight.'

Jim's grief seems closer to the surface. A stricken expression crosses his face when he talks about Alex's body, in the glacier on Shishapangma. He imagines it 'in the fetal position'. His firstborn son. The image brings a sadness that will shadow him for the rest of his days.

On the anniversary of Alex's death, Jim and Dottie hike up to the summit of one of the Blue Smoky Mountains. They take a picnic, some candles to light, and Alex's photograph. 'The view is expansive – mountains in all directions – like the places Alex loved. It's a beautiful fall day. The grass is tall and dry. We lay back, look at the clouds, and remember him.'

11

The Brilliance Beyond

‘*T*he important message,’ said Cherie Bremer-Kamp, ‘is that through unspeakable tragedy, life goes on. You don’t want it to at first, but it does. The sun keeps rising in the morning and going down at night. The flowers – God damn those flowers! – keep blooming.’ The voice was brave, but tears spilled down her cheeks. She wiped them away with the tiny stumps that were her fingers.*

When her hands were whole, Cherie Bremer-Kamp was a Himalayan mountaineer. She had a dream to climb Kangchenjunga with her husband, Chris Chandler. To make the first winter ascent of the mountain’s north face. In the winter of 1984/5, accompanied by a Tamang climber, Mongol Sing, they began the hardest climb of their lives.

Stormbound for days on the mountain, Chris and Cherie talked about the impoverished villages they had passed through on their way to base camp. They tossed around ideas on how they might help the people of the area. Perhaps they could raise funds to improve the water and sanitation systems. Perhaps they could build a clinic, a school.

After almost fifty nights on the mountain, patiently waiting out wild storms and devastating winds, the trio finally reached a high point of 26,000 feet. The morning of their summit attempt, as they prepared to leave camp, Chris began coughing badly, spitting out blood-streaked sputum. He seemed unable to put on his crampons. When Cherie bent down to help him, he told her he'd gone blind. As doctor and nurse, Chris and Cherie both understood these symptoms. High-altitude sickness. Pulmonary and cerebral oedema. Fear surged through Cherie; the adrenaline that rushed through her body, she believes, constricted the blood vessels in her extremities and caused her hands to freeze. She tore off her gloves to look at them. They were 'white and marble-like'. When she clapped her hands, the sound was like 'banging two pieces of wood together'.

Chris's only hope was to get to a lower altitude, fast. But he could barely walk and Cherie's hands had lost all feeling. Their progress was painfully slow. Hours of stumbling and sliding down the mountain, and they'd lost only a thousand feet of altitude. As darkness closed around them, Cherie and Mongol hacked out ledges in the hard snow. Chris was confused, restless and afraid. Cherie managed to settle him into his bivvy bag, and tied him to an ice axe. But he was lying on some rope she needed; when she asked him to roll over so she could get it, he slid off the ledge. In panic he tried to stand up and run. His feet got tangled in the bag. As he fell over he lost consciousness. While she was moving him back to the ledge, Cherie realized he had stopped breathing. She tried frantically to revive him, but Chris was gone.

Cherie spent the night of 15 January 1985 lying in shock on the side of Kangchenjunga, a few feet away from her husband's body. Her hands were frozen into 'rigid claws'. She couldn't feel her legs. She was drawn to follow Chris, 'to seek out where he had gone.' But by morning she had made her choice. She stood up. She left Chris where he was, 'in dignity, with his pack and ice axe beside him, gazing out over the vast Tibetan plateau'. She could not face the idea of burying his body in a crevasse.

It took Cherie and Mongol two more days and nights to reach base camp. By then, both were seriously frostbitten. One of their support team set off to run the mountain trails to Tapeljung, from where he intended to send a telegram requesting a helicopter rescue. On the way he passed through Ghunsa, the highest permanent settlement on the route to Kangchenjunga. The villagers were in the middle of an important religious festival. But they remembered Chris and Cherie, who had stopped there on their way up the mountain and provided what 'band aid' medicine they could to those in need. Almost half of the villagers left immediately, and trekked up to the base camp. In large straw baskets slung on their backs, they took turns carrying Cherie and Mongol 7,000 feet down steep, switch-backing trails. 'All I can remember is being in this basket,' said Cherie, 'and hands reaching up to stop me falling out, into the chasm below.' The villagers carried them as far as Foley, at 10,800 feet, to a place where a helicopter could land. They refused all offers of money. Cherie insisted that she wanted to repay them. What did they need the most? A school, they said. Healthcare. As they carried her to the helicopter, Cherie vowed she would return to these people, and bring to life the plans she and Chris had dreamt of on the high slopes of Kangchenjunga.

Fulfilling her promise was a long, tough journey. Back in Seattle, she faced not only a mountain of grief over the death of Chris, but also the trauma of disability. She spent five pain-riddled months in the hospital, undergoing ten operations. She lost a third of each foot. Her fingers were removed, save for stumps of bone which were grafted with skin from her thighs and buttocks.

Waiting for her operations, Cherie began to write. Clutching a pen between dead, blackened fingers, she filled page after page with spidery scrawl. She felt compelled to record her extraordinary experience on the mountain, 'before it escaped me, before it dissipated'. And she needed to confront what had been unfinished business with Chris Chandler. Theirs had been a passionate but deeply troubled relationship. Chris was prone to outbreaks of uncontrollable anger. When these erupted, he frequently lashed out at Cherie. On several occasions, she feared for her life. Even while they were climbing on Kangchenjunga, where she was utterly vulnerable, literally with nowhere to run, he beat her. After one foray up the mountain, they were on their way to base camp when fog moved in. For a while they lost their way. Cherie was tired, and moving slowly. Sensing Chris's mood darken, she tried to joke, to defuse his anger. It didn't work. When she stopped to rest, and took off her rucksack, he attacked her. He beat her around the head and back. He threw the rucksack at her. Then he threw the ice axe. It missed her and hit a rock; the impact sent sparks into the night.

When he died, her confusion about this side of their relationship only intensified her grief. 'I had been denying it when Chris was alive,' she said. 'Each time I just hoped it wouldn't happen again, but of course it did, again and again. A big part of the writing process was about starting to deal with it. I can remember struggling to write each part down. I'd finish a page and put it away. The next day I'd read it and just curl up in shame. But the process of putting it on paper was a way of releasing it. And I wanted people to know who Chris was, all of him, and still be able to love him. He wasn't a monster. He had demons.'

Her book, *Living on the Edge*, was published in 1987. More than the story of an expedition, it is a painfully honest account of an abusive relationship, and its destructive cycles. A book, begun as a personal catharsis, which ultimately helped villagers half a world away on the high slopes of Kangchenjunga.

Throughout the writing and the operations, she had struggled with her desire to climb again. She kept wondering if she would be able to hold an ice axe. A Spanish climber she'd heard of had lost both his hands to frostbite, but had gone back to climb K2, with some help. Could she return to climb Kangchenjunga, with her damaged hands and feet? Finally, she decided such desires weren't healthy for her. 'I resolved to take that energy and convert it not to what was in the past, but to the here and now. To the living rather than the ethereal.'

Eventually she went home, to the boat where she had lived with Chris Chandler. 'It was terrible at first,' she said. 'I'd have friends over, I'd cook breakfast for them and I'd drop the frying pan. The food would end up on the floor and I'd be so overwhelmed I had to go and lie down. It was like someone had beaten on me.'

Grief over her double loss turned into clinical depression. Anti-depressants didn't help, and neither did therapy. Her doctors starting talking about electro-shock treatment. Going back to work as a nurse only made things worse. Every loss she witnessed reminded her of her own tragedy; when she did CPR on a patient, it transported her back to that terrible night on Kangchenjunga, and her futile efforts to save Chris. After six months, she quit; by then she knew what she needed to do. Cherie came up with her own cure. 'I went to my therapist and said, "This might sound crazy, but I want to go to Kangchenjunga with my kids."' The therapist agreed. In 1989, she set off with her son and daughter, aged thirteen and fourteen, and trekked up to Kangchenjunga base camp. The last time she had been there, the area was locked in winter snows. Now it was the monsoon. 'There were waterfalls everywhere. We were knee-deep in flowers. The Bharal sheep were rutting; there were eagles swooping down; it was like this huge celebration of life. That was the beginning of my healing.' Best of all was reconnecting with the people of Ghunsa, and confirming her promise to help them. 'I'd brought a Godzilla bottle of antidepressants with me. Once I got to Kangchenjunga I stopped taking them. I've never taken one since.'

She founded the Kangchenjunga School Project. All the promotion for her book, all the publicity around her tragedy she linked to raising funds and gaining sponsors. The project's first task was to build a nine-room school in Ghunsa, outfit a medical clinic and train a local Buddhist monk to act as a 'barefoot doctor'. With generous support from The Himalayan Foundation, the Himalayan Fair, Jon Krakauer, and other individuals, more initiatives followed. The building of a school and clinic in Folay, a Tibetan refugee settlement close to Ghunsa; the installation of solar-powered vaccine refrigerators in seven health posts across the Tapeljung district; a preschool run by local women, using Montessori methods; the training of a maternal health worker in Ghunsa.

At the time of writing, Nepal is gripped by Maoist insurrections. Cherie worries for the people she knows there, and acknowledges the risk to the project. 'It's like a sand mandala,' she said. 'So easily swept away.' Whatever happens, however, the deeper effects of her work can't be destroyed.

Cherie admits that her commitment to the people of the Kangchenjunga area, and the redirection of her energies that it involved, was key to her recovery from the tragedies that beset her in 1985. 'It's not just been about giving to the villagers,' she said. 'It's been a real exchange.' Now, as well as running the project, Cherie works in a liver transplant unit in San Francisco. She is happily married to Rob Rowlands, who has embraced her work in the Kangchenjunga area. Her children are grown, and doing well. She is close to her grandchildren. She no longer climbs, but she still takes risks – she shrugs off the fact that a few years ago she broke six ribs, her clavicle, and her pelvis in a mountain bike crash, and more recently fractured a bone in her thumb while skiing. 'Some people look at my hands and say, "You're a stupid woman." I say, "Excuse me! Go back to your shopping mall and your television. That's your life. Mine's a bit different."'

While she was recovering from the emotional blow death and maiming had delivered, Cherie wrote, 'Despair is not necessarily such a bad thing, for when all hope is gone, there is no fear. From that deep despair, a beauty is born and new possibilities can arise.' But that was two years after Chris Chandler died. After she'd slowly clawed her way from the blackness of despair, towards the light.

That blackness is something Andy Parkin knows well. On a warm summer day in 1984, the renowned British climber had a brutal fall. He was guiding a client up the Riffelhorn in Zermatt, when the rock they were attached to broke away from the cliff face. The client dropped about six feet and hurt his toe. Andy fell thirty feet and landed on his side on a rock slab. He has no memory of the impact, only of lying on the ground and thinking, I'll have a breather first, then I'll get up.

But that wasn't to happen for a long while. He had landed with such force that his pelvis broke in thirteen places, his heart came out of its casing, his spleen ruptured, his elbow was badly smashed, one of his arms was broken and his ribs were cracked. For the first week after the accident, the doctors weren't sure if he'd survive. Andy was unaware of this. 'All I was worried about was whether or not I'd be fit again in time for climbing the following winter.' He pulled through, but the doctors had bad news for him. Calcification had developed in his hip and right elbow, fusing them both. Climbing, they said, was something he would never do again. For Andy it was 'a crushing blow'.

'When you're climbing,' he said, 'you dream up the worst-case scenarios and think about what you would do if they happened. You owe it to yourself to be prepared. Except you think you're preparing for when it happens to someone else, like your climbing partner. I honestly never thought it would happen to me. Once, when I was climbing in Yosemite, I jokingly declared I wasn't going to see thirty. The accident happened within a month of my thirtieth birthday. I had time in hospital to reflect on that.'

He spent a couple of years in and out of hospital. To help pass the time while he lay immobilized, he returned to a passion from his childhood: painting. In his early teens he had thought about the possibility of art school. Then he discovered climbing, and it took over his entire life. Now, painting was his 'only option' and he threw all his energies into it. Quite literally, he painted himself out of despair and into a new career.

In 1986 Andy had his first exhibition, in Chamonix, France. Every painting there had been done on an easel at the side of his bed.

A year and a half after the accident, doctors tried to cut away the calcification in Andy's hip. The operation wasn't successful; his mobility could not be improved. 'From that moment on,' said Andy, 'I decided to create my own body.' From his home in Chamonix he started 'hobbling around the mountains on crutches', camping on glaciers for five days at a time. He was living like a climber, but he couldn't climb. Instead, he sketched and painted. His paintings of the Alps began to sell in France, England, the States. He branched into sculpture. In 1989, on the Mer de Glace, with the French sculptor Phillipe Vouillemoz he created a massive work of art from garbage left behind by climbers and skiers, to raise awareness of the impact of both sports on such a fragile environment. Three years later, in the Chamonix valley, he collaborated with six sculptors and a number of other artists on a project called Espacé Endangé. Using materials washed out of the glacier in the river, Andy created a huge elephant. He described it as 'an endangered species, from human detritus'. In his studio he crafted smaller sculptures. Figures of bronze wire that leapt and ran. A mountain made of stained glass. Delicate pieces that expressed what the accident had taught him. 'Life is so ephemeral. It's a tenuous affair.'

From the devastating accident that almost took his life, Andy Parkin emerged as an internationally renowned artist. 'For a while art became a substitute for climbing,' he said. 'I was lucky to have it to turn to. For climbers I'd say it's good to cultivate something else you can develop, with a lot of energy and passion, in case the worst happens.'

The 'worst' – forever losing the ability to climb – didn't happen to Andy. In 1988, a group of friends who were planning a Himalayan expedition had invited him to join them on the trek to Makalu base camp. He had no intention of climbing; his rucksack was stuffed with painting supplies. The two-week walk-in to the mountain was a struggle for him. His leg muscles, unaccustomed to such prolonged use, were in agony. Once at base camp, however, he decided to try climbing a nearby 'easy little peak' of 6,000 metres. To his astonishment, he succeeded. 'Next I found myself at over 7,400 metres on Makalu with Greg Child. I hadn't brought any high altitude gear with me. All my clothing was old, from before the accident. I was on the mountain, sewing up my gloves, gluing up my boots. Suddenly I was thinking, Maybe I can do this again.'

Proving the doctors wrong, Andy fashioned a new climbing technique, learning how to get up mountains and rock walls in a unique, lopsided fashion. His friend Paul Pritchard described watching him climb in India: 'His right arm and leg would always move first and then pull his thin ripped torso up a stop to allow his left limbs to locate the nearest edge or pocket. It seemed to me the movement of a very graceful crab.'

Since his success on Makalu, Andy has climbed to 8,300 metres on the North Ridge of Everest without oxygen. He's climbed Shivling, Broad Peak and put up two new routes on K2. Over the past decade he's been regularly drawn to Patagonia, where he's soloed his 'hardest ever new routes'. Only in the mountains, he says, does he feel entirely normal. 'In harsh survival situations I forget about my hip and my elbow, because the rest of my body is suffering all the time as well.'

But his art remains an essential part of his life. Because of it, he sees mountains differently. His climber's eye still sees the mountain as a network of lines and routes to the top. His painter's eye notes the play of light, and the details that make up the daily lives of the people and animals living in the shadow of that mountain. Before a hard climb, he uses his painting to tune into his surroundings, to 'centre' himself for the hard task ahead. When he's pinned down by storms, he passes the time by painting on the inside walls of his tent. Most importantly, he values what his art has given him. 'If I could wave the magic wand and go back to that fateful day, and not take my client to that particular mountain . . . everything could be very different. Obviously, if I could get my body whole again, that would be marvellous, I'd sacrifice almost anything for that. But at the same time, if I could have it all back again, would I be willing to lose what I've gained? I've got a richness of life now. I'm no longer that tunnel-vision climber I used to be. I'd like to think I'm a better person.'

And still a climber. Unlike Charlie Houston, who made a conscious decision, a year after surviving a legendary epic on K2, that climbing was no longer an option for him. It was his second attempt on the yet-unclimbed peak. He was the leader of the expedition, and its doctor. In the spring of 1953 he set off for the mountain with fellow Americans Bob Bates, George Bell, Bob Craig, Art Gilkey, Dee

Molenaar and Pete Schoening, and a British army officer, Tony Streather. By early August they had established their high camp at 7,800 metres, and were poised for the summit. Then a storm moved in, trapping them for ten days. Unable to keep their stoves going, they survived on snow mixed with powdered milk and jam. Soon, they were suffering from dehydration and hunger, as well as the effects of being at altitude for so long. Art Gilkey, a twenty-seven-year-old geologist from Iowa, was particularly badly affected. He had great pain in one leg, and was unable to stand or walk. Charlie Houston diagnosed thrombophlebitis – blood clots – in his legs, which moved into his lung. As the weather continued to pin them down, Art's pulse rose to a dangerously high rate and he was coughing up blood. Charlie went though 'agony' at the decisions he faced. 'I felt guilty, because I was a doctor and I couldn't do anything for him. I knew Gilkey was going to die if we stayed there. I was pretty certain that he would die if we tried to take him down. I knew all of us were nearly at the end of our strength. Those last few days were a terrible period for me, knowing that one or more of us would die.'

One thing was certain – they were giving up hopes of the summit in order to try, at all costs, to get Art Gilkey down the mountain. 'It was a moral decision,' said Charlie. 'The only one that we could consider. The only one I would make today if I had to do it again.'

Avalanche danger made it impossible for them to descend the way they had come up. They started down in a storm, over an unexplored rock rib, lowering Gilkey, who was tightly wrapped in a cocoon made of an anorak and a sleeping bag. After four hours, they came to a difficult pitch. Craig went first, and was almost swept away by a small avalanche. He unroped, and crossed the slope to their intended bivouac site. Next they lowered Gilkey for about thirty feet on Pete Schoening's rope, which Pete anchored with his ice axe behind a rock. The others started down behind them. Then George Bell slipped. As he fell, he slid into Streather, Houston and Bates, knocking them off in what Houston describes as 'a domino effect.' Tumbling head over heels down the mountain, the four men's ropes somehow got tangled up with Pete Schoening's. Astonishingly he summoned the strength to hold the rope, and their accumulated weights, saving all of their lives.

'I only vaguely remember the fall,' said Charlie. 'I do remember lying on the rocks and Bates shouting at me, "If you ever want to see your wife and kids again, get up and climb." I was semi-conscious for the next twelve hours.'

In various stages of shock and injury, the team regrouped, and set up a couple of small tents. Then Bates and Streather returned to collect Art Gilkey from where Pete Schoening had left him firmly anchored. He was gone. The slope on which he'd been lying looked 'swept clean' as if by an avalanche. Art, the rope, the axe that had held it to the snow, had all disappeared.

'It's been suggested that it wasn't an avalanche,' said Charlie. 'That Art set himself free because he knew how desparate our situtaion was. But none of us ever thought that was true. I had given him a shot of morphine part of the way down, so he wasn't completely conscious. And he was wrapped up so tightly, mummy style, it's doubtful he could have pulled out the belay and ice axe.'

Charlie recalls little of these events. His memory only begins the next morning. When the team set off down the mountain, he took the lead. 'Something that we all saw immediately, but never mentioned to each other until we had our twenty-fifth reunion, is that we began climbing down through blood and tissue and bits of a sleeping bag and ropes. We had about fifteen to twenty minutes of climbing down through this debris. It was Art's funeral.'

It took them four days to struggle the two vertical miles down the mountain. Even when they reached the safety of base camp their journey was far from over, as they still faced a long, gruelling trek through rugged valleys. 'During that walk I remember thinking, After what has happened, nothing in the world will ever bother me again,' said Charlie. 'But of course, that's not true.'

He returned home, 'still traumatised', to his wife and three small children, and his medical career. He threw himself into his commitment to co-writing a book with Bob Bates about the expedition. And he started thinking about a return to K2 in 1955.

In the summer of 1954, Charlie was out for dinner when he heard a radio news report that a group of Italians had made the first ascent of K2. A few days later, he went missing from his home in Exeter, New Hampshire. A policeman found him forty miles away, wandering lost and confused, suffering from transient global amnesia. When Charlie's memory returned, he took a holiday to recover. With his wife and children he set off for their summer cottage by a lake. As he was driving there, to his horror he kept seeing blood. Huge pools of it, all over the road ahead.

A flashback? Delayed post-traumatic stress? Whatever the cause, by the following year he was making plans to return to K2. Then, in the autumn of 1954, he suddenly decided he couldn't go ahead with the climb. 'I said, "I've got a wife and three kids. I have patients. I have responsibilities. I'm not going."'

He revoked his permit. And he never climbed again. It was an abrupt end to a long and impressive career in the mountains. A career that had begun at the age of twelve, with climbs in the Alps. That had taken him to Alaska, where he did the first ascent of Mount Foraker. To Nanda Devi with H.W. Tilman and others, in 1936. Up to 7,900 metres on K2 two years later and, in 1950, on an exploration of the southern approach to Everest with Tilman and his father, Oscar Houston. He had been a true pioneer, an explorer. Climbing was a huge part of his life and now, suddenly, it was all over. 'Once I had quit the big mountains I quit climbing completely,' he said. 'I just lost interest in it. Having been in the Olympics I wasn't going to be satisfied with county competitions. I turned to other things.'

Those 'other things' included building an early model of the artificial heart, and continuing clinical studies, begun during the Second World War, on the effects of high altitude. Along with Herb Hultgren, a Stanford cardiologist, he co-discovered HAPE – high-altitude pulmonary oedema. He did pioneering work in setting up group practices, and was medical director of the Aspen Health Center at the Aspen Institute for Humanistic Studies. During the first year of the Peace Corps, Houston took on the position of director in India. By the time he left, the volunteer force of six had swelled to five hundred. He was recalled to Washington to create the Doctors' Peace Corps, and he helped to set up a medical school in Jalalabad in Afghanistan. In Vermont, he became involved in the university's newly formed Department of Community Medicine. He wrote a number of books, edited more and contributed to many journals and magazines. Turning ninety in August 2003, he is completing a film which chronicles his Himalayan career and his high altitude research.

All these achievements, he says, were another form of exploration. 'I'm always ahead of the curve, looking beyond the horizon. As soon as I arrive somewhere, I want to go someplace else.'

Only once has he returned to the high mountains. When he was seventy-seven, a film project took him to Nanga Parbat, with Chris Bonington. He never went further than Base Camp. It was an emotional time for him. 'On the way out,' he recalled, 'I sat down on a rock in the moonlight and looked at the mountains. I thought, You know, I really miss this. Chris was very sensitive. He didn't say a word. He sat down and put his arm around me.' Charlie's voice caught; he paused for a few seconds, composing himself. 'And that,' he said eventually, 'was the end of it.'

Everyone finds their own ending. Linda Wylie rejected the one that Annapurna had given her: Anatoli Boukreev's death. They had planned to work on a book together, and she determined to go ahead with that. She gathered together all his papers and diaries, and had them translated from Russian into English. Painstakingly, she worked through those literal translations, making selections and rewriting them in Anatoli's voice. 'The book was totally necessary for me,' she said. 'I had to circle in his words for a while. It was like listening to him, having a long conversation with him.' *Above the Clouds* took her two years to complete. By then, she was under financial pressure to go back to her normal job as a nurse practioner. But she wanted to get away from the States, to a place where she felt more in tune with Anatoli. In 2001 she applied to the Peace Corps for a post in Kyrgistan. Then September 11 happened, and Kyrgistan was closed. A two-year post came up in Kiev, in the Ukraine. She accepted it immediately. 'Kiev is the start of Russia. I went there because I was longing to hear Toli's voice again, to feel his manners . . . I knew a special Russian but I recognise breezes from him in conversations with a taxi driver, from strangers I meet on the street . . .'

An unexpected bonus of her new life was learning the history of the Ukraine. It has helped to put the deaths of Anatoli and her lover who died before him into some sort of perspective. 'I've lost two people, but in the Ukraine, my God, they lost more than anybody in the Second World War. Before that, there were the horrible purgings by Stalin. Generation after generation of people have been taken out. The Ukrainians have survived a desperate history and yet they continue to find a reason to live, to express a passion for life.'

Even when her contract in Kiev is up, Linda has no plans to return to the US. She seems to have absorbed Anatoli's restless spirit, his love of experience rather than material possessions. 'I travel like a pack rat,' she said. 'With a few sticks and stones.' The house she built near Santa Fe, the home that was the centre of her life for fifteen years, means little to her now. Leaving it recently, not expecting to be back again for a year, she walked out without a backward glance, as if she was going for coffee at a neighbour's. Just as Anatoli would have done. 'When a person you love dies,' she said, 'something of you dies with them. And something of them lives on in you.' In the summer of 2002 she travelled to the Caucasus to climb Mount Elbrus, at 5,642 metres Europe's highest mountain. And she did it alone. 'It's not a hard mountain,' she wrote, 'but it was work and I had to pay attention. It was glorious.' She sensed Anatoli close to her. Above 5,000 metres, she felt strong, and happy.

Ask mountaineers why they climb: invariably they say that it makes them feel alive. It allows them to live in the moment. Ask those bereaved by climbing accidents if anything positive has emerged from the tragedy, and, in one way or another, they usually echo the climber's sentiment. If they love someone, they tell them. If they have a gift to give, they give it now . . . just in case. They take nothing for granted. 'I can tell you what Death has taught me,' says Terres Unsoeld, in her one-woman play *Making My Way in the Dark*. 'It's taught me to hold on to life and make each moment count.' Her twenty-one-year-old sister, Nanda Devi Unsoeld, died on her namesake mountain. Three years later, when Terres was twenty, her father, Willi Unsoeld, was killed in an avalanche on Mount Rainier. And what did she do after this double tragedy? 'I started living life with a vengeance . . .'

I understand that sentiment. Learning of Joe Tasker's death stripped away my desire to live for the future. My life became the past and the present. I lived from moment to painful moment, an intense, vivid and extreme existence where nothing mattered and anything was possible. That intensity, I now realise, was Joe's legacy to me. It compelled me to follow his example, taking from life what I wanted and needed, shaping it to my dreams, experiencing it to the fullest, knowing that the end can come suddenly, without warning. Joe's death jolted me alive.

Select Bibliography

Ashenburg, Katherine — *The Mourner's Dance*, MacFarlane Walter and Ross, Canada, 2002

Attig, Thomas — *How We Grieve*, Oxford University Press Inc, New York, 1996

Bonington, Chris — *Boundless Horizons*, Weidenfeld & Nicolson, London, 2000

Bonington, Chris and Clarke, Charles — *The Unclimbed Ridge*, Hodder & Stoughton, London, 1983

Bremer-Kamp, Cherie — *Living on the Edge*, David & Charles, Newton Abbot, 1987

Boukreev Anatoli, Edited by Linda Wylie — *Above the Clouds*, St Martin's Press, New York, 2001

Breashears, David — *High Exposure*, Canongate, Edinburgh, 1999

Boardman, Peter — *The Shining Mountain*, Hodder & Stoughton, London, 1978
Sacred Summits, Hodder & Stoughton, London, 1978

Campbell, Joseph

The Hero with a Thousand Faces, Fontana Press, London, 1988
The Power of Myth, Bantam Doubleday Dell Publishing Group, New York, 1988

Camus, Albert

The Myth of Sisyphus, Penguin Books, London, 2000

Curran, Jim

High Achiever, Constable Robinson, London, 1999
K2: Triumph and Tragedy, Hodder & Stoughton, London, 1987

Child, Greg

Postcards from the Ledge, Mountaineers Books, Seattle, 2000
Mixed Emotions, Mountaineers Books, Seattle, 1993
Thin Air, Patrick Stephens Ltd, Cambridge, 1988

Csikszentmihalyi, Mihaly

Flow, Rider, London, 2002
The Evolving Self, HarperPerennial, London, 1994

Diemberger, Kurt

The Kurt Diemberger Omnibus, Mountaineers Books, Seattle, 1999

Douglas, Ed and Rose, David

Regions of the Heart, Penguin Books, London, 2000

Gillman, Peter and Leni

The Wildest Dream, Headline, London, 2001

Franz, Marie-Louise

The Problem of the Puer Aeteus, Inner City Books, Toronto, 2000

Hankinson, Alan, editor

Changabang, William Heinemann, London, 1975

Herzog, Maurice

Annapurna, Pimlico, London, 1997

Hill, Lynn

Climbing Free, HarperCollins, London, 2002

Hillman, James

The Soul's Code, Bantam, London, 1997

Hornbein, Thomas

Everest: The West Ridge, Mountaineers Books, Seattle, 1998

Houston, Charles and Bates, Robert	*K2, The Savage Mountain*, McGraw Hill, New York, 1954
Knapp, Ronald J.	*Beyond Endurance: When a Child Dies*, Schoeken Books, New York, 1986
Krakauer, Jon	*Eiger Dreams*, Pan, London, 1998 *Into Thin Air*, Macmillan, London, 1997
Messner, Reinhold	*To the Top of the World*, Mountaineers Books, Seattle, 1998
McDonald, Bernadette Amatt, John	*Voices from the Summit*, National Geographic Books, Des Moines, 2000
Outside	*The Best of Outside: The First, Twenty Years*, Villard, New York, 1997
Petit, Philippe	*On The High Wire*, Faber and Faber, London, 2003
Potterfield, Peter	*In the Zone*, Mountaineers Books, Seattle, 1996
Pritchard, Paul	*Deep Play*, Baton Wicks, London, 1997 *Totem Pole*, Constable Robinson, London, 2000
Reinisch, Gertrude	*Wanda Rutkiewicz: A Caravan of Dreams*, Carreg Limited, 2000
Scott, Chic	*Pushing the Limits*, Rocky Mountain Books, Calgary, 2000
Simpson, Joe	*Touching the Void*, Jonathan Cape, London, 1988 *The Beckoning Silence*, Jonathan Cape, London, 2002
Summers, Julie	*Fearless on Everest: The Quest for Sandy Irvine*, Weidenfeld & Nicolson, London, 2000
Stokes, Brummie	*Soldiers and Sherpas: A Taste for Adventure*, Michael Joseph, London, 1988
Tasker, Joe	*Savage Arena*, Methuen, London, 1982 *Everest the Cruel Way*, Eyre Methuen, London, 1981

Todhunter, Andrew — *Fall of the Phantom Lord*, Bantam Doubleday Dell Publishing Group, New York, 1998

Twight, Mark — *Extreme Alpinism*, Mountaineers Books, Seattle, 1999
Kiss or Kill, Mountaineers Books, Seattle, 2001

Ullman, James Ramsey — *Straight Up*, Doubleday, New York, 1968

Unsoeld, Terres — *Making My Way in the Dark – Sex, Death and Love with no Intermission (a woman's journey)* Unsoeld Unlimited Productions; terresu@aol.com

Vause, Mike, editor — *Rock and Roses*, Mountain n' Air Books, California, 1990

Venables, Stephen — *A Slender Thread*, Hutchinson, London, 2000

Washburn, Barbara — *The Accidental Adventurer*, Epicenter Press, Seattle, 2001

Weathers, Beck — *Left for Dead*, Little, Brown and Co, London, 2000

Webster, Ed — *Snow in the Kingdom: My Storm Years on Everest*, Mountain Imagery, 2000; www.mntimagery.com

Weihenmayer, Erik — *Touch the Top of the World*, Hodder & Stoughton, London, 2001

Whittaker, Tom — *Higher Purpose*, Lifeline Press, Washington D.C., 2001

Jim Wickwire with Bullit, Dorothy — *Addicted to Danger*, Simon & Schuster, New York, 1999

Worden, William — *Grief Counselling and Grief Therapy*, Routledge, London, 1991
Children and Grief, Guildford Press, New York, 1996